WHERE TO WATCH BIRDS IN TURKEY, GREECE AND CYPRUS

HAMLYN BIRDWATCHING GUIDES

WHERE TO WATCH BIRDS IN TURKEY, GREECE AND CYPRUS

HILARY WELCH, LAURENCE ROSE,
DEREK MOORE, BILL ODDIE AND HARRY SIGG

HAMLYN

First published in 1996 by Hamlyn,
an imprint of Reed Consumer Books Ltd
Michelin House, 81 Fulham Road,
London SW3 6RB and Auckland, Melbourne,
Singapore and Toronto

ISBN 0 600 582 329

A CIP catalogue record for this book is available from the British Library

Page Design by Jessica Caws
Maps by Andrew Thompson

Printed in the UK by Clays, Bungay, Suffolk

CONTENTS

INTRODUCTION 7

TURKEY 12
BIRDWATCHING AND ARCHAEOLOGY 16
MOUNTAIN PASSES 18
WEST AND SOUTH COASTS 19
Terkos Gölü (Durusu Gölü)| 20
Bosphorus 20
Rumelifeneri 22
Büyük Çekmece Gölü 23
Uludağ 23
Uluabat Gölü (Ulubat Gölü, Apolyont Gölü) 24
Kocaçay Deltası 25
Manyas Gölü (Kuş Gölü) 26
Marmara Gölü 26
Çamaltı Tuzlası 27
Küçük Menderes Deltası 27
Büyük Menderes Deltası and Bafa Gölü 28
Dilek Yarımadası, Samsun Dagı 30
Güllük Korfezi 31
Köyceğiz Gölü and the Dalyan Deltası 32
Akseki area 33
Göksu Deltası 34
Çukurova Deltası 38
Belen and Topboğazı Geçidi 41
BLACK-SEA COAST 42
Abant Gölü 42
Yedigöller Milli Parkı 43
Soğuksu Milli Parkı, Kızılcahamam 44
Sarıkum Gölü 45
Kızılırmak Deltası 45
Yeşilırmak Deltası 48
Yedikır Barajı 48
Kaz Gölü 49
Tödürge Gölü, Hafik and Yarhisar 50
Sivrikaya, Kaçkar Dağları 51
İspir 52
Borçka and the eastern Pontics 52
Erzurum Ovası 54
CENTRAL ANATOLIA 56
Işıklı Gölü 57
Karakuyu Gölü 57
Acıgöl 58
Burdur Gölü 59
Yarışlı Gölü 60
Karataş Gölü 60
Gölhisar Gölü 61
Eğirdir Gölü 61
Kovada Gölü 62
Beyşehir Gölü 62
Karamıkbataklığı 63
Eber Gölü and Akşehir Gölü 64
Çavuşçu Gölü 64
Balık Damı 65
Gölbaşı Gölü (Mogan Gölü, Mugan Gölü) 66
Çöl Gölü 66
Kozanlı Saz Gölü and Samsam Gölü 67
Kulu Gölü (Düden Gölü) 68
Bulak Gölü, Ağabeyli and Tersakan Gölü 69
Eşmekaya 70
Hotamış Sazlığı and Süleymanhacı Gölü 71
Ereğli Sazlığı 73
Seyfe Gölü 74
Tuzla Gölü (Palas Gölü) 76
Sultan Sazlığı 77
Demirkazık 79
SOUTH-EAST 81
Gavur Gölü 82
Işıklı and Durnalık 83
Birecik to Halfeti, the Fırat (Euphrates) Vadigi 85
Ceylanpınar 88
Cizre 88
Yüksekova 89
EAST 90
Kuyucuk Gölü 90
Ağrı Ovası 91
Iğdır Ovası 91
Saz Gölü 91
Murat Vadigi, north of Bulanık 92
Nemrut Dağı 93
Sodalı Gölü (Arın Gölü) 95
Çaldıran Sazlığı 95
Erçek Gölü 96
Van wetlands 97

GREECE 100
Evros Delta 104
Dadia-Soufli forest 106
Avas Gorge 108
Lake Mitrikou (Lake Ismardia) 109
Porto Lagos 110
Thracian Lagoons 112
Eastern Rodopi 121
Nestos Delta 121
Nestos Valley and the central Rodopi 124
Strymon delta 125
Lake Kerkini 126
Angelochori and Epanomi Lagoons 128
Lakes Volvi and Koronia 129
Kassandra Peninsula 130
Cholomontas Mountains and Sithonia Peninsula 130
Mount Athos Peninsula 132
Axios Delta 132
Aliakmon delta 134
Alyki Kitros lagoon 134
Mount Olympus 135
Voras Mountains 136
Prespa Lakes 137
Lakes Petron, Vegoritis, Cheimaditis and Zazaris 139
Lake Kastoria 140
Vikos-Aoos national park 140
Pindos Mountains 141
Metóra 143
Kalamas delta and Gorge 143
Acherondas Gorge and Souliou mountains 145
Amrvrakikos gulf 145
Lefkas and Lake Voulkorio 147
Akarnian mountains 147
Klissoura Gorge 148
Mesolongi wetlands 148
Delphi 150
Mount Parnassos 151
Mount Iti 152
Sperchios Delta 152
Cape Araxos 153
Mykenai and Lake Stymfalia 154
Southern Pelopponese 154
Central Corfu 155
Northern Corfu 156
Southern Corfu 157
Zakynthos and the Strofades 158
Athens City 159
Marathon marshes 160
Northern Evvia 160
Southern Evvia 161
West Crete (Chania) 161
Samaria Gorge 162
Central Crete 163
Lesithi Plateau 164
Crete: offshore isalnds and headlands 164
Naxos 165
Northern Sporades 166
Limnos 166
Lesbos: Kallonis Bay 167
West Lesbos 169
Agiassos 170
Samos and Fourni 170
Kos 171
Chios 172

CYPRUS 174
Akrotiri salt-lake 179
Phassouri reedbeds 181
Paphos headland 183
Mavrokolymbus dam 184
Coral bay and Ayios Yeorios 185
Polis, Lachi and the baths of Aphrodite 185
Asprokremos dam 187
Kensington cliffs and Quarry Beach 188
Larnaca salt-lake 189
Paralimni lake 190
Cape Greco and Aya Napa 190
Akhna reservoir 191
Kouklia and Dhiarizos valley 192
Troodos mountains 192
Akamas peninsula 193
Paphos forest 194
Lara 195
Curium beach 195
Cape Aspro 196
Larnaca seafront 196
Athlassa dam and forest 197
Cape Koruçam 198
Gecitköy reservoir 199
Gönyeli and Kanliköy reservoirs 200
Gülseren and Glapsides wetlands 201
Lake Mehmetcik 203
Kirpasa peninsula east from Dipkarpaz, with the Klidhes islands 204

BIBLIOGRAPHY AND FURTHER READING 206
LIST OF SPECIES 207
INDEX 213

INTRODUCTION

The romantic lure of sun, sand and archaeology has long attracted tourists to Turkey, Greece and Cyprus. The birds are a less well-known attraction, yet there are many species here which are seen nowhere else in Europe and many opportunities for birdwatchers to make exciting discoveries.

Migration ifs legendary, yet nowhere is it regularly monitored. In Turkey White Storks and raptors can be seen in hundreds of thousands, whilst in Cyprus and the Greek islands migration of small birds is truly phenomenal. There the killing of migrants – from Bee-eaters to Blackcaps – continues on a heart-rending scale, with an estimated 8,000,000 annually in Cyprus alone.

In winter the wetlands hold 1,000,000 to 1,500,000 waterbirds. These include 10,000 Greater Flamingos in Cyprus, more than 100 Lesser White-fronted Geese in Greece, and around 10,000 White-headed Ducks at one site in Turkey, the largest wintering concentration in the world. Breeding birds at many wetlands are unsurveyed, although we do know that Turkey's wetlands hold the largest breeding population of Marbled Ducks in Europe, and in Greece about 200 pairs of Audouin's Gulls nest on offshore islands.

Both Greece and Turkey are excellent for raptors, with 26 species recorded in Greece including 2800 pairs of Eleonora's Falcons, the largest population in the world. They also hold large populations of Olive-tree and Rüppell's Warblers, and Masked Shrike, all species with very restricted global ranges. Turkey, because of its position, has many edge-of-range specialities – White-breasted and Pied Kingfishers are two of a long list of species seen nowhere else in Europe, and there are doubtless more to be discovered. Cyprus has the only endemic breeding species – Cyprus Pied Wheatear and Cyprus Warbler.

Only in recent years have national conservation bodies started to emerge and fight for the survival of these natural riches. Their major weapon is the Important Bird Areas in Europe. Ironically, the vast majority of the information in that book was drawn from the notebooks of foreign, holidaying birdwatchers. We shouldn't be surprised. Birdwatching, unlike hunting, is not a tradition activity amongst the locals – the number of Turkish birdwatchers still barely reaches double figures – so visiting birdwatchers continue to be a major and valuable source of data. We hope this book will stimulate you to join in the fight – visit this exciting area, and pass your records on. Contact the relevant national society if you would like guidance over where to go and what to do to help most.

Bird names in this book follow those used in Lars Jonsson's *Birds of Europe* (published by Helm), arguable the best field guide for the area. Sites are based on those listed in Important Bird Areas in Europe, concentrating on those which are good for birds and birdwatching. Some new areas, several of them potential IBAs, are included, but some of the original IBAs are already disappearing.

ACKNOWLEDGEMENTS

TURKEY

I have never been sure why I agreed to write about birdwatching sites in Turkey when my knowledge at the start was so pitifully minimal, but it seemed like a good idea at the time! To have produced this book at all I am therefore indebted to OSME for giving my initial interest in Turkey and for sending me there in 1989, thereby starting my friendship with DHKD; Jo Hemmings for cajoling me into saying 'yes' over an expensive lunch; Murat Gergin for providing us with 'special price' yet very reliable hire cars; Geoff Welch for providing encouragement from start to finish, finding the birds, and driving many thousands of rally-style kilometres on the promise of new birds at the next site, only to have to count yet more Coots for DHKD; the Turks for being so friendly and unperturbed by our strange behaviour, wherever we went; Sunay Demircan for sharing his knowledge of the Kızılımak delta and feeding us on home-produced honey and cream; Sancar and Sibel Bariş, for their friendship and confession that even they regularly get lost in the Kızılımak delta; Gürdoğar and Arzu Sarıgul for sharing their home in the Menderes with us and laying on 11 species of raptor over their disabled VW. Hasan Günen for our true Turkish welcome to the Göksu and for somehow buying us a meal despite having only 60,000 Turkish Lira in his pocket; Nergis Yazgan for her open and welcoming hospitality at Polonezköy; Gernant Magnin for his irrepressible and infectious sense of fun and for his amazing maps of Turkey's IBAs; Murat Yarar for unearthing information from the DHKD IBA files, housing us in Gürdoğar's flat and introducing us to Turkish sticky buns; Tim Collins and the many others who submitted their Turkish bird records to OSME and thus made this book possible; John Faldbord and Vincent van den Berk for checking over final texts and sharing the benefit of their own experience; my parents for translating large amounts of German text so willingly, despite the marital tension this inevitably created and Guy Kirwan for putting at my disposal his incomparable knowledge of Turkey's birds together with large amounts of his time.

Finally, thanks are due to the authors of *Important Bird Areas in Europe*, Richard Grimmett and Tim Jones, and especially to Max and Aygün Kasparck and A. Ertan who compiled the accounts which provided the inspiration for this book.

Hilary Welch

GREECE

The following friends and colleagues provided invaluable information and comments: Graham Burton, Brendan Godley, Dionyssia Hatzilakou, Doug Ireland, Hans Jerrentrup, Myrsini Malakou and Georgios Katsadorakis, Bob Malsom and Ben Ross, Olympic Airways, John O'Sullivan and Sarah Brennan, Costas Papakostandinou, Kostas Pistolas, Andy Simpson, Kevin Standring, Georgia Valaoras, Stella Vareltzidou, Kostas Vassilakis, Ann Whitehouse.

Laurence Rose

BirdLife International

BirdLife International is a worldwide partnership of organizations working for the diversity of all life through the conservation of birds and their habitats.

The partners in BirdLife International are like-minded national conservation organizations, which represent BirdLife in a country or specific territory. Where there is no Partner, an organization or individual may become a BirdLife Representative. BirdLife is represented in more than 100 countries worldwide.

Birds are the entry point for BirdLife, providing it with a focus for all elements of its strategy. However, the organization recognizes broader environmental objectives. It adopts the rationale of shared responsibility for the global environment and the sustainability of the use of the world's natural resources.

BirdLife International pursues a programme of:

SCIENTIFIC RESEARCH AND ANALYSIS to identify the most threatened bird species and the most critical sites for the conservation of avian diversity, for setting global priorities for bird conservation.

FIELD ACTION to address these priorities, ranging from community-based integrated land-use and management projects to species recovery programmes, all benefiting wildlife and humans.

ADVOCACY AND POLICY DEVELOPMENT to promote sustainability in the use of all natural resources and the conservation of biodiversity, by targeting intergovernmental agencies, decision-makers, community leaders, non-government organizations and individuals.

NETWORK BUILDING to expand the global partnership of conservation organizations (especially in developing countries and Central/Eastern Europe) and promote worldwide interest in, and concern for, the conservation of birds and, through that, for wider environmental issues.

An example of BirdLife's work is the Important Bird Areas (IBA) programme. Sites of important for birds throughout the world are being identified on strict, standardized criteria; IBAs in Europe and the Middle East have already been identified, programmes are underway in Africa, and currently being developed for Asia and the Americas. BirdLife's goal is to identify the world's Important Bird Areas by the year 2000. BirdLife also takes action for the priorities identified, as demonstrated by the successful programmes for the protection of Important Bird Areas in 31 countries in Europe.

BirdLife International has its headquarters in Cambridge (UK), and regional offices in Brussels (Belgium), Washington DC (USA), Quito (Ecuador), and Bogor (Indonesia).

How to use this Guide

Each country is introduced by a map or maps showing the locations of the sites covered. It should be remembered, however, that the maps in this guide are meant to complement, not replace, more detailed maps available in the areas concerned.

A section with general information follows, with advice on such things as how to get there, when to go, climate, accommodation, public transport, language and currency. There are background details on each country's importance for birds and details of bird conservation organizations and their work.

The section on Habitats covers the key habitat types of he various regions and the kinds of birds that inhabit each. Importance for Birds highlights endemic races, edge-of-range species which are difficult to find elsewhere in Europe and rarities.

Seasons details the weather and birdwatching highlights throughout the year.

Each entry begins with a general description of the site, (some in Turkey and Greece are accompanied by maps), and the typical and interesting birds found there. Timing explains which time of day and which seasons will be most productive. Species picks out the specialities of each site and Access explains where the site is, how to get there and whether you need permission.

Code of conduct for birdwatchers

When birdwatching in Turkey, Greece and Cyprus behave as you would anywhere else. Remeber the Code of Conduct for Birdwatchers. Well-behaved birdwatchers are an important lobby for nature conservation, and there are ample opportunities to set a good example by respecting habitats, laws and the rights of local people.

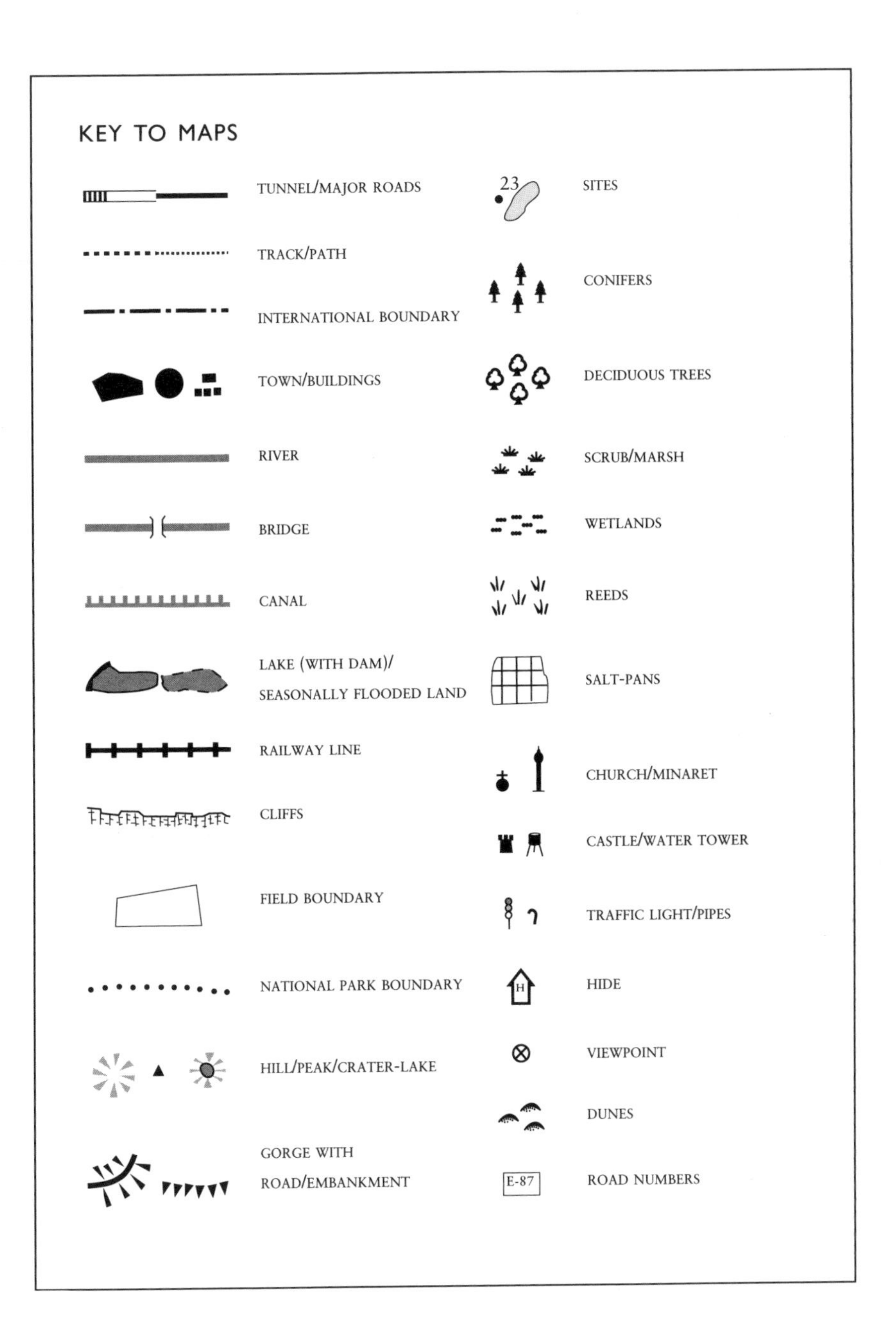
KEY TO MAPS
TUNNEL/MAJOR ROADS
TRACK/PATH
INTERNATIONAL BOUNDARY
TOWN/BUILDINGS
RIVER
BRIDGE
CANAL
LAKE (WITH DAM)/
SEASONALLY FLOODED LAND
RAILWAY LINE
CLIFFS
FIELD BOUNDARY
NATIONAL PARK BOUNDARY
HILL/PEAK/CRATER-LAKE
GORGE WITH
ROAD/EMBANKMENT
23
SITES
CONIFERS
DECIDUOUS TREES
SCRUB/MARSH
WETLANDS
REEDS
SALT-PANS
CHURCH/MINARET
CASTLE/WATER TOWER
TRAFFIC LIGHT/PIPES
H
HIDE
VIEWPOINT
DUNES
E-87
ROAD NUMBERS

TURKEY

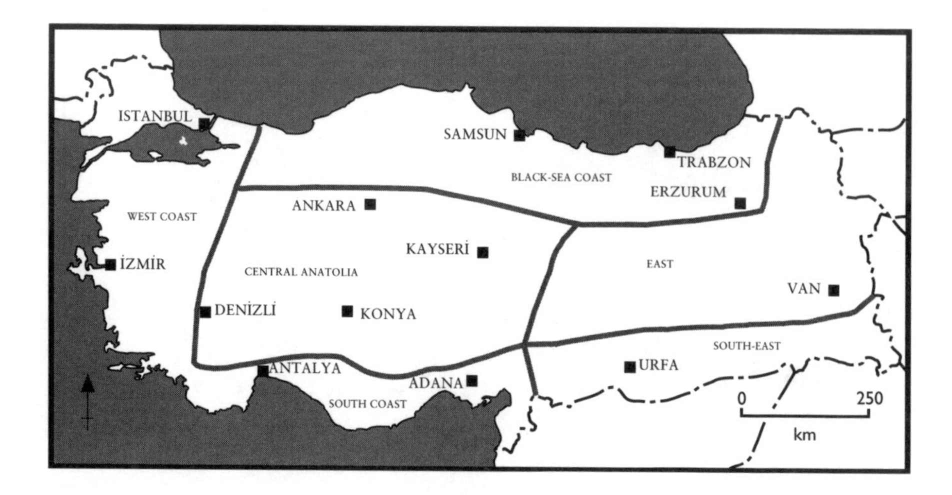

Turkey is a vast and wonderful country with huge, sweeping landscapes and stunning scenery. Birdwatching can be breathtaking, particularly on the impressive wetlands – if you want to find the Marbled Ducks or just enjoy the Ruddy Shelducks don't forget your telescope!

For day-to-day information I recommend the most recent edition of the *Rough Guide*. This contains good, reliable information on everything from accommodation to national holidays. Do check the dates of Ramadan before your visit. Also note that travellers' cheques can be exasperating and expensive to exchange in Turkey. Try taking some cash – dollars or sterling – particularly if you will be away from tourist centres.

Everywhere you go you'll find Turks very friendly and keen to talk to you and offer cups of çay, even when you have no language in common. Less friendly are the fearsome-looking Anatolian sheepdogs which frequently accompany flocks of grazing sheep and goats and are trained to kill wolves. They are best treated with respect and avoided.

Sadly, visiting large parts of eastern Turkey is currently not advisable because of the unstable political situation (the *Rough Guide* gives more information on this). Thus there are 14 sites marked with an ✖ here as they are in areas which are considered unsafe; for these I have relied on information published by others. Before visiting any of these eastern sites – even with an organized tour – contact your local embassy and/or the Foreign Office.

I have used the Turkish names for all of the sites as these are, after all, what you will see on road signs and maps. In some cases sites have alternative names and I have given these as well where I know them. A translation of the Turkish words used in the text and, especially, on the maps is given below.

adası	island	*kale*	castle
barajı	reservoir, dam	*korfezi*	marshes
bataklıgı	marshes	*küçük*	small, little
büyük	large, greater	*milli parkı*	national park
çay	tea	*orman, ormanı*	forest
dağ, dağları	mountain(s)	*ovası*	plain,
deltası	delta	*pansiyon*	guest house
geçidi	(mountain) pass	*sazlığı*	marshes
gölü, göl	lake	*Şehir Merkezi*	town centre
hüyük	artificial mound, makes an excellent viewpoint in a flat landscape	*tuzlası*	saltpans
		vadigi	valley
		uarımadası	peninsula

A Turkish phrase book will help you with the pronunciation.

IMPORTANCE FOR BIRDS

Because of its position, at the junction of the Asian, European and African continents, Turkey is very rich in birds. Of greatest importance are its many wetlands with significant populations of globally threatened species – Dalmatian Pelicans, marbled, Ferruginous and White-headed Ducks – and huge concentrations of waterfowl on passage and in winter including an amazing 250,000 Coots. These wetlands – with their technicolor Greater Flamingos, Ruddy Shelducks and Red-crested Pochards, backed by snow-capped mountains – are the very essence of Turkey.

At the continent junctions soaring migrants are concentrated in their thousands – principally pelicans, storks and raptors – and even away from these sites migration is a big feature of birdwatching throughout Turkey, spring and autumn.

But for many birdwatchers Turkey's greatest attractions are its many specialities – the restricted and edge-of-range species such as Caucasian Black Grouse, Caspian Snowcock, Striated Scops Owl, Radde's Accentor, Red-tailed Wheatear, Greenish Warbler, Great Rock Nuthatch and Grey-necked Bunting. There are also 21 endemic breeding subspecies!

GETTING THERE AND GETTING AROUND

Getting to Turkey is easy, with regular flights to Istanbul and internal ones to many large cities. Public transport can also take you to the birdwatching sites – the bus service is excellent – but for finding your way around them you need a car, although the energetic and ingenious may manage without.

Road maps are continually improving – I currently use the *Euro Atlas of Turkey*, published by Verlag (Germany), scale 1:800,000 – but they are still inadequate away from the major routes. A compass can be very useful.

Driving in Turkey is always interesting, but avoid Istanbul by picking up your hire car at the airport. Other road users are a hazard, but also varied and often entertaining.

Turkish roads should be treated with respect, oven old metalled ones can be riddled with exhausting pot holes. Many are stone-finished and good, but after rain some turn into a quagmire. A car with a determined driver at the wheel can go almost anywhere, but in wet weather always check dubious section of road by walking them first (particularly if you are miles from anywhere), and keep away from dirt tracks. If you do get irretrievably stuck seek assistance – the Turks get stuck so often they will probably know you need help before you ask – but don't forget to offer some payment. If your request gets a cold response make sure they understand you are a birdwatcher, not a hunter. At some sites – the Kocaçay delta and Marmara Gölü are two – locals are strongly anti-hunting.

CONSERVATION

After you have enjoyed Turkey and its birds, pass your records on by filling in some site recording forms (available from DHKD or OSME).

DHKD Bird Section, PK18, 80810 Bebek-Istanbul, Turkey, tel 90 212 279 0139/0140, fax 90 212 279 5544. The Turkish Society for the Protection of Nature is a non-governmental organization which promotes and protects IBAs. With only a handful of birdwatchers in Turkey, information from visiting birdwatchers if always gratefully and enthusiastically received.

OSME, c/o The Lodge, Sandy, Bedfordshire SG19 2DL, UK. The Ornithological Society of the Middle East is run by volunteers and publishes Sandgrouse, a journal which collates and disseminates information on the regions's birds. The Society publishes a Turkey Bird Report and welcomes records. OSME publications can be purchased from the address above.

SEASONS

Many of Turkey's wetlands are large and very shallow, with the area of each fluctuating naturally between a spring maximum and an autumn minimum. In years of little rain or periods of drought wetlands may dry up altogether, sometimes for several years, only to reappear when the rains return. More worryingly, however, some wetlands have disappeared permanently following systematic and efficient drainage whilst others, much reduced in size by drainage, are now under enormous pressure from the people who still depend on them for their livelihoods (Hotamiş is a recent example). Thus you may find some sites no longer match the descriptions in this book, although not all changes will necessarily be permanent.

Spring Before Easter weather can be unpredictable but is often good on the west and south coasts where many winter birds are still present (Smew,

Great Black-headed Gull), and good numbers of early migrants are to be seen (White Stork, Garganey, Ruff, hirundines). By mid-April the winter birds have gone, migrants are passing through, breeding birds are setting up their territories and the mountain areas are becoming accessible. The last migrants arrive in May (Black-headed Bunting is one of the last).

Summer Hot, with lots of tourists, and the best time for mountain birds and flowers. Some small migrant birds leave (Bimaculated Lark, Red-tailed Wheatear, Black-headed Bunting) or become difficult to find, wader migration is underway, White Storks start to leave.

Autumn The weather gradually cools down, and return migration is underway, with Lesser Kestrels, Rollers and Bee-eaters leaving in early September and raptor migration throughout the period.

Winter Usually cold (very cold on the central plateau), often with snow or rain; most tracks are impassable. Huge numbers of waterbirds on the wetlands.

BIRDWATCHING SITES

There are so many sites to include that the accounts have had to be short. I have concentrated of providing detailed and unambiguous information on access wherever possible – it's no good knowing an area has marvellous birds if you can't find the site! Distances given from or to towns are measured from the road sign which indicates you are just entering or leaving the town. However, roads (and place-names) change fast in Turkey, so if the directions have become inaccurate, please let me know.

The bird information for each site is very variable – it may be limited to one visit 30 years ago or comprehensive and up-to-date – but all of the sites have been included for good reason and are worth visiting, so don't be put off if the bird list doesn't provide you with the encouragement you require! Much still remains to be discovered about birds and sites in Turkey.

Seldom mentioned in the bird lists are species which are widespread and common in the right habitat, even though they may be exciting and new for unseasoned travellers. These include: White Stork, Little Egret, Ruddy Shelduck, Marsh Harrier, Long-legged Buzzard, Black-winged Stilt, Kentish Plover, Little Stint, Syrian Woodpecker, Bee-eater, Roller, Hoopoe, Calandra, Crested and Shore Larks, Isabelline and Black-eared Wheatears, Moustached, Great Reed and Olivaceous Warblers, Rock Nuthatch, Penduline Tit, Red-backed and Lesser Grey Shrikes and Cretzschmar's, Black-headed and Corn Buntings.

Sardinian Warbler

COMBINING BIRDWATCHING WITH ARCHAEOLOGY

For those who want to see Turkey's archaeological riches as well as its birds, there are many sites where the two activities can be combined, including those below. Birdwatching is likely to be best in spring.

Assos and Patara

36°18N 29°18E

The archaeological sites along the Aegean and Mediterranean coasts present good opportunities for birdwatching, both of characteristic breeding species such as Scops Owl, Hoopoe, Woodlark, Red-rumped Swallow, Subalpine, Sardinian and Bonelli's Warblers, Golden Oriole, Hawfinch and Cirl Bunting and of passage migrants such as Alpine Swift. Assos on the Aegean coast near Ayvacık and the area around the sites at Xanthos, Letoon and Patara, *c.* 60 km south of Fethiye, are both good examples. Letoon is a strange mixture of archaeological remains, mimosa swamp and greenhouses, and Patara, with its silted-up harbour, extensive dunes, and largely unexcavated and scrub-covered remains holds particular promise.

SPECIES

- ◆ *Middle Spotted Woodpecker* In cork-oak forest, particularly on the Aegean coast.
- ◆ *Olive-tree Warbler* In open coastal scrub, especially olive groves and oak woodland.
- ◆ *Krüper's Nuthatch* Common and often easily seen in pines.
- ◆ *Orphean Warbler* Shy, preferring taller vegetation and wooded hillsides.
- ◆ *Sombre Tit* Regular wherever there are trees.

Sumela Monastery

40°42N 39°40E

The monastery clings to a cliff face high above the Altındere valley, 54 km south of Trabzon on the Black Sea. It is surrounded by an area of forest where, if you can escape the crowds of tourists, some characteristic mountain and forest birds of this region can be seen, including the elusive Black Woodpecker.

SPECIES

- *Dipper* Along the stream below the monastery.
- *Green Warbler* A popular site for this species although it probably occurs in suitable habitat throughout the Black-Sea region. Present until early September but easiest to find in spring.
- *Red-breasted Flycatcher* Breeds in the valley below the monastery.

Nemrut Daği

37°59N 38°45E

Not to be confused with the crater-lake of the same name near Van Gölü, Nemrut Dağı lies south-east of Malatya and is famous for the stone heads on its peak. The mountain's slopes have an unusually rich and varied flora because there is little or no regular pasturing; characteristic birds such as Shore Lark, Tawny Pipit, White-throated Robin, Snow and Crimson-winged Finches can be seen here, along with more localized species.

SPECIES

- *Red-tailed Wheatear* A rather nondescript, inconspicuous wheatear, look on the stony slopes.
- *Cinereous Bunting* Prefers areas with a few bushes.

Cappadocİa

38°30N 34°30E

The amazing landscape of Cappadocia covers a large area and provides many opportunities for birdwatching. In the popular Göreme area (east of Nevşehir) typical species include Montagu's Harrier, Black-bellied Sandgrouse, Calandra and Bimaculated Larks, White-throated Robin, Finsch's Wheatear, Rock Thrush and Rock and Cretzschmar's Buntings, with Little Ringed Plover on the Kızılırmak River at Avanos. Other places, less populated by tourists, are also worth a look and include the wooded gorge of the Ihlara valley, the mountain passes and pastures of Sekkin Boğazı (between Güzelyurt and Gölcük) and the rocky slopes above the caves at Soğanlı.

SPECIES

- *Dipper* Along the Melendiz river in the Ihlara valley.
- *Red-fronted Serin* This and other mountain species can be seen on the rocky slopes close to the road at Soğanlı.

MOUNTAIN PASSES

Many roads in Turkey cross high mountain passes and all of these will provide opportunities to see a range of mountain species without having to climb the mountain. Scree slopes can be productive for birds like Black Redstarts and Red-fronted Serins as the rock crevices provide many places to search for food, and the same areas are favoured by Ring Ouzels for nesting. Sheer cliff faces and gorges are favoured by Crag Martins and are the places to search for Wallcreeper. The sparsely vegetated mountain slopes and plateaus are home to Alpine Accentors, Snow Finches and Rock Buntings. Any reasonably high passes are wort investigating but those best known by birdwatchers (because they lie on the route between birdwatching sites) are: **Erciyes Dağ** (38°33N 35°30E) The Kayseri–Develi road passes below the peak and runs close to Sultan Sazlığı. This is the most westerly known breeding area for Radde's Accentor, and Shore Lark, a bird regularly encountered in mountain areas, is extremely common. **Sertavul Geçidi** (36°57N 33°47E, 1610 m) On the Konya–Silifke road above the Göksu Deltası. This is a good area for seeing birds of prey (especially vultures), and Krüper's Nuthatch is common among the pines. **Gezbeli Geçidi** (38°15N 36°03E, 1960 m) A lesser-known pass and only passable during the summer months, but another area where Radde's Accentor has been seen. **Ovitdağ Geçidi** (40°38N 40°46E, 2600 m) Above the Caucasian Black Grouse site at Sivrikaya. The speciality here is undoubtedly Caspian Snowcock, which can be seen along with other species with restricted ranges in Turkey such as Twite and Crimson-winged Finch.

TIMING

Mountain birds are generally easiest to find in May and June as the snows retreat and the birds display, but many species can be seen in the area around the snow-line throughout the year.

SPECIES

- *Lammergeier, Griffon, Egyptian and Black Vultures* The vultures are true mountain birds with Lammergeier, in particular, only occurring in the wildest terrain.
- *Golden Eagle* A mountain bird which will often move to the lowlands in winter when food is scarce.
- *Alpine Chough, Chough and Raven* The three crows of the mountains. Be warned that young Choughs have short, yellow-orange bills!
- *Water Pipit* Can be surprisingly common at high altitude.

WEST AND SOUTH COASTS

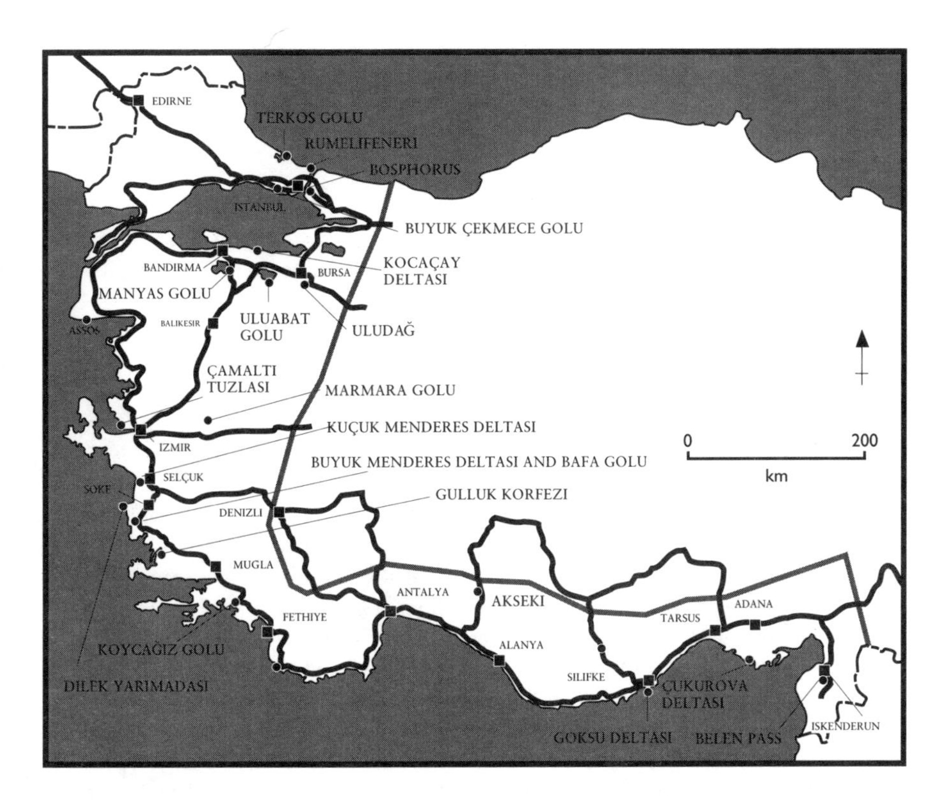

The west and south coasts of Turkey are the most touristed, so for convenience are grouped together here, along with the sites in European Turkey (Thrace). For Thrace the list of sites is certainly incomplete, and it is inadvisable to birdwatch close to the Greek border in the wonderful but dangerous Meriç delta (the Turkish name for the Evros delta).

The west and south coasts have some spectacularly rugged scenery. In summer the climate is hot and dry, but for those who cannot cope with excessive heat late March/early April can be pleasant. The birdwatching can be excellent too – with a mix of winter birds and early migrants.

Some birds typical of this region and in some cases unlikely to be seen elsewhere in Turkey include: Cory's Shearwater, Spotted Eagle (in winter), Eleonora's Falcon (summer visitor), Black Francolin, Purple Gallinule, Great Spotted Cuckoo, White-breasted Kingfisher, Middle Spotted Woodpecker, Red-rumped Swallow, Yellow-vented Bulbul, Rufous Bush Robin, Cyprus Pied Wheatear, Fan-tailed, Graceful, Upcher's, Olive-tree, Subalpine, Rüppell's and Orphean Warblers, Krüper's Nuthatch, Woodchat and Masked Shrikes, and Cretzschmar's Bunting.

TERKOS GÖLÜ (DURUSU GÖLÜ)

41°19N 28°32E

A lake on the Black-Sea coast, north-west of Istanbul, surrounded by wooded and farmed hills, dunes and areas of reed and flooded woodland. The lake is a reservoir for Istanbul, so water levels can be very low in summer or during droughts, especially at the western end.

This site deserves investigation, but this involves driving a lot of roads not marked on any map! There is no access to the dunes, which are part of a stabilization project.

TIMING

The wide variety of habitats should provide year-round interest and its position on the Black-Sea coast, near the Bosphorus, makes it well situated for migration.

SPECIES

- *Osprey, Little Bittern and Night Heron* Possibly breed.
- *White Stork and migrating raptors* Spring and autumn.
- *Black-throated Diver, Yelkouan Shearwater and waterfowl* On the sea in winter.

ACCESS

The lake is about one hour's drive from Istanbul. **Terkos west** Follow the TEM west from Istanbul and take the road to Çatalca. After Subas,ı, follow the road to the right towards Durusu and after 3.7 km turn left to Karacaköy and continue a further 20 km or so. Before Ormanlı is an area of wet woodland, rough grass and farmland bordering the river – this is flooded at times of high water and can be a good area for birds. At the junction just east of the road bridge over the river, take the road signposted to Hisarbeyli and Celepköy. At Celepköy, turn right and almost immediately left down an unmade track. After less than 1 km the track forks; both forks lead to views over the lake. Return to Celepköy and drive south on the tarmac road through Örencik – beyond here you can turn east to Durusu. **Terkos east** This can be reached from Istanbul on the road signposted to Habibler from the TEM – fork right in Arnavutköy – the roads to Durusu from here are marked onmaps of the area. The lake can be viewed from the roadside north of Durusu. This road continues to the coast at Karaburun where there are good views of the sea from the lighthouse. From Karaburun a made-up track follows the coast westwards and goes through a conifer plantation (part of the stabilization project); you can drive as far as a gate, beyond which there is no entry. A track to the left just before the gate is worth exploring in spring and autumn for migrant passerines.

BOSPHORUS

41°00N 29°00E

The wooded hills and narrow straits of the Bosphorus form a migration corridor between Europe and the Middle East used by hundreds of thousands of birds each year. Most obvious are the storks and birds of prey

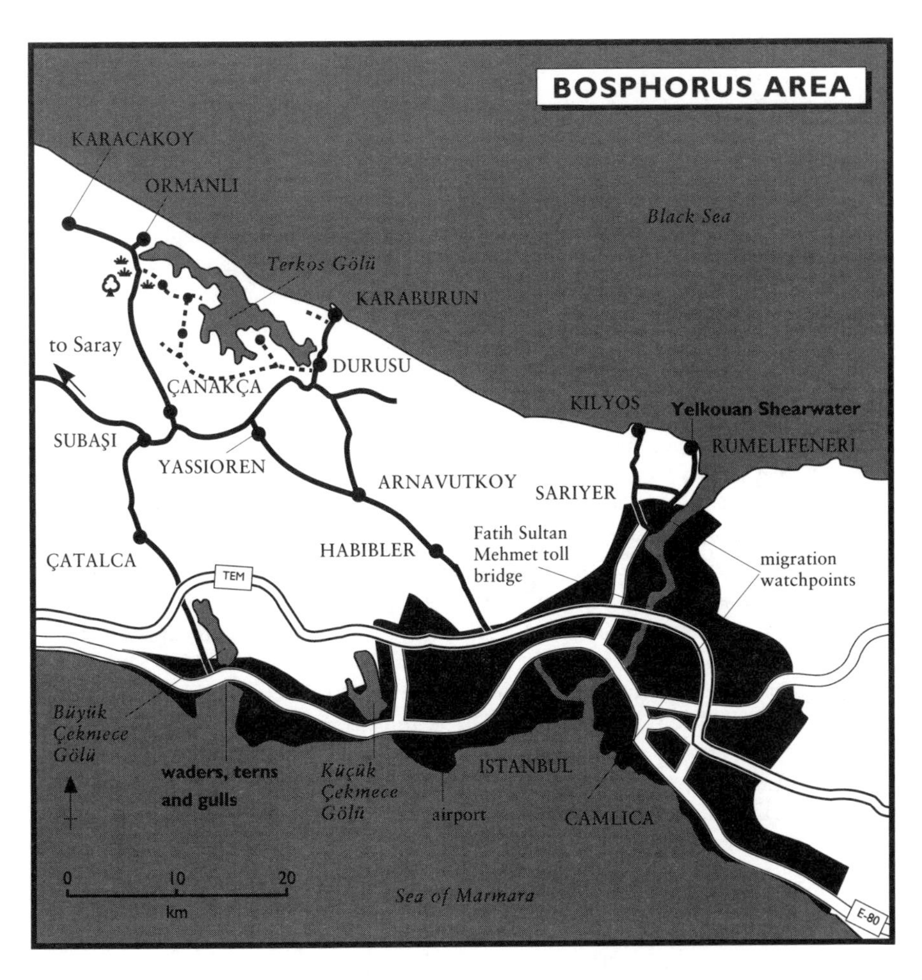

which migrate during the day – more than 20 species of raptor have been recorded. Small birds, too, use the route with Bee-eaters heard (less often seen!), and warblers, flycatchers and buntings stopping off to feed and rest during the day before resuming their migration at night. Alpine Swifts are common over Istanbul for much of the year and Laughing Doves are well-established. Another speciality is Pallid Swift.

The birds' routes will vary according to the weather conditions, so you may find that the roof of your hotel provides the best views! Birds can be seen from mid-morning to mid-afternoon at Çamlıca, but at Sarıyer they tend to start moving earlier and finish later.

TIMING

Autumn migration is the best-known with the greatest variety of species in the first half of September, but good numbers of birds could also be seen here in the spring. The Dardanelles, at the western end of the Sea of Marmara, are little known and would also be worth investigating.

SPECIES

Annual maxima:

- *White Stork* August–mid-September – 207,000.
- *Black Stork* September–early October – 6000.
- *Lesser Spotted Eagle* September – 17,000.
- *Buzzard* Mid-September–mid-October – 30,000.
- *Levant Sparrowhawk* Middle two weeks of September – 7000.
- *Honey Buzzard* Mid-August–mid September – 23,000.

ACCESS

Çamlıca Take the southern suspension bridge to the east side of the Bosphorus – Küçük Çamlıca is straight ahead and Büyük Çamlıca to your left, both hills can be recognized by their many radio masts. Take the third exit after the bridge (signposted to Çamlıca) and keep heading towards the radio masts until you find more signs near the bottom of the hills. **Sarıyer** *c.* 15 km north of central Istanbul on the western side of the straits. Follow the signs to Sarıyer to a T-junction with traffic lights on the edge of the Bosphorus. Turn left, and after 1 km take another left turn at more traffic lights. Turn right at the next T-junction and, after 50 m turn left up a small side street opposite a mosque. Bear left at the first fork and then continue uphill for 2 km until you reach another T-junction at the top. Turn left – after 600 m the road ends at a recreation ground with a sign 'Kocatas Parkı'. Views are good from here, but the area is rapidly being built up. Search of the hills in this area would probably reveal a good alternative watchpoint.

RUMELIFENERI

41°14N 29°06E

At the north-west end of the Bosphorus an old fort stands guard over the Black-Sea entrance to the straits. From the fort's elevated position makes there are good views of the Bosphorus and the Black Sea, providing an opportunity for quiet seawatching close to Istanbul.

TIMING

Very little is known about how birds use the Black Sea, but the largest numbers and greatest variety of birds will probably be present in winter, i.e., November–March, with Black-throated Divers regular.

SPECIES

- *Cormorant and Shag* Both can be seen here.
- *Kittiwake* A rare bird in Turkey, has been seen nearby in January.
- *Yelkouan Shearwater* Should be common outside the breeding season.

ACCESS

Take the road north out of Istanbul through Sarıyer and towards Kilyos; Rumelifeneri is 14 km from the centre of Sarıyer (don't take the road which follows the Bosphorus – there is an army camp on it just north of Sarıyer). Between Sarıyer and Kilyos take the right turn signposted to Rumelifeneri. On reaching Rumelifeneri the road forks; the right fork leads down to the harbour (gulls) and the left goes to the fort.

Büyük Çekmece Gölü

41°02N 28°32E

The westernmost of two lakes lying on the edge of Istanbul and the Sea of Marmara surrounded by fields, factories and houses. In the south, the small area of water between the dam and the Sea of Marmara is shallow, and usually holds a few waders and feeding gulls and terns.

TIMING

In summer and early autumn, water levels can be low and birds few. In winter the lake is used by divers, ducks and geese whilst in spring and autumn migrating raptors and storks stop to rest and feed. The lake is most easily watched from the west side, so for the best light avoid early mornings.

SPECIES

◆ *Smew* Probably regular in winter.

◆ *Mediterranean Gulls* Regular with 10,000-plus recorded in March 1995.

◆ *Red-footed Falcon* On passage – April–June and August–October.

ACCESS

Head west out of Istanbul, following the old main road to Edirne (D-100) along the Bosphorus and bypassing the airport to the south. As you approach Büyük Çekmece, ignore the signposted turning and continue to the bottom of the hill where the road crosses the channel connecting the lake to the Sea of Marmara. Turn right before the channel, immediately after the sign indicating that you are leaving Büyük Çekmece. Park, and scan the area between the road bridge and the dam from the Roman bridge.

To see the main lake, return to the Edirne road and, after crossing the channel, take the first right, signposted to Mimarsinan and Çatalca. Take the first available right turn to look over the area immediately north of the dam. The northern end of the lake can be seen from the minor road which goes off to the right just before the Çatalca road crosses the TEM and snakes around below the raised motorway.

Uludağ

40°04N 29°11E

At 2543 m, Uludağ is the highest mountain in western Anatolia. It lies south-east of Bursa and is the nearest and most accessible site to Istanbul for seeing mountain species. The habitat is very varied with Mediterranean maquis, mixed deciduous woodland, coniferous forests and alpine meadows, and a fauna and flora typical of the Black-Sea region. More than 11,000 ha is a national park but the summit is the most important winter-sports centre in Anatolia and is also disturbed by small-scale tungsten mining in the same area. Typical species above the tree-line are Shore Lark, Water Pipit, Alpine Accentor, Rock and Blue Rock Thrushes, Chough and Alpine Chough, with Wryneck, Black Woodpecker and Firecrest in the forested areas. Tengmalm's Owl has been heard here in the ancient fir forest, and 27 species of birds of prey recorded including Egyptian Vulture, Goshawk and Lesser Spotted and Golden Eagles.

TIMING

Snow cover can last into May and winter can start as early as October, so the best time to visit is late May–September.

SPECIES

- *Lammergeier* Nests but can be difficult to see.
- *Pallid Swift* A regular summer visitor to this area.
- *Krüper's Nuthatch* Common in the forest areas along the road.
- *Red-fronted Serin* A bird of the tree line, sometimes seen near the hotels, but more often found feeding on the scree slopes or the tungsten mine waste heaps. This is the westernmost edge of its range.

ACCESS

Roads to the mountain are signposted from Bursa. Alternatively, a cable-car goes from Bursa as far as Sarıalan, ending at a high alpine meadow. From here a path of 6 km or so (about two hours) leads up to the hotels at the summit.

A good circular walk of three hours or so starts from the hotels. the Initially the path follows the road eastwards beyond the hotels, as far as the tungsten mine. Turn south and then west here, following the mountain ridge as far as the 2096-m peak of Pasaray, directly above the hotels. From here take the path down the mountain and back to the road. Pay attention to the weather as it can change rapidly.

ULUABAT GÖLÜ (ULUBAT GÖLÜ, APOLYONT GÖLÜ)

40°12N 28°40E

A large and attractive lake, with several small islands and extensive areas of reed. It is excellent for birds yet surprisingly little visited by birdwatchers despite being only about 3 hours from Istanbul. Along the south-western side, where the river flows into the lake, there are large wet-meadows, reedbeds and extensive areas of tamarisk; elsewhere the lake is surrounded by olive groves and farmland, and small patches of marsh.

Breeding birds include Pygmy Cormorants, Little Bitterns, Night, Squacco and Purple Herons, Spoonbills, Montagu's Harriers, Collared Pratincoles, Spur-winged Plovers, Whiskered Terns and Penduline Tits.

TIMING

There is a good variety of birds to see all year round. In winter there are many thousands of waterfowl with Pochard and Coot both numerous, and Great White Egret and Smew regular.

SPECIES

- *White and Dalmation Pelicans* Seen in good numbers throughout the year but not known to breed.
- *Red-footed Falcon* Can occur in large numbers on autumn passage.
- *Great Snipe* May be regular on autumn passage.
- *Great Black-headed Gull* Recorded in March 1993, and likely to be a rare winter visitor.

ACCESS
From Bursa, take the first left turn to Akçalar immediately after the lake comes into view. This goes round the east and south sides of the lake and gives good, views although the birds may be distant. Doggedly follow the roads which hug the shore and you will circuit the lake to join the raised track which runs down its western side from the village of Uluabat – a round-trip of 69 km. Alternatively, the western track is easily found from the main road – from the east, cross the river and immediately turn left into Uluabat, then left again. The track follows first the river and then the lake shore, and provides good views.

Along the northern shore, the tarmac roads to Eskikaraağaç and Gölyazı both lead to the lake and give good views over various bays.

With birdwatching possible all around the lake, plan your route according to the light.

Kocaçay Deltasi

40°22N 28°30E

This varied delta, backed by hills and overlooking the Sea of Marmara, is divided in two by the Kocaçay river. The western side is wooded, and its lake – Dalyan Gölü – is surrounded by wet woodland and scrub-covered dunes. Rufous Bush Robins and Masked Shrikes breed in the scrub. The eastern side is more open, and its lake – Arapçiftliği Gölü – is flanked by hills and dunes. Wetland birds include Pygmy Cormorant, Ruddy Shelduck and Gull-billed Tern. The combination of wetland and mature woodland provides a rich habitat and breeding birds include Black Stork, White-backed Woodpecker and Golden Oriole, and a variety of raptors including Honey Buzzard and Lesser Spotted Eagle.

Despite its proximity to Istanbul the Kocaçay is surprisingly little known and underwatched. It requires time and exploration on foot to appreciate fully.

TIMING
There are birds to see all year, but after rain exploration of the delta can be extremely difficult as many tracks are impassable.

SPECIES
◆ *White Pelican and White Stork* Fly over in flocks on migration.
◆ *Bewick's Swan* A flock of 14 was recorded here in March 1995.

ACCESS
Eastern delta From Karacabey take the road north signposted to Bayramdere. Turn right 10 km north of Karacabey (just before a cemetery) to Hayırlar and Harmanlı. Over the river a surfaced track heads north, eventually swinging east along the southern edge of Arapçiftliği Gölü. For closer views there are unsurfaced tracks which go nearer to the lake at its western and eastern ends, but you may have to walk. **Western delta** 9.5 km farther along the main Karacabey road, the road bends left away from the river take the track which goes off to the right here. Drive as far as you can and then walk for views of the southern edge of Dalyan

Gölü. Back on the main road continue westwards past the Pheasant breeding-station to the coast at Yeniköy. Here, take the track off to the right at the local timber yard, and follow this as far as you can. Bear left, keeping to the dunes, as the tracks in the woodland are generally too wet to be passable. At the end, the vegetation opens out giving views over the eastern end of the lake.

MANYAS GÖLÜ (KUŞ GÖLÜ)

40°10N 28°00E

A large lake with a small national park, known as Kuşcenneti, ('Bird Paradise'), in the wooded north-east corner. An observation tower looks over a mixed heron and cormorant colony with Pygmy Cormorant, Night, Squacco and Purple Herons, Little Egret, Glossy Ibis and Spoonbill. The reed-fringed southern shore at the mouths of the Kocaçay and Karadere rivers is probably the most productive area of the lake outside the national park.

TIMING

To see birds in the breeding colony visit from March – June. In winter the lake is used by thousands of wildfowl. The observation tower, open from 8 a.m.–5 p.m. for a small charge, looks south, so visit at the beginning or end of the day for the best light. Avoid weekends and holidays.

SPECIES

- ◆ *White Pelicans* In May, migrating birds rest in fields in the south-east.
- ◆ *Dalmatian Pelican* Nests on artificial platforms visible from the tower.
- ◆ *Smew* Regular in winter with a record count of more than 500 in 1995.

ACCESS

The road to the national park and observation tower is signposted off the Bandırma–Balıkesir road, 18 km south of Bandırma. The southern side of the lake can be explored by turning right in Aksakal towards Manyas; various tracks and banks lead to the lake edge from this road. Daskyleion, an archaeological site just west of Ergili, is on a hill and provides a good vantage point for birdwatching over the lake.

MARMARA GÖLÜ

38°41N 28°00E

A shallow, attractive lake surrounded by hills, 90 km east of İzmir. There are wet-meadows and reedbeds in the north and east. Breeding birds include Ruddy Shelduck, Ferruginous Duck, Short-toed Eagle, Black-winged Stilt, Spur-winged Plover and Gull-billed Tern.

TIMING

In the summer or during droughts water levels in the lake can be low and the lake may dry out altogether. For the best light, birdwatch in the north-east corner in the morning.

SPECIES

◆ *Black-necked Grebe and Dalmatian Pelican* Good numbers in winter.

◆ *White-tailed Eagle* Can be seen in winter.

ACCESS

For the north shore take the Kemerdamları road out of Gölmarmara. After *c.*12 km the lake comes into view; watch from the road and hills. Farther on, the roads around Kemerdamları and the dyke at the east end of the lake provide more views; the roads can be impassable after rain. For the south and west of the lake take the Tekelioğlü road from the Gölmarmara–Salihli road. You can birdwatch from the west and east of the village.

Çamaltı Tuzlası

38°27N 26°52E

An area of bays, lagoons, saltmarshes and saltpans on the coast between İzmir and Foça with excellent birdwatching all year. Homa Dalyan, the largest of the lagoons, is designated a 'Bird Paradise' and has an information centre and two marked visitor routes. Greater Flamingos can be seen here all year with 100–200 pairs breeding. Ruddy Shelducks, Black-winged Stilts, Avocets, Spur-winged Plovers and Caspian Terns also breed.

TIMING

Large numbers of waterfowl and waders in winter, including several thousand Greater Flamingos.

SPECIES

◆ *Dalmatian Pelican* Resident with largest numbers in winter.

◆ *Pygmy Cormorant* Occurs in winter.

ACCESS

From the main coast road (E-87) north of İzmir take the turn to Sasallı in Çiğli. This road leads to the main gate through the fence surrounding the saltpans – tell the people on the gate that you have come to birdwatch and you will be allowed in. The information centre and main birdwatching area around Homa Dalyan are a few kilometres north of the gate. Birdwatching is not encouraged on the saltpans between the gate and the information centre as the area is still being worked.

Küçük Menderes Deltası

37°58N 27°17E

Wetland at the mouth of the Küçük Menderes river, west of Selçuk. The best remaining area lies north of the river and consists of farmland (including rice fields), two small lakes and large areas of reed and tamarisk.

TIMING

In summer and times of low rainfall the wetland area may be very small. When conditions are right breeding birds can include Little Bitterns, Purple Herons, Ruddy Shelducks, Little Crakes and Collared Pratincoles. In winter the birds are badly disturbed by hunters.

SPECIES

- *Cory's and Yelkouan Shearwaters* May be seen moving along the coast in the evenings in spring.
- *Eleonora's Falcon* A regular summer visitor.
- *Great Spotted Cuckoo and Masked Shrike* Occurs on migration and may stay to breed.
- *Orphean Warbler* On the scrubby hillsides.

ACCESS

Drive west out of Selçuk, passing Ephesus on your left, and head towards the beach at Pamucak. When you reach a roundabout turn right towards Seferihisar and Gümüldür. Cross the river and the wetland lies on both sides of the road – mainly reed and tamarisk. A track crosses the road 1.4 km beyond the bridge, just north of the hill Ada Tepe, and gives access on foot to varied wetland habitat on both sides of the road. About 600 m farther on take the right turn to Zeytinköy; this will lead you through cultivated wetland areas and back to Selçuk. Much of the eastern part of the delta can be viewed from this road, particularly if water levels are high. Other tracks are accessible only when water levels are low. Tracks heading east out of Zeytinköy will take you in the direction of the two lakes.

Büyük Menderes Deltasi and Bafa Gölü

37°34N 27°15E

The Büyük Menderes national park is a large and attractive wetland on the Mediterranean coast south of İzmir, between Selçuk and Milas. Most of the floodplain is cultivated for cotton but many areas of interest remain with lagoons, meadows and marshes in the valley and two lakes farther inland. A wide variety of birds can be seen here, particularly during migration.

The wetland divides into three areas: **the delta** where the main areas of interest are the lagoons along the coast with breeding Stone-curlews, Mediterranean Gulls, Gull-billed and Caspian Terns, and the marshes and oxbows along the old course of the Menderes holding Little Bittern, Little Crake and Great Reed Warbler; **Bafa Gölü** (Çamiiçi Gölü on some maps) a beautiful lake tucked into the mountains with often-excellent wader-watching along its western shore (Collared Pratincoles breed here) and **Azap Gölü** a small lake and area of floodplain north of Bafa Gölü with large patches of reed holding breeding Bitterns.

TIMING

The delta is at its best during spring migration and the breeding season (April–June), whilst in winter (December–March) a good variety of waterbirds can be seen (although many of the tracks are then impassable to vehicles). Lighting is a major consideration – the northern end is best in the early morning, whilst Bafa Gölü and Azap Gölü are at their best in the afternoon and evening.

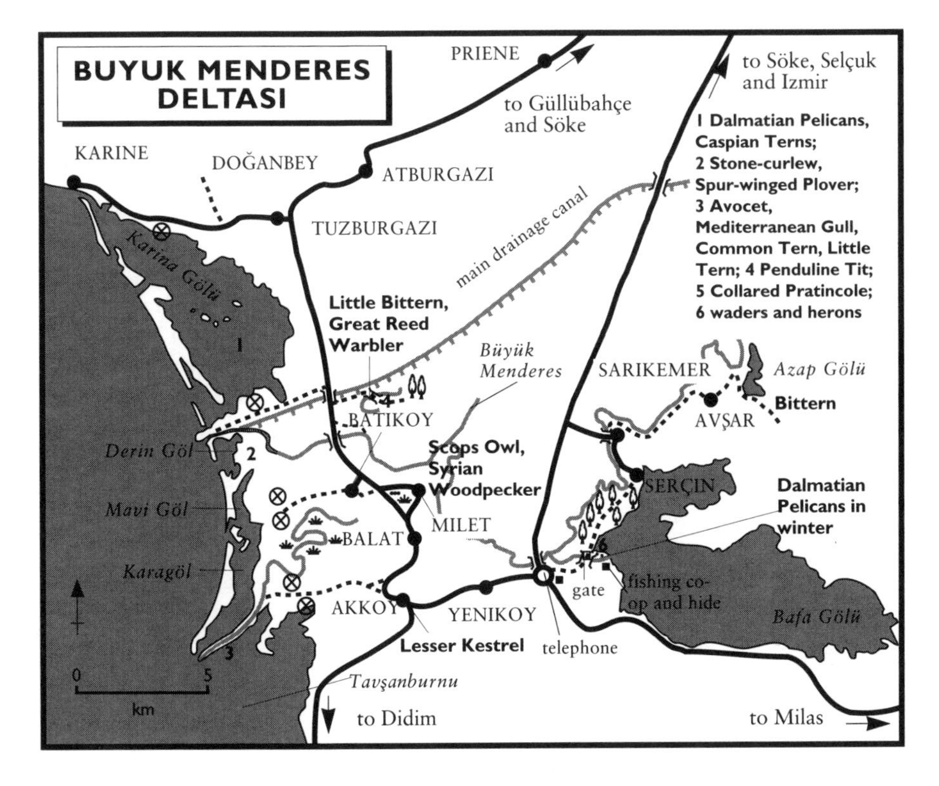

SPECIES

- *Dalmatian Pelican* Nests on the islands in Karina Gölü and are present in good numbers in winter; they can often be seen on Bafa Gölü.
- *White-tailed Eagle* Often seen in the area.
- *Lesser Kestrel* Nests in several villages in the delta, notably Akköy and Serçin, returning from their wintering-grounds in late March.
- *Eleonora's Falcon* Can regularly be seen in summer.
- *White-fronted Goose and Hen Harrier* Winter visitors, with Great White Egret and Glossy Ibis often numerous at this time.

ACCESS (see map)

Warning! All the tracks marked on the map which lead west from the main road are unsurfaced and often impassable after wet weather.

The delta From the north take the turn signposted to Priene off the main coast road just south of Söke. Initially this road follows the bottom of the mountains, but after 20 km, beyond Atburgazı it swings south to cross the delta. NORTHERN DELTA AND KARİNA GÖLÜ NORTH Fork right through Tuzburgazı for views over some fresh-water marshes and the northern end of Karina Gölü. The road ends at Karine. This road can be a good place for seeing raptors. KARİNA GÖLÜ SOUTH Take the main road south across the delta, and after 7 km you reach a bridge crossing the main drainage canal; turn right just before the bridge and follow the canal to the sea for views of the southern end of Karina Gölü. MENDERES

OXBOWS Return to the main road, cross the bridge and turn left, following the canal and then swinging right towards some large eucalyptus trees. After 1.5 km park by a bridge which crosses the first of a series of reed-fringed oxbows, and birdwatch along the track for *c.* 1 km from here. MENDERES RIVER About 1 km south of the main drainage canal a short track goes off to the left just before a bridge (over the Menderes). The track goes through mixed habitat which can be good for such passerines as Cetti's Warbler, Penduline Tit and Spanish Sparrow. MİLET The area between the main road and Milet floods when the water is high and, as the water drops in spring, can be very good for migrants and species such as Squacco Heron. Scops Owl, Syrian Woodpecker and Hoopoe breed in the trees around the car park and tourist shops. BATIKÖY Opposite the turning to Milet, a dirt track goes west, passing south of the village of Batıköy. Drive down here as far as you can for views over a fresh-water wetland to the south, and the central part of the delta to the north. TAVŞANBURNU Continue south from Milet and after 6 km turn right, immediately before Akköy. This track leads to views over the southern lagoons and bays of the delta.

Bafa Gölü Continue through Akköy (stop to look for Lesser Kestrels) and take the left turn to Milas. After 7 km cross the main coast road at a roundabout, going straight over down the stone track opposite. The maquis bordering this track is rich in wildflowers and at its best in early spring. After 2.7 km park next to a bridge over a canal. Walk across the bridge and follow the north side of the canal to the lake or, if water levels are high, look for birds on the lake from the south side of the canal. For more views of the lake return to the bridge and drive through the gate (generally not locked), following the eucalyptus-lined stone track along the top of the floodbank to Serçin. Views of the lake are distant but in late spring/summer birds such as Collared Pratincole can be seen along here.

Azap Gölü Azap Gölü lies 13 km north of Serçin. After a wet winter the wetland area may start below the village of Avşar. If the cotton fields between the village and the river flood they can be excellent for migrants in May/June when the water level drops. Watch the lake from the road. Avşar is a particularly good village for nesting White Storks.

DİLEK YARIMADASI, SAMSUNDAĞI

37°40N 27°10E

A mountainous peninsula lying between the Büyük Menderes and Kuşadası. The high peaks, sheer cliffs and deep canyons, areas of maquis and mixed pinewoods are little disturbed by people.

TIMING

It is cooler in the mountains than in the delta below in summer, but spring or autumn when temperatures are more comfortable are best for an all-day visit. Birds and flowers are at their best in spring from late March to June. Many birds of prey nest in the mountains with Short-toed, Booted and Bonelli's Eagles and Peregrine amongst the species present.

SPECIES
- ◆ *Middle Spotted Woodpecker and Masked Shrike* Nest where there are mature trees.
- ◆ *Blue Rock Thrush and Rock Nuthatch* In the barer rocky areas
- ◆ *Subalpine, Rüppell's and Orphean Warblers, Hawfinch, Rock and Cirl Buntings* All birds of the vegetated mountain sides and scrub.
- ◆ *Krüper's Nuthatch* Where there are pines

ACCESS
Although a national park, a large part of the north-western end of the peninsula is a military zone, so explore from the south. From Priene westwards, tracks go up into the mountains from most of the villages, with the one from Doğanbey recommended (*see* map under Büyük Menderes); the turning to Doğanbey is 3.5 km after Tuzburgazı, with the old village lying 1.8 km up the hillside. From the village – which consists of old Greek houses being restored as holiday homes – a well-defined track goes into the mountains, initially through old gardens and maquis where many passerines can be seen. A full day can easily be spent walking in the mountains; ask locally for information regarding routes and the state of paths.

Güllük Korfezi

37°15N 27°38E
An area of saltmarsh and reedbed, created from silt deposited by the River Değirmen, lying at the head of Güllük Körfezi between Bodrum and Milas. Between the south-west corner of the marsh and the mouth of the bay a row of hills gives an excellent overview of the southern corner. It also provides a good watchpoint for visible migration and is itself a good area for passerines. Sadly the marshes are disappearing fast, with much of the once-winding river canalized, and an airstrip under construction. It is difficult to know whether any wetland will remain around the edges of the airstrip and at the mouth of the bay, but as the bay seems to act as a funnel to migrants in spring the area will probably always be of some interest to birdwatchers and is still worth a look if you are in the area.

TIMING
Probably best in spring, late March–early June, but the area is little known.

SPECIES
- ◆ *Spring/summer* Eleonora's Falcon, Black-winged Stilt, Stone-curlew, Spur-winged Plover, Pied Kingfisher and Bee-eater.
- ◆ *Migration* Glossy Ibis, Osprey, Alpine Swift.
- ◆ *Winter* Great White Egret, Pygmy Cormorant.

ACCESS
From Milas take the turning to Bodrum and after 14.2 km turn right to Güllük. Follow this road for 4.1 km, along the southern edge of the marsh and past turnings to Ekinanbarı Köyü and the airstrip (both of which are possible tracks to explore the area in more detail later) and, just before entering Güllük, turn right on the brow of a hill immediately after the Jandarma (police station). Follow this track for 1.8 km, bearing

right whenever you have a choice, until the way becomes deeply rutted. Continue on foot, still heading for the end of the peninsula, eventually following only an ill-defined path through olive trees and a prolific growth of giant fennel, until you come out at the head of the bay with excellent views over what remains of the marsh.

KÖYCEĞİZ GÖLÜ AND THE DALYAN DELTASI

36°55N 28°40E

On the Aegean coast 70 km west of Fethiye, this beautiful area has a rich variety of habitats: a river, fresh-water lake, marshes, brackish delta with many reed-fringed channels, flooded liquidamber forest, sand dunes, coastal habitats, pine forests, maquis and mountains. The beach at İztuzu is famous for its nesting Loggerhead Turtles and to protect them from disturbance the beach is closed at night from May–October. A good range of typical species can be seen around the archaeological site at Kaunos including Roller, Rufous Bush Robin and Rüppell's Warbler. In the marshy areas look for Little Bitterns, Purple Herons, Cetti's and Great Reed Warblers, and Penduline Tits where there are larger trees.

TIMING

Work according to the light. The Dalyan area can be a very disappointing place for birds as it is very disturbed by tourists, particularly from June–September. However, there can be exciting falls of small birds during migration as well as raptor-movements. Köyceğiz Gölü is important for waterbirds in winter.

SPECIES

- *Night Heron* Passes through in spring and probably breeds.
- *White-tailed Eagle* Is regularly seen in summer.
- *Red-footed Falcons, Hobbies and Eleonora's Falcons* Pass through in good numbers on passage.
- *Scop's Owl* Regularly heard in and around Dalyan.
- *White-breasted and Pied Kingfishers* Breed in small numbers.

ACCESS

Köyceğiz is signposted off the main road. Drive into town and turn right to Çandır, along the lake's western shore. After Köyceğiz the road passes through a marshy area. This is probably the best birdwatching area and the most likely place for seeing White-breasted and Pied Kingfishers. Farther on, there are views of the southern end of Köyceğiz Gölü between Hamitköy and Küçükkaraağaç.

For Dalyan, turn off the main Fethiye road at Ortaca, taking the Şehir Merkezi turn, and follow the signs. In Dalyan it is possible to take a boat trip through the marshes out to the beach; this gives a good impression of the area although it can be a very frustrating way of birdwatching! However, you may be lucky and see a Nile Soft-shelled Turtle. Alternatively, a boat trip into Köyceğiz Gölü stopping off at Gedova

Sombre Tit

Tepesi – an island at the southern end of the lake – can be excellent for seeing the waterfowl in winter.

From Dalyan the road signposted to İztuzu goes round the edge of Sülüngür Gölü and then enters an area of pine forest; for access to the beach continue on – if the barrier is down the beach is closed – or take the track off to the left just before the barrier, and birdwatch in the pine forests up the slopes of Bozburun Tepesi for species such as Krüper's Nuthatch. There is a splendid view of the whole wetland from the top.

Akseki area

37°05N 31°50E

Akseki is a village lying in well forested mountains just off the 695 road which runs to the coast from Beyşehir. Lying within easy reach of the tourist resort at Antalya, Akseki has become a popular area for seeing a variety of species such as Olive-tree, Rüppell's, Orphean and Bonelli's Warblers, Sombre Tit, Krüper's Nuthatch and Cretzschmar's Bunting along with a range of migrants. But the areais best known for its woodpeckers with at least seven species recorded including Wryneck, Grey-headed (occurring alongside Green) and the very localized White-backed; Middle Spotted is probably the commonest.

TIMING

April–early June provides the best birdwatching with breeding birds singing and easier to find, and migrants moving through. The White-backed Woodpeckers can be very elusive. They are seen most regularly in late June/early July, and should also be possible to find in March and April when they are setting up territories.

ACCESS

There are four known places to explore in the Akseki area.

Migrants Walled plantation Fom the south turn left down a track signposted to İbradı, *c.* 500 m before the turn to Akseki. Drive for 1 km and a stand of large, mainly deciduous, trees is obvious on your left. **Akseki graveyard** Take the road to Akseki, and in the village turn right just before the road is split by a line of trees. At the far end, turn right again down a road signposted to Dutluca and three other villages, and the walled graveyard can be seen stretching for 300 m along the right-hand side of the road.

Woodpeckers AKSEKİ OLD ROAD Drive through Akseki and head north on the old main road past the rubbish dump. 8 km after leaving the village (from the last mosque) a track goes off to the left on a right-hand bend; explore the forest along this track. BEYŞEHI'R ROAD About 16 km north of Akseki on the main 695 road take the main left fork signposted to Beyşehir and Konya. 2.5 km from the fork is an excellent area of open forest; the area on the left-hand side of the road is recommended.

GÖKSU DELTASI

36°20N 33°59E

The Göksu river meanders down a spectacular gorge to the Mediterranean at Silifke. Its sediment has created a rich 15,000-ha delta, with fresh- and salt-water marshes and lagoons, scrub-covered dunes and sandy beaches. Extensive rice-growing – has also created a rich habitat. With more than 330 bird species recorded, the Göksu delta is one of the most important bird areas in Europe or the Middle East. In 1990, the delta was declared a Specially Protected Area (SPA) in recognition of its importance.

The western half of the delta is rich in birds and is dominated by two lagoons, Akgöl and Paradeniz. Akgöl is and extensively vegetated with fringing reedbeds where egrets and herons nest. Marbled Ducks breed here (easiest to see from the second half of June when they have young), along with Ferruginous Ducks and Purple Gallinules and a variety of waders and marsh terns pass through on passage. Black Francolins and Graceful Warblers are resident in the scrub-covered dunes. Paradeniz Gölü is more saline, virtually unvegetated and has fewer birds, but they are easier to see! It usually holds gulls and waders of a different range of species from those at Akgöl. In early spring birds may include Greater Sand Plover and Slender-billed Gull and in winter hundreds of Pygmy Cormorants and Common Cranes. North of the lakes, the rice paddies can be excellent for birds from May–September; in autumn all three crakes are present, with Water Rails in their hundreds and Kingfishers very common.

An impressive number of rarities have been recorded. One-offs include Great Northern Diver, Yellow-billed Stork, Crab and Lesser Sand Plovers, Spotted Sandpiper and Paddyfield Warbler, with more frequent records of Great Snipe and Terek Sandpiper, and Cyprus Pied Wheatear a seemingly regular spring overshoot in March and early April. Red-breasted Goose, Great and Little Bustards and Great Black-headed Gull have all been recorded in winter.

TIMING

The weather in the delta is wet and mild in winter and hot and dry in summer, but it is humid throughout the year and suffers from frequent high winds, especially in winter. There is a good selection of birds to see

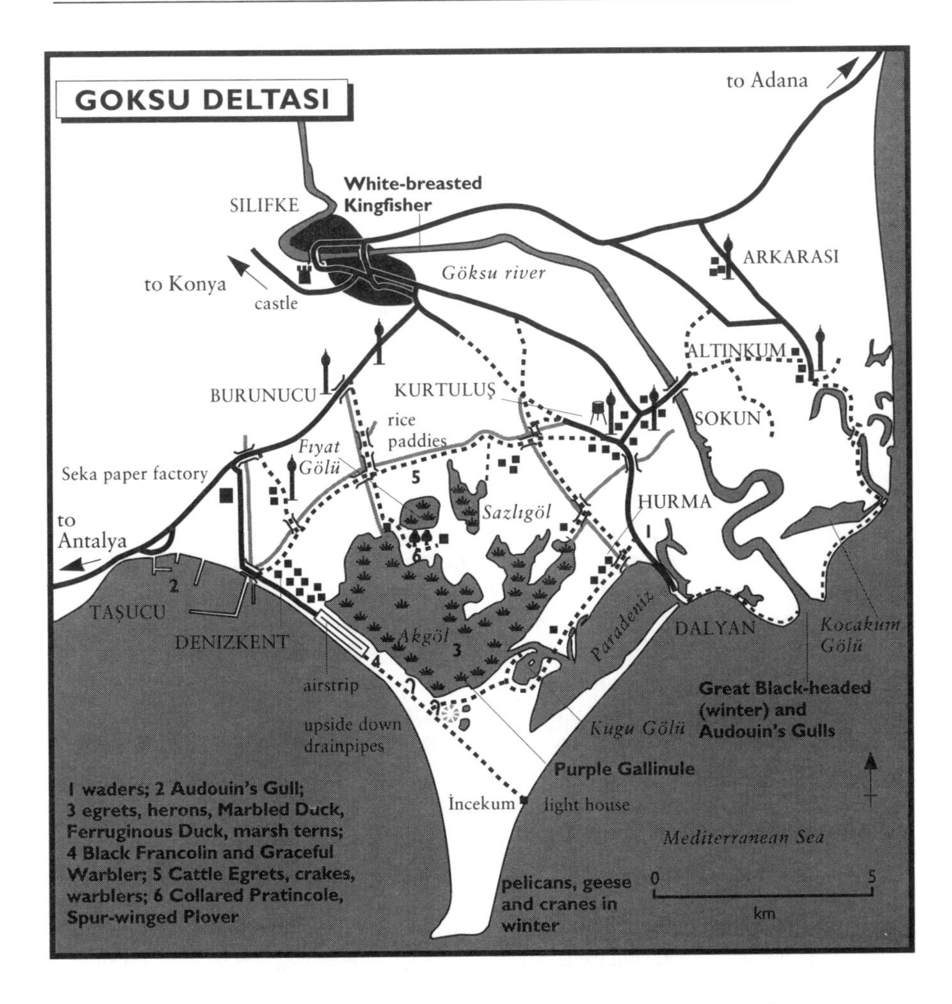

at any time of year but the weather is probably most comfortable in spring and autumn, which coincides nicely with the migrations periods.

Autumn tends to be the more spectacular period with White Pelicans, White Storks (maximim 20,000 at roost) and eagles. But spring, particularly the early period in March and April, should not be ignored – migrating Glossy Ibis, Marsh Harrier and Common Crane can occur in their thousands. Some of the more regular species on migration include Greater Flamingo, Corncrake, Broad-billed and Marsh Sandpipers, Whimbrel, Great Spotted Cuckoo, Red-throated Pipit and Rose-coloured Starling. Mosquitoes can be a problem at any time of year so come prepared!

SPECIES

- *Dalmatian Pelican* An occasional winter visitor.
- *Cattle Egret* Probably the best site in Turkey for seeing this species with flocks of more than 100 recorded on the paddyfields.
- *White-tailed, Spotted and Imperial Eagles.* Regular winter visitors.
- *Eleonora's Falcon* Summer visitor, even seen regularly in Taşucu.

- *Lanner and Saker* Seen irregularly throughout the year.
- *Kingfisher, White-breasted and Pied Kingfishers* All occur.
- *Yellow-vented Bulbul* A typical bird of orchards and gardens.

ACCESS

To see the whole of the delta you need to stay at least two days and to explore the area thoroughly you need your own transport. The best and closest base is Taşucu (camping is not allowed in the delta).

Taşucu To make the most of your visit, try to visit the DHKD project office first. It is in an old building opposite the harbour, between a restaurant and the bookings office for the Cyprus ferry, and is open from 8 a.m. until at least 10 a.m. daily. Staff here should be able to tell you what birds have been seen recently and provide you with up-to-date information about access. Don't forget to let them have your bird records when you leave. HARBOUR Check the pier for roosting Audouin's Gulls.

Akgöl and dunes Drive east out of Taşucu and after 2.2 km turn right after the Seka paper factory, following the signs to Liman. The road follows a drainage canal, usually dry, which it crosses after 2.6 km. Turn right towards the beach, skirting the holiday village of Denizkent, and follow the well-marked road/track along the coast. Beyond the houses the track widens into a short airstrip; from here there are scrub-covered dunes. These hold many breeding birds in spring and, in season, many migrants; since they border the south-west edge of Akgöl they also provide convenient high points from which to survey the lake. Black Francolins are present all year and in April and May the males call loudly from any convenient hillock. It is easy to lose your bearings in the flat landscape of the delta and vertical landmarks become important – the water tower at Kurtuluş, the various mosques, and the abandoned, half-finished building between Akgöl and Paradeniz Gölü are all useful reference points. Along the south-east edge of Akgöl a series of tall pipes, their tops curled over like shower heads, are spaced at regular intervals alongside the stone track which leads from Denizkent to the light-house on İncekum. Counting from the south-east end of the airstrip, the second pipe stands just before the largest dune which provides the best view of the lake and İncekum, and marks a track on the left which leads around the southern tip of Akgöl to a more open area with closer views of the lake. Here, if you are patient, you might see Purple Gallinules – early mornings or evenings are best, although they can be heard moaning anywhere around the lake, at any time. This track leads past a fisherman's hut to a small open lagoon called Kugu Gölü, and provides views of the south-west end of Paradeniz Gölü. When water levels are low it is possible to drive along this track and cross a bridge to Paradeniz Gölü and Hurma. If you have time and the weather is conducive, seawatching either from the light-house or, if you can face the walk, the end of İncekum cape can sometimes be rewarding. The cape is also a daytime winter roost site for pelicans, geese and cranes.

Rice paddies and marshes Return to Denizkent and at the bridge bear right round the back of the holiday village, following a major canal. This farm track takes you past fields and connects with a network of tracks and dykes – it is easy to get lost! Look for the rice paddies, at their best from May to late September and lying between Akgöl and the main track. If you can find a well-defined track between the paddies, go for walk in search of birds such as crakes and warblers, but you need either waterproof footwear or to go barefoot, it will be very wet and muddy. 3.9 km from Denizkent you reach a crossroads. Turn right here along the canaland drive slowly to the reedbeds at the end which mark the back edge of Akgöl – birdwatch as you go. A track to the left just before a building leads to some tall trees and a fisherman's hut. This can be a good area for Collared Pratincoles and Spur-winged Plovers (a very common breeding bird in the delta). Return to the crossroads and turn right, continuing on the original track for a further 3.7 km to a small village followed by another junction of tracks and canals. Take the right-hand-most track and continue until you reach a minor track and canal branching off to the right; this leads to another fisherman's hut at the extreme north-east of Akgöl and further possibilities for birdwatching. Return to the main track and turn right for Paradeniz Gölü.

Paradeniz Gölü At the end of the track you reach a T-junction and the fishing village of Hurma. Turn right and follow the track along the northern edge of Paradeniz Gölü. Proceed with caution as this track deteriorates and can be impassable after rain. Return to Hurma and continue to a T-junction with a more major track. From Kurtuluş (which lies to the left) to the coast at Dalyan (which lies to the right), there are various pools and wet fields next to the road which can be excellent for waders in spring and autumn, with thousands of storks resting here on their migration in autumn.

Dalyan, beach and river mouth At Dalyan a gate across the road will more often than not be opened by the locals – if not you will have to walk but beware of the dogs! From here there is a view down the length of Paradeniz Gölü and you can walk through to the beach where more waders can be seen along the shoreline. A walk east along the beach from here to the Göksu River mouth takes about 45 minutes and is often worth the effort. A series of pools just in from the beach together with the beach itself are used by a variety of waders, terns and gulls, including Greater Sand Plovers, and Audouin's Gulls are regularly seen at the river mouth along with Nile Soft-shelled Turtles in the river itself. Great Black-headed Gull has been seen here in recent winters.

Eastern delta East of the Göksu, the delta is more heavily farmed and access is a great deal more difficult and confusing. Many tracks are deeply rutted mud and totally impassable by vehicles for much of the year. However, if you have time and a good sense of direction, the easiest access is via the bridge which can be reached from Sökün. Look for White-breasted Kingfishers near the river. Another area for White-breasted Kingfishers is on the edge of Silifke. Take the Mersin road out of Silifke and 2 km from the bridge turn right down a track to the river, just west of a Shell garage. As many as three pairs have been seen along the river between here and the bridge in Silifke.

Silifke Castle The castle in Silifke provides a good although distant overview of the delta – useful for getting your bearings. There are birds around the castle, too, with Griffon Vulture sometimes drifting over, and Sardinian Warbler and Wallcreeper both winter visitors. Another area to try for passerines is on the hillsides above the delta. At the Seka paper factory a small road heads north into a gorge where birds such as Eagle Owl, Blue Rock Thrush, Upcher's Warbler and Rock Nuthatch may be seen.

Çukurova Deltasi

36°45N 35°25E

The huge delta of the Ceyhan, Seyhan and Berdan rivers lies on the coast south of Adana on a major migration flyway around the north-east corner of the Mediterranean. The Seyhan river is one of the best places in Turkey for seeing White-breasted Kingfishers; other relatively localized specialities such as Black Francolin, Yellow-vented Bulbul and Graceful Warbler are common in the delta. During migration birdwatching can be spectacular, particularly in the eastern half of the delta, with White Pelicans and White Storks flying over in flocks of several hundred birds at a time and large numbers of waders on the lagoons and oxbows. In winter the delta's wetlands hold tens of thousands of wildfowl.

TIMING

With hot dry summers and mild wet winters the delta is most pleasant to visit in early spring (March–mid-May) when migration is underway but before the weather gets too hot. The autumn migration period, as yet little known, probably runs from late August to October.

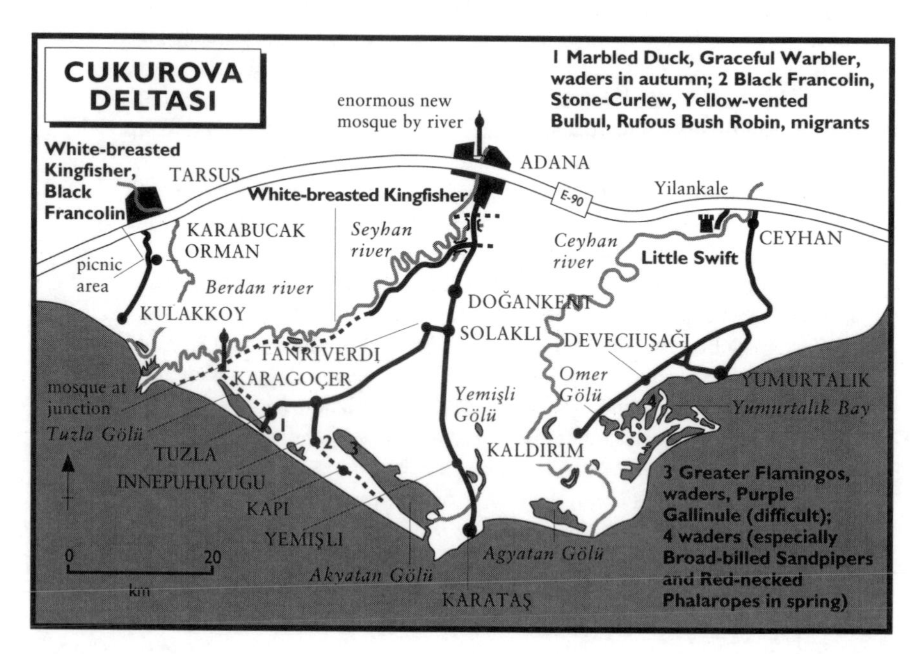

SPECIES

- *Greater Flamingo* Largest numbers present in winter, with more than 10,000 recorded on Akyatan Gölü.
- *Marbled Duck* Most numerous on migration in April, with several pairs breeding on the coastal wetlands.
- *White-headed Duck* Winters in good numbers with 900 in 1990.
- *Little Crake* A spring migrant in good numbers; it probably breeds.
- *Black-winged Pratincole* Small flocks may occasionally be seen on migration in September.
- *Bee-eater and Roller* Common migrants in spring, with small numbers breeding.
- *Calandra Lark* A very common breeding bird.
- *Red-rumped Swallow* A common breeding bird in the delta.
- *Dead Sea Sparrow* Breeds in small numbers. Search for their round nests in Spanish Sparrow colonies.

Some scarce but regular migrants include Great Snipe, Terek Sandpiper, Red-necked Phalarope, Great Black-headed Gull (wintering), Citrine Wagtail, Thrush Nightingale and Pied and Cyprus Pied Wheatears.

ACCESS

The delta is 50 km from north to south with a 150 km long coastline. The birdwatching possibilities described here concentrate on the central delta south of Adana, but for those with time to spare there are many other good areas, particularly in the eastern delta.

Western delta, Tarsus KARABUCAK ORMAN A varied eucalyptus plantation with a picnic area and trails in the western delta. From the west on the E-90 turn right after the first traffic lights, 500 m beyond the Tarsus sign; from the east turn left 1.1 km after the Şehir Merkezi turn. The junction is signposted, and lined with mature eucalyptus trees. The picnic area is 4 km south of the junction, with parking outside the fenced recreation area. A short circular track goes round an area of plantation and marsh opposite. Listen for the raucous cries of the White-breasted Kingfishers and look for them perched high in the trees or on telegraph poles. Black Francolins also occur and the area can be full of singing Nightingales in spring. Avoid weekends when the area can be busy.

Central delta The turning to Karataş, from the main Mersin-Guziantep in Adana, is signposted, but easier to spot are the bridge over the Seyhan River, and a huge new mosque on the river's west bank; the turn to Karataş is on the east side of the river. Once you've turned keep the river on your right, and head due south on a major-looking tarmac road. SEYHAN RIVER A wide river with steep banks and oxbows – the best area for White-breasted Kingfishers. 3.6 km after leaving Adana (8.3 km from the E-90), the road crosses a large canal. Turn right along a dyke the south side of the canal which runs parallel with the Seyhan River virtually all the way to the sea. Stop and birdwatch in any good-looking habitat; there are various oxbows and in several places the river comes close to the road. TUZLA GÖLÜ AND OXBOWS When water levels are low these can hold numerous waders including stints, Broad-billed and Marsh Sandpipers. The oxbows are also good for Marbled Ducks and Graceful Warblers. After driving 42 km along the dyke from Adana you reach a village; turn left after the mosque and this track leads along the north side of Tuzla Gölü to Tuzla (10 km). Turn right in Tuzla to see the eastern end of the lake. Take the road north out of Tuzla and in Karagöçer turn right on the tarmac road to Innepühüyügü (easily missed). Turn right in Tuzla to see the eastern end of the lake. Continue to the sea and a track which runs east along the dunes to a new holiday resort passes many small wetlands, always holding a variety of waterfowl. Take the road north out of Tuzla and in Karagöçer turn right on the tarmac road to Akyatan. Stop frequently to scan the various creeks and oxbows. INNEPÜHÜYÜGÜ An area of scrub, cultivated dunes, marshy areas and plantation between Innepühüyügü and Kapı, next to Akyatan Gölü. Species include Stone-curlew, Black Francolin, Yellow-vented Bulbul, Rufous Bush Robin and migrants. The Black Francolins generally prefer the wheatfields. The track is impassable to cars beyond the plantation. AKYATAN GÖLÜ A large, shallow lagoon, one of only two known sites in Turkey for Purple Gallinule. Waders include Collared Pratincole and Greater Sand Plover. Thousands of waterfowl winter here. The lagoon is best and most easily watched from the south-west corner near Innepühüyügü; light is best in the afternoons (There is only limited viewing from the eastern end at Karataş). Where the birds are will depend entirely on water levels – over the course of the summer the lake area shrinks by two-thirds. YEMİŞLİ GÖLÜ A shallow fresh-water lake 3 km south of Yemişli, on the Adana–Karataş road, holding water only in winter and spring. This can be a frustrating site to birdwatch, with the ducks and herons hidden in the dense vegetation in the centre of the wetland, although many waders – especially Kentish Plovers – use the large expanse of mud around the lake edge as the water drops. Scan it from the road.

Eastern delta DEVECIUŞAĞI AND YUMURTALIK BAY A large complex of lagoons, surrounded by saltmarsh and mudflats, divided by a dune ridge

White Stork

covered with open pinewoods – an excellent area and worth a visit if you have time to explore. It is best for waders and in spring when Broad-billed Sandpipers and Red-necked Phalaropes occur in good numbers. YILANKALE A castle commanding an excellent view over the Ceyhan plain with breeding Little Swifts, Blue Rock Thrushes and Rock Nuthatches. Wallcreepers can occur in winter. It is signposted off the E-90, 3–4 km west of Ceyhan and 3 km south of the road. Garages on either side of the junction help to identify the turn, but the castle (on a hill in the river plain) is clearly visible. There is a small charge for parking but otherwise access is free. In spring, a morning visit can be good for watching migration.

BELEN AND TOPBOĞAZI GEÇİDİ

36°30N 36°12E

Lying opposite the Çukurova delta, across the Gulf of İskenderun, the 750-m-high Belen Pass provides a passageway through the Nur Dağları range for birds following the migration corridor up the Rift Valley around the eastern Mediterranean. Thousands of raptors, storks, pelicans and Spoonbills have been recorded here in autumn, but there is still very little known about how and where birds cross the Gulf; the spring migration, although recorded in the Çukurova, is virtually unstudied here.

TIMING

The only detailed information is from August and September 1976, with White Storks occurring in good numbers from early August. From what is known at other migration watchpoints, movement probably continues into November, especially of the larger birds of prey. The bulk of the migration tended to occur – or to be most easily seen – between 10 a.m. and 1 p.m. A visit at any time from mid-March–mid-May could be productive.

SPECIES

Counts in 1976 were: White Pelican (6200), Black Stork (3300), White Stork (83000), Spoonbill (590), Honey Buzzard (16,000), Black Kite (500), Egyptian Vulture (870), Short-toed Eagle (730), Levant Sparrowhawk (2950) and Booted Eagle (590).

ACCESS

The 'best' place to watch migration still has to be established. In autumn the birds seem to prefer the north-eastern side of the pass, but as the pass itself is 10 km across at its widest and the mountains present no great barrier on days of good upcurrents, where they cross is probably controlled by the weather and their starting point.

Choosing a good place to watch from is therefore largely a matter of luck. The 1976 count site was described as 'the head of a short steep-sided ridge in the centre of the pass above and just west of Belen, at about 600 m'. Another possibility is to drive up to the pass and 400 m beyond it take the track which goes off to the left on a right-hand bend. This leads up the mountainside (although you can only drive a short distance) where there are various possible viewpoints.

BLACK-SEA COAST

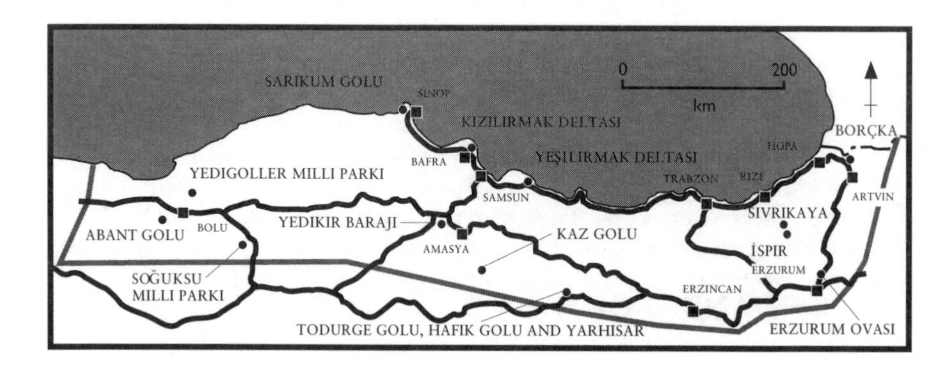

The Black-Sea coastlands are quite unlike any other region of Turkey. Uplands dominate and run in an almost unbroken chain from hills in the west to the impressive Pontic Alps in the east. Moisture-laden winds off the Seack Sea hitting these mountains create a mild wet climate on the northern slopes. This equable climate is good for farming – between highly populated Rize and the Georgian border more than 50 per cent of the land is cultivated. Farther inland the steep mountainsides are heavily afforsted, with alpine vegetation at higher altitudes.

Birdwatching in the region is varied and exciting with the extensive delta of the Kızılırmak at its centre. In the mountains in the north-east the Caucasian Black Grouse is the most elusive yet sought-after speciality, and birds of prey are common – particularly when their numbers are augmented by tens of thousands of migrating birds in spring and autumn.

Typical and in many cases special birds of the region include Caspian Snowcock, Black Woodpecker, Barred, Marsh and Green Warblers, Mountain Chiffchaff, Red-breasted and Semi-collared Flycatchers, Twite and Scarlet Rosefinch.

Abant Gölü

40°38N 31°29E

A river valley with mixed woods south of the old Istanbul–Ankara road (E-80) west of Bolu. The river valley between the main road and the lake can be excellent for birds and holds one of the most westerly known populations of Green Warblers. Other birds recorded in this area, most of which probably breed, include Honey Buzzard, Black Stork, Golden Eagle, Black Woodpecker and Krüper's Nuthatch.

TIMING

Visit in May and June when the birds are singing and easiest to find.

SPECIES

- *Collared Flycatcher* Occurs on migration
- *Bullfinch* An endemic subspecies which is not often seen in Turkey.

ACCESS

The road to Abant is signposted 12 km west of Bolu. The road follows the river valley which for the first 12.5 km is wide and open. After Dereceören, the valley narrows and the sides become steeper and more heavily wooded. Birdwatching in the trees along the riverside anywhere from here onwards can be productive.

YEDİGÖLLER MİLLİ PARKI

40°58N 31°45E

Few birdwatchers visit the extensive mature mixed forests in and around Yedigöller national park yet these are full of promise. The park lies in gently mountainous terrain north of Bolu. The park is popular with locals, so avoid weekends and holidays.

TIMING

A visit in spring should be rewarding with Grey-headed, Black and Middle Spotted Woodpeckers, Green Warbler and Red-breasted Flycatcher all present. The roads into the park can be inaccessible in wet weather.

SPECIES

- *Raven* On the rocky crags above the forest.
- *Honey Buzzard, Goshawk and Buzzard* Seen on in June and probably breed. Several other birds of prey probably occur.
- *Marsh Tit* Common here, in Turkey this species is restricted to the Black-Sea coastlands.

ACCESS

The park can be approached on stone tracks from north of Mengen in the east (50 km) or from Bolu in the south-west (42 km): both routes are well signposted. The Mengen road has the better surface and approaches

Black Vulture

Yedigöller from the valley below, the last few kilometres following a narrow river valley. The Bolu road approaches the forest from higher up, with excellent views over large areas of forest from several points – the last one, less than 1 km inside the park entrance, has a wooden platform and – watch for displaying birds of prey in spring.

SOĞUKSU MİLLİ PARKI, KIZILCAHAMAM

40°28N 32°29E

The Soğuksu national park is 86 km north of Ankara, south-east of Kızılcahamam, and includes steep rocky hills, forested mountain slopes, river valleys and open scrub. This variety of habitats, together with its position between the vast forests of the Black Sea and the steppes of Central Anatolia results in a good range of species: Black Vulture is of particular note.

South of Kızılcahamam, where the road crosses the Kirmir river, a rubbish dump on the riverside includes carcases from the abattoir and these attract scavenging raptors – Black Kites and Egyptian Vultures have been seen here and Black Storks are regular.

TIMING

Best from April–September; particularly good for migrant raptors in September – virtually every species that occurs in Turkey has been recorded here and a large proportion of them breed.

SPECIES

- *Woodpeckers* Seven species have been recorded of which Wryneck, Grey-headed (only one record) and Black are the most difficult to see.
- *Short-toed Treecreeper* More common than Treecreeper.
- *Warblers* Include Wood (on migration), Bonelli's and Olivaceous.
- *Sombre Tit* Common, as are Hawfinch and Scarlet Rosefinch.

ACCESS

Turn off the E-89, Gerede–Ankara road into Kızılcahamam, following the yellow signs to Soğuksu. The park entrance is on the far side of the town and you may be asked to pay a small entrance fee; follow the road for 1.4 km from here to the park restaurant where the road forks. Turn right for the picnic area where Krüper's Nuthatch is regularly seen. Take the left fork for the circular route around the park. For 3.5 km the track climbs the mountainside in a series of hairpins and then arrives at a more open area with views to the south and a major track going off to the left which takes you out of the park. Go straight on and follow the road for a further 3.4 km, bearing left at the next fork. Eventually you will reach a ridge joining two peaks with excellent views over the forest to the north and north-east. This is probably the best area for Black Vultures and general raptor-watching. The track continues round the park.

For the abattoir, drive south out of Kızılcahamam and look for the petrol stations on the right, just after the bridge. From here you can observe the river and the dump without disturbing the birds. You can cross the river to get closer, but the birds generally use an area which is screened and visible only from the garages.

Sarikum Gölü

42°01N 34°51E

A small lake lying on the Black-Sea coast 20 km west of Sinop. Around the lake are dunes, grazing marsh, reedbeds, coniferous plantations and extensive areas of mature deciduous forest. Little known by birdwatchers.

TIMING

Sarıkum should be good for birds at any time of year, but a visit in spring would be best for the woodland areas. White-tailed Eagle and Smew have both been seen in winter.

SPECIES

- Great White Egret (winter), Lesser Spotted Eagle, Hobby, White-fronted Goose (winter), Greylag (winter), Red-crested Pochard, Ferruginous Duck, Lesser Spotted Woodpecker and Hawfinch.

ACCESS

Follow the coast road west from Sinop and take the right turn signposted 'Sarıkum 3 km' along the eastern side of the lake; this gives the best views of the water areas. Drive through Sarıkum: keep bearing left and you eventually reach a bridge. Birdwatch in the dunes for migrants. Continue over the bridge and after 600 m turn left. This track runs through woodland and finally peters out at an area of grazing marsh.

Kizilirmak Deltasi

41°40N 36°00E

The Kızılırmak is the longest river in Turkey, and its delta, lying between Sinop and Samsun, is the largest and most important wetland on the Black-Sea coast. About 80 per cent of the land is farmed traditionally with the remainder – more than 10,000 ha – natural habitats. The main area of interest lies east of the Kızılırmak river, with large areas inaccessible.

Sarıkamış grazing marsh, flooded in winter and early spring and – passage waders and wagtails. **Cernek Gölü** a large lake surrounded by reed- and sedgebeds – ducks, passage terns and Little Gulls, waders in spring and autumn. **Reedbeds** breeding Common Cranes, Dalmatian Pelicans and Spoonbills. **Dunes** migrants, breeding Stone-curlews. **Liman Gölü** diving ducks and sawbills in winter. **Yörükler** flooded forest with breeding Black Storks, Lesser Spotted Eagles, Nightjars, Rollers, woodpeckers, Golden Orioles and Red-breasted Flycatchers. **Kızılırmak River** sand and gravel banks, and migrants, nesting plovers and terns.

TIMING

Birdwatching in the wetland areas is best between dawn and about 10 a.m. – after this the sun makes viewing very difficult. Migration periods provide exciting birdwatching and the greatest variety of species. In April/May these include Honey Buzzard, Red-footed Falcon, Common Crane, Broad-billed Sandpiper, Red-necked Phalarope, White-winged Black Tern, Citrine Wagtail, Red-throated Pipit and Rose-coloured Starling. August and September are good for waders, depending on water

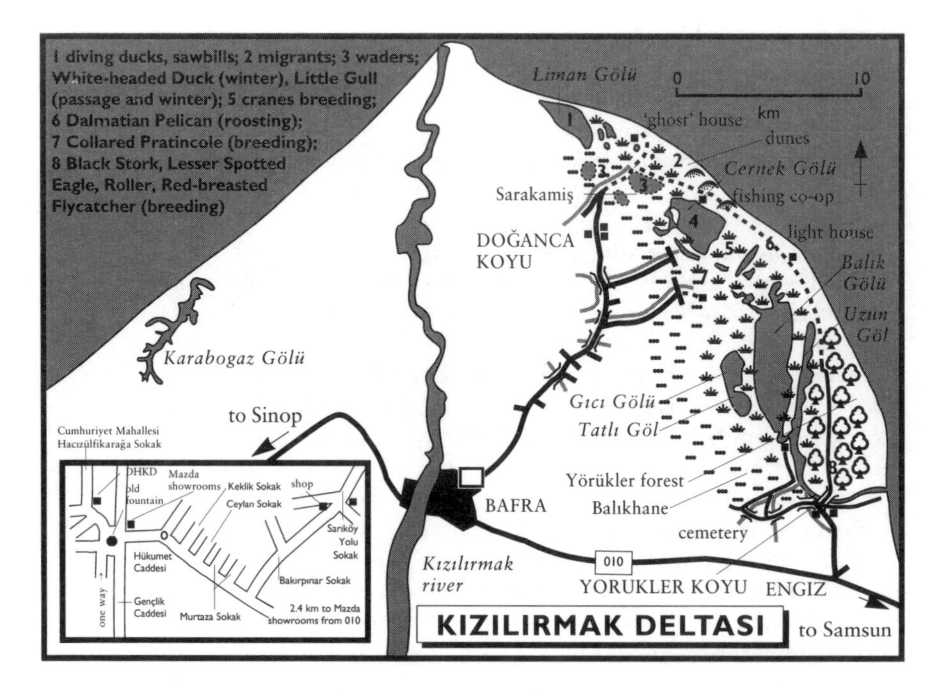

levels. In winter there are large numbers of wildfowl, Black-throated Divers on the sea, a good chance of Smew and Great Black-headed Gull.

SPECIES

- More than 300 species have been recorded in the delta with numerous Turkish rarities (including Bewick's Swan, Wilson's Phalarope, Olive-backed Pipit and Little Bunting) and about 120 breeding species.
- *Dalmatian Pelican* Present all year.
- *Bittern* Breeds in good numbers and is easy to see in spring.
- *Great White Egret* As many as 200 in November–March.
- *Osprey* Summers and has bred in the past.
- *Little Gull* Present September–March, with thousands in late winter.
- *White-headed Duck* Present September–June with the highest numbers in February/March on passage. Could breed.
- *Black-winged Stilt, Collared Pratincole, Gull-billed Tern* All breed.

ACCESS

Because of the large number of roads and tracks it is easy to get lost in the delta. The best way to get around the area is a 4-wheel drive vehicle or a bicycle, but a car is adequate when the tracks are dry. The delta is open at all times, but before you visit go to the DHKD office in Bafra for up-to-date information on access and what birds have been seen. The office is at 16 Cumhuriyet Mahallesi Hacızülfikarağa Sokak (*see* map), tel (in Turkey) 0362 542 5522, fax 0362 542 6177 and is open 9 a.m.–6 p.m. on weekdays and 1 p.m.–6 p.m. at weekends. For advance information write to Sunay Demircan, DHKD Kızılırmak Delta Project, PK 38, Bafra 55410 Samsun.

Kızılırmak Delta east East of the river turn north into Bafra from the main Samsun–Sinop road at the turning marked 'Şehir', by the Hilmi Bayrak mosque. From the Mazda showrooms follow the directions on the map. The road leads to Sarakamış, Liman Gölü (a fair walk from the Ghost House), Cernek Gölü and extensive areas of scrub-covered dunes. In spring the two tracks running east from the Bafra–Doğanca road provide views over pools and areas of wet grazing marsh.

Balık Gölü/Yörükler forest Leave the Samsun–Sinop road at Engiz (or Ballıca), turning north at the grey-blue minaret next to the main road. After about 50 m turn left, signposted to Yörükler, and after a further 3 km you reach a crossroads at Yörükler village; turn left for Balık Gölü and right for the forest. BALIK GÖLÜ from the crossroads drive 1.6 km to the next canal, cross it and turn right. Cross a larger canal and turn right again. Along the track are occasional views of the lake, and good areas of scrub. YÖRÜKLER FOREST from the crossroads follow the road through the village and turn left opposite the mosque. The road crosses a major canal and enters the forest where there are various tracks to explore. You can continue north on the main track to Cernek Gölü, but it is often wet and impassable immediately south of the lighthouse. **Kızılırmak River** Before and after migration the delta can be generally quiet and it can be productive to drive along one of the two tracks which run one either side of the river to the sea. It is easiest to start from where the main Samsun–Sinop road crosses the river; here you can choose which side according to the light. On the east side, tracks lead from the mouth of the river along the coast to Liman Gölü. **Karaboğaz Gölü, Kızılırmak Delta west** Travelling west on the Samsun–Sinop road, turn right *c.* 100 m after crossing the river, towards İkiztepe Orenyeri, Sahilkent and Emenli. After 3.4 km turn right again at a canal with an unfinished bridge standing in the

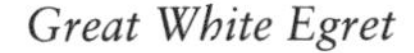

Great White Egret

middle. 2.7 km further on take a left turn to Emenli and eventually this track settles to follow the Emenli canal – keep the water on your left. An area of rice fields alongside the track can be good for birds when wet. The track ends at the north end of Karabogaz Gölü. The lake can be checked from the fisheries buildings, or you can hire a boat with the local fishermen to explore the area more thoroughly. The surrounding scrub is good for passerines on migration. Best visited early in the morning.

YEŞİLIRMAK DELTASI

41°17N 36°50E

A largely drained river delta on the coast east of Samsun. The Yeşilırmak no longer has the large wetlands of the nearby Kızılırmak, but still has areas of interest – particularly the paddyfields in the east.

TIMING

Herons are a speciality of the Yeşilırmak with particularly large numbers in September when migrating flocks can be seen.

SPECIES

- *Hobby* Breeds and can be very common on passage.
- *Cattle Egret* One of two sites in Turkey where they are seen regularly.
- *River Warbler* Has been recorded twice in June, and the delta is probably an important area for migrating passerines.

ACCESS

The delta is a mass of roads and tracks, few of which are marked on any map. There may be remaining wetland areas to be discovered, but it is less frustrating to head for the eastern side of the delta at Terme. On the coast road from Samsun, pass the turn into Terme at S,ehir Merkezi, and a few metres farther on turn left along a made-up track which follows the west bank of a wide canal. Follow this track down to the sea (walk the last few hundred metres) to sandbars at the river mouth for herons, gulls and terns. Alternatively, leave the canal where the made-up road leaves the top of the bank. Bear right when you have a choice and then turn right after crossing a small canal. This track takes you down to the sea and dunes.

YEDIKIR BARAJI

40°48N 35°35E

This 593-ha reservoir lies on the northern edge of the Central Plateau, north of Amasya, in an open landscape of farmed and uncultivated steppe, backed by mountains. Although Yedikır is only just over the mountains from the Kızılırmak delta, the range of species has a distinctly Anatolian flavour with birds such as Greater Flamingo, Ruddy Shelduck and Penduline Tit. In 1989 it was declared a 'bird paradise', fenced and protected from hunting. It is exceptionally easy to work, but do avoid the weekends.

TIMING

Probably worth a visit at any time of year with the greatest variety of species – including waders – during migration.

Moustached Warbler

SPECIES
- *Osprey* On passage in autumn.
- *Short-eared Owl* Hunts along the reservoir banks in winter.
- *Calandra Lark* Common in the surrounding steppe.

ACCESS
The reservoir is signposted off the Samsun–Amasya road just south of Suluova; follow the signs to the lake, a drive of about 7 km. The road follows a high bank round three sides of the reservoir, giving excellent views. Shallow pools on the outside of the reservoir in the south and south-west can be observed from the bankFor closer views, tracks go down the outside of the bank at two points on the south and east sides.

Kaz Gölü

40°17N 36°10E
A 300-ha reed-filled lake between Tokat and Zile. In areas with a good variety of vegetation – standing and cut reed, open water and scrub – 'sit and wait' birdwatching can be productive, particularly for crakes, rails and small birds. It is seldom visited by birdwatchers and will probably soon disappear as a result of extensive drainage works.

TIMING
Little and Baillon's Crakes and Bluethroat have been recorded on spring passage. Moustached and Great Reed Warblers and Penduline Tit all breed.

SPECIES
- *Squacco Heron* The most common heron in a reedbed colony.

ACCESS
The reedbed is visible north of the minor Zile–Pazar road. A track along a bank east of the reedbed is the best place for birdwatching, its entrance lies 25 km east of Zile and about 500 m west of Hacıpınar. A variety of habitats along the track includes tall trees, cultivated and grazing land, reedbed and ditch. In winter water levels can be appreciably higher.

TÖDÜRGE GÖLÜ, HAFIK AND YARHISAR

39°53N 37°30E

In its upper reaches, east of Sivas, the Kızılırmak River is fed by several tributaries running through meadows and farmland are creating a series of seasonal wetlands and lakes.

TIMING

April–June is best for the breeding birds with Red-necked Grebe, Ruddy Shelduck, Red-crested Pochard, Black Kite, Crane and Citrine Wagtail among the highlights. Mid-August–October should have a variety of waders, and later large numbers of wildfowl.

SPECIES

◆ *Black-winged Pratincole* A recent record in September.
◆ *Common Crane* Several pairs breed with 200-plus birds in autumn.
◆ *Great Bustard* Has been seen in recent years and may breed nearby.
◆ *Gull-billed and White-winged Black Terns* Flocks on passage.

ACCESS

The main E-88 Ankara–Erzurum road passes through the area. There are three known centres of interest (*see* map) and other places probably remain to be discovered. **Hafik** From the west, turn left following the signs into town and then left at the T-junction. Take the next right, signposted to Gölgazinosu (nightclub); after the mosque the road forks – both lead to the lake with the left turn giving raised views. Back on the E-88 farther to the east a road heads south over the Kızılırmak and leads to an area of floodplain; this is worth investigating, particularly in spring. **Yarhisar** Lies south of the E-88 *c.* 10 km east of Hafik. The first lake,

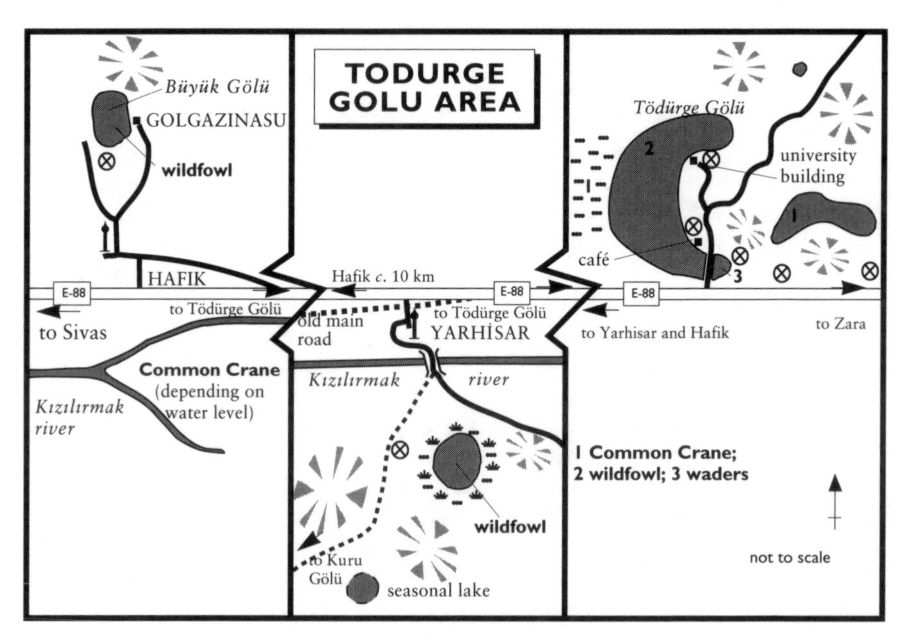

although less than 2 km from the main road, is only visible after crossing the Kızılırmak. The seasonal lake marked farther south may hold water and birds in spring and, if it does Kuru Gölü may be worth investigating. Kuru is marked on maps and (according to locals) lies farther along this track, but you will have to walk. **Tödürge** The main water areas are visible from the road with access as shown on the map. The wetlands east of the main lake is usually the best area.

SIVRIKAYA, KAÇKAR DAĞLARI

40°40N 40°44 E

The Kaçkar mountains form a high and formidable barrier between the north-eastern Anatolian plateau and the Black Sea, connecting in the east with the Caucasus. Caucasian Black Grouse, which is restricted to this area and the Caucasus, occurs in the dense Rhododendron scrub on the northern slopes. The mountains are a popular trekking area, and several days' walking and camping in the mountains is the best way to see the birds and other wildlife.

TIMING

May and June are best for Caucasian Black Grouse, when the males are displaying, sometimes in groups of 10 or more.

SPECIES

- *Lammergeier and Griffon Vulture* Regular in the Sivrikaya area.
- *Caspian Snowcock* Most easily seen above Ovitdağı Geçidi.
- *Shore Lark, Alpine Accentor, Chough, Alpine Chough, Snow Finch, Twite, Rock Bunting* All common in rocky alpine areas.
- *Wallcreeper* Seen regularly on the road up to the pass.
- *Red-fronted Serin and Crimson-winged Finch* Typical birds of high altitude.

ACCESS

Sivrikaya is a small village on the north side of the mountains, on the Rize–İspir road. Above the village are conifer plantations and large areas of Rhododendron scrub, with mountain pastures and bare crags above the treeline. Access can be a problem before June, with snow and/or landslips sometimes blocking the pass from İspir to the south. If in doubt, approach Sivrikaya from the north.

Between the village and the pass there is a variety of habitats, and a walk can be productive. For species such as Marsh and Green Warblers, Mountain Chiffchaff and Scarlet Rosefinch take the track which goes out from behind the mosque, and cross the stream to explore the meadows, rhododendron scrub and conifers on the other side. If the weather is clear and you can see across the valley try looking for the Caucasian Black Grouse from the road. 5 km south of Sivrikaya is an area of Rhododendron scrub on the west side of the valley; scan the grassy areas around the bushes and with persistence you will see them. If conditions are right this can be the easiest and best way to see the birds. The crags and screes here are also favoured by Caspian Snowcock and Wallcreeper.

The alternative for Caucasian Black Grouse is to get higher up, above the conifers, and be on site for dawn, either by camping overnight or by climbing while it is still dark. The best known track starts at the cemetery, 800 m south of the mosque, and climbs the hill-side to the north-east. Follow the path uphill for about two hours and you arrive at a deep gully with Rhododendron scrub on both sides; this is a popular Caucasian Black Grouse area. When the weather is poor you should only attempt this walk with the help of a guide as it is east to get lost. Ask for Mustafa Sarı, the local guide, in the Sivrikaya coffee-house. You will have to pay for his services but he knows the mountains and the birds well. If accessible, a walk from Ovitdağı Geçidi up the mountains to the south can be excellent for mountain birds, with Caspian Snowcocks even heard and seen here at 3 p.m. on a hot September afternoon!

İSPİR

40°28N 41°00E

İspir is a village lying in the Çoruh river valley in the Kaçkar mountains. Many migrants pass over the mountains in spring and autumn, avoiding a long flight over the Black Sea by taking a route around its eastern shore, and then follow the river valley, which acts as a funnel and concentrates the birds still further. Any agricultural areas provide valuable places for birds to feed, but the orchards along the river between İspir and the Rize–Erzurum road can be especially productive. An even better reason for making a stop at İspir is to see the Griffon Vulture colony. There is also a good chance of Lammergeier and Black Vulture here.

TIMING

Roller, Semi-collared Flycatcher, Golden Oriole and Rose-coloured Starling are among the more regular migrants seen in spring.

SPECIES

- *Imperial Eagle, Blue Rock Thrush and Chough* and other mountain species may be seen near the vulture colony.

ACCESS

Approaching İspir from the west, turn left over the bridge and follow the Yusufeli road. After 5.5 km the road goes through a tunnel; park after the tunnel and the colony can be seen up on the crags to the right.

BORÇKA AND THE EASTERN PONTICS

41°20N 41°30E

The damp and mountainous terrain of the eastern Black Sea is possibly the best area in Turkey for watching migration. From Hopa to Rize the river valleys provide a relatively hospitable migration corridor between the Black Sea and the Caucasus, used each year by many thousands of migrating birds. Migration was first documented here in 1976 with a phenomenal 380,000 migrating raptors recorded, including 137,600 Honey Buzzards, 5775 Black Kites and 205,000 Steppe Buzzards. The

Egyptian Vulture

locals have known of this annual spectacle for generations and from Rize eastwards the tradition of trapping migrating Red-backed Shrikes to catch migrating Sparrowhawks, with which to hunt migrating Quail is still practised each autumn.

Migration can be seen from almost anywhere, but the Fırtına river mouth at Ardeşen, and Hopa have been productive in spring. For good numbers of birds in autumn, rain and low cloud are essential; on clear, sunny days the birds fly high and pass unseen.

Artvin, an amazing village built on the sheer mountain sides *c.* 30 km south of Borçka, is worth a stop to look at its rubbish dump – Lammergeiers are regular here – and the forests above the town hold Grey-headed Woodpeckers.

TIMING

Autumn visits should be worthwhile from August through till late November, with mid-September–mid-October probably the best time for seeing large numbers of birds. In late autumn the weather may prohibit access or at least limit the number of days on which birdwatching is possible. In spring April and May are probably best.

SPECIES

Many species use this migration route in large numbers but the raptors are undoubtedly the most impressive. As well as those already mentioned the following have all been recorded: Egyptian and Griffon Vultures, Short-toed Eagle, Marsh, Hen, Pallid and Montagu's Harriers, Goshawk, Sparrowhawk, Levant Sparrowhawk (largest numbers in spring – end of April), Long-legged Buzzard, Lesser Spotted, Spotted, Steppe, Imperial, Golden and Booted Eagles, Osprey, Lesser Kestrel, Red-footed Falcon, Hobby, Saker and Peregrine.

- ◆ *Bee-eater* Can be seen (and more often heard) in large numbers on migration along with many passerines.
- ◆ *White-backed Woodpecker* Occurs, probably in areas of mature forest on the mountainsides, probably only in small numbers.

ACCESS

The Çoruh river valley north of Borçka is a good place to start, if only to discover what the birds are doing before moving to your chosen spot.

This valley concentrates migrating birds in autumn, but wind direction plays a large part in the numbers of birds you will see – regular raptor-watchers consider westerlies to be most productive.

Entering Borçka from the Arhavi direction, take the right turn sign-posted to the hospital (Hastane), 900 m south of the bridge over the Çoruh. Follow the road uphill, bearing right when faced with a choice: it soon deteriorates into a rough stone track. The best viewpoint is 5.5 km from the main road, where there is a large open area to park. A short walk along a path to the end of the hill gives good views up the valley to the north, and also out to the west and south. However, a bulldozer working here in 1994 may have signalled a change.

Erzurum Ovasi

39°59N 41°15E

Erzurum, eastern Turkey's largest city, stands at 1950 m on an open plain surrounded by mountains. It is a bleak area with bitter, six-month winters and a summer too short for many crops or even trees to grow. The vast plain north of the town, approximately 520 km^2, is traditionally used for grazing livestock and was once largely marsh. Canals now drain much of it but several large areas of seasonal wetland remain, attracting a variety of birds to stop on migration and a few to nest. The mosquitoes can be particularly vicious here in summer!

TIMING

Spring is likely to be best, when water levels should be high. In May, thousands of White-winged Black Terns can be seen, with an amazing 15,000–20,000 counted on 13 May 1993. Herons and waders seem to be commonest in early spring and so are probably largely passage birds.

SPECIES

- *Purple Heron* Sseen in good numbers in early spring.
- *Saker* Seen at Şikköyü in June
- *Ruddy Shelduck* Large flocks of more than 1500 in June.
- *Quail* Very common in late June, it presumably breeds.
- *Common Crane* Breeds.
- *Lapwing* The most common nesting wader.
- *Armenian Gull* Seen regularly, usually in small numbers.
- *Citrine Wagtail* A few pairs breed.

ACCESS

Drive from Erzurum on the Artvin road until the main drainage canal crosses it. From here you can scan the area either by birdwatching from the road, or by walking in either direction along the northern side of the canal. To the east you soon have to turn north and walk parallel with the road along the edge of a side canal. To the west it is a fair and sometimes muddy walk to the southern Sitavuk marshes, but the views are good.

The area which generally holds most water and birds is near Şikköyü, reached via a left turn off the Artvin road on the outskirts of Erzurum.

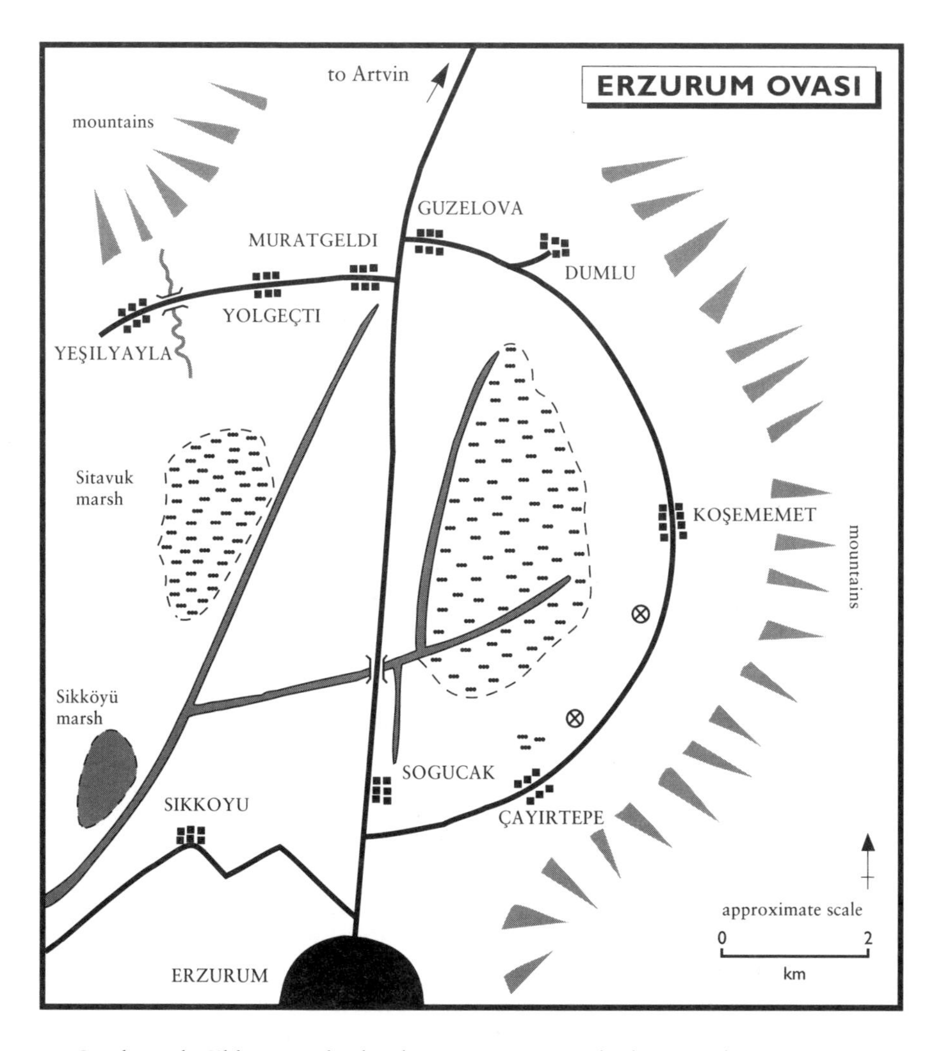

Go through Şikköyü and take the most important-looking track across the fields to the canal (lying to the north-west), and cross the canal to the marshes on the other side. Farther north along the Artvin road, a right turn to Çayırtepe skirts the eastern edge of the marsh and rejoins the main road at Güzelova. The best views of the marsh can be obtained between Çayırtepe and Köşememet. From Güzelova head back south on the main road towards Erzurum and turn right towards Yeşilyayla. After Yolgeçti stop where the road crosses a small stream (nearer Yeşilyayla than Yolgeçti), and walk along the western (Yeşilyayla) side of the stream for reasonable views of the Sitavuk marshes to the south. NB A major new road which was being built to the north of Erzurum in 1994 cuts through the southern end of the plain near Şikköyü and may have affected the marshes in this area.

I am grateful to John Faldborg for all the information on this site.

CENTRAL ANATOLIA

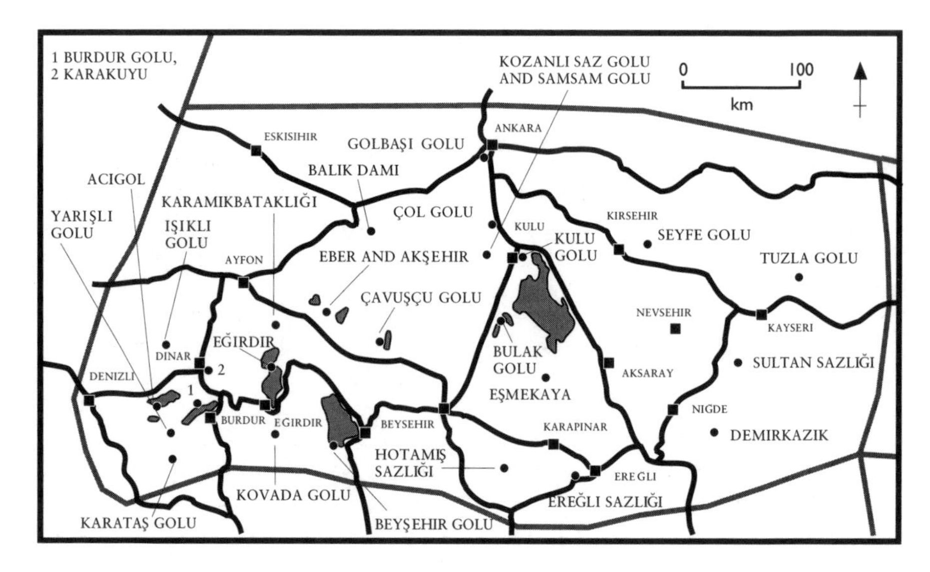

Central Anatolia is an elevated basin of open, rolling country surrounded by mountain ranges. In the south-west mountains dominate, but on the central plateau the landscape is very open with seemingly endless fields of crops interspersed with original steppe, and the few towns and villages clustered along streams, sheltered from the weather by belts of poplars and willows.

The region's wetlands are typically shallow, with widely fluctuating water levels and thus a high salinity. Because of their saltiness many wetlands are also very open – with no fringing vegetation. The wetlands are created by the winter and spring rains, with maximum levels in May rapidly dropping during the hot, dry summer, sometimes drying up altogether. This even applies to Tuz Gölü, which at 1100 km^2 dominates the plateau.

In spring many migrants pass through these wetlands with large numbers of species such as Garganey, Ruff, Little Stint and White-winged Black Tern. On the saltlakes breeding birds include Mediterranean and Slender-billed Gulls and Gull-billed Terns, and occasional Greater Flamingos, whilst those wetlands with extensive reedbeds may hold species such as Black-necked Grebe, White-headed Duck and Whiskered Tern. By September extensive areas of very shallow water and soft mud provide ideal conditions for feeding waders – including Greater Sand Plover and Broad-billed Sandpiper, if you're lucky. On the barren fringes Asian Short-toed Larks (*Calandrella cheleensis niethammeri*, an endemic subspecies occurring only in Central Anatolia) are very common – Lesser Short-toed Larks, which they resemble, do not occur here. In milder winters (in cold winters even the saltlakes freeze over), these wetlands hold tens of thousands of wildfowl. Other characteristic birds of this region are White-fronted Goose (large numbers in winter), Lesser Kestrel, Red-footed Falcon (a common migrant), Calandra and Short-toed Larks and Citrine Wagtail (a migrant that breeds on some wetlands).

Işikli Gölü

38°16N 29°55E

A fresh-water lake at the spring of the Büyük Menderes river, south-east of Çivril. This site provides a mix of lake, marsh and mountain birds, with such highlights as Spotted Eagle and Red-fronted Serin. After a wet winter, there are marshes in the north-west and south-east.

TIMING

The area is excellent for birds all year, with huge numbers of waterbirds in winter and a good variety of breeding species.

SPECIES

- *Breeding* Black-necked Grebe, Little Bittern, Squacco and Purple Herons, Ruddy Shelduck, Ferruginous Duck, Griffon Vulture, Golden Eagle, Gull-billed and Whiskered Terns and White-throated Robin.
- *Migration* Glossy Ibis, Red-footed Falcon and Little Crake.
- *Winter* Pygmy Cormorant, White-fronted Goose, Red-crested Pochard and Ferruginous Duck.

ACCESS

The lake is 26 km north of Dinar on the Çivril road. The best birdwatching is in the south and east, with the lake easily watched from the road between Gümüsşu and Beydilli, and from a hüyük 2 km north of Gümüsşu, in the south-east. For closer views of the lake and reedy islands in the southern corner, turn off the main road in Gümüsşu, head south-west past the mosque, and after 6 km cross a wide channel flowing into the lake. This waterway is excellent for waders and herons and tracks down both banks make the area very easy to observe. The tracks continue for several kilometres in both directions along the lake shore.

The lake and marshes in the north-west seem to be full of birds yet are frustratingly inaccessible. However, 6 km south of Gümüsşu around Gokgöl, an area of seasonally flooded wetland, much of it reedbed, can be excellent when wet with some pools easily viewed from the road. The road to İşaklı, 3.8 km south of Gümüsşu, runs along the northern edge of this area and may provide possibilities for birdwatching.

Karakuyu Gölü

38°06N 30°15E

A small L-shaped lake immediately south-east of Dinar encircled by motorways and a railway line. The lake itself is enclosed by a bank topped with a good track; this is excellent for observing the whole area but is also a legacy of drainage schemes. The southern part of the lake is covered with extensive but sparse reed growth; water levels fluctuate widely. This lake has been largely dry in recent years (although it was wet in spring 1995) so has been seldom visited by birdwatchers and little is known about what birds occur here. It is so easy to get to and to work that it is worth a look in passing.

SPECIES

A typical range of waterbirds; birds seen on one visit in March included Great White Egret, Pintail, Garganey, Long-legged Buzzard, Ruff, Snipe, Black-tailed Godwit and Little Gull.

ACCESS

Karakuyu is most easily reached from the 650 road which runs down the east side of the area to Keçirborlu and the lake can be seen from this road. Three access tracks make a full circuit of the whole area very straightforward. The description below starts from the northernmost of these.

Travelling from the north look for a minor track crossing the main highway with the left turn leading to Burunkaya village. Turn right and follow this for 1 km across open fields, turning right again before reaching some buildings clustered around the railway line. 2.5 km farther on, cross a small canal and turn left towards the lake, across the railway line. On reaching the raised track around the lake you can circuit the area to left or right. The right-hand track runs along or near the lake shore for 9 km before rejoining the main road 6.5 km south of the Burunkaya turn. The left-hand track also follows the lake shore and passes an area of rough marsh outside the retaining bank which can hold a variety of waders. After 5 km the track rejoins the highway at a small village. This turning is marked by a green DSİ sign (DSİ Karakuyu Depolaması) 2 km south of Burunkaya. Some of the tracks, particularly those across the farmland at the northern end of the lake, may be impassable after rain.

ACIGÖL

37°49N 29°52E

This is the second most saline lake in Turkey – second to Tuz Gölü which is eight times saltier than sea water. Its dazzling blue-green water, fringed in the north by a wide band of salt, can be seen from the Denizli–Dinar road between Çardak and Dazkırı. Springs along the southern edge of the lake create fresh-water marshes and the best areas for birds.

TIMING

Greater Flamingos nested in 1993 and appear to breed here irregularly. Records from the 1970s and 1980s indicate that the largest numbers of birds use the area in the post-breeding period with 1800 Black-necked Grebes, 4000 Common Cranes, 1700 Little Stints and 6000 Avocets.

SPECIES

- *Golden Eagle* Breeds in the surrounding mountains.
- *Common Crane* Most often seen from the main Çardak–Dazkırı road.
- *Great Bustard* May still breed in the surrounding steppe, particularly in the north-east, although there are herds of sheep and goats everywhere.
- *Marsh Sandpiper* Regular on spring passage.

ACCESS

It is possible to drive right round the lake on surfaced tracks. The best views are from the track along the south-east side, with the best birdwatching in the eastern half of the lake where there are fresh-water springs, between Başmakçı and Gemiçköyü. The rocky slopes south of this track hold species such as Eagle Owl, White-throated Robin, Finsch's Wheatear, Blue Rock Thrush, Sombre Tit, Rock Nuthatch, Red-fronted Serin, and Cirl and Rock Buntings.

South of Acıgöl, surrounded by mountains, lies the small shallow lake of Akgöl (or Çorak Gölü – 37°41N 29°45E). More often than not this is dry and birdless but it can be worth a look in wet years. Access round the lake is improving by the year and most roads in the area are not yet marked on the maps. From Acıgöl (via Çaltı), turn left on reaching the lake and drive along the northern shore. The birds tend to be rather distant, using the deepest and least disturbed area of water in the south-east where access and viewing are difficult.

Burdur Gölü

37°43N 30°15E

A classically beautiful lake of the south-west Anatolian lake district with steeply shelving shores and a backdrop of mountains. This is currently the most important site in the world for White-headed Ducks with huge numbers here from September–April – the record was 10,927 in January 1991.

At the south-western end of the lake is the last remnant of what was once an extensive area of marshes, now virtually all drained and farmed but worth a quick look in passing. If there is any water Ruddy Shelducks can be numerous here.

TIMING

For White-headed Duck visit September–April but there is a good variety of birds to be seen on and around the lake all year.

SPECIES

- *Black-necked Grebe* Thousands in autumn.
- *Pochard and Coot* Along with White-headed Duck these are the most numerous waterfowl in winter – more than 85,000 Coots were counted in January 1989.

ACCESS

The lake is 130 km north of Antalya, just north of Burdur. Birdwatching is best along the north-west side, from the road and various tracks. The band of farmland and steppe between the lake and mountains can hold holds such birds as Quail, Bee-eater, Calandra Lark and Lesser Grey Shrike.

For the marshes, from the Burdur–Yes,ilova road take the Yazıköy turning round the southern end of the lake and the first left after the second bridge, signposted to Kumluca. In Kumluca (3 km) the road forks to the right and goes uphill; after 300 m park on the left and look out east over the remaining marshes.

Yarışli Gölü

37°34N 29°58E

A small, attractive lake west of Burdur and north of Kocapınar. The water is shallow and saline, with no emergent vegetation, and is favoured by Greater Flamingos, dabbling ducks and waders. There are meadows and arable land around the gently shelving lake shores in the south and west, rising to hills and low mountains. This is a small site and easy to work.

TIMING

At its best in winter and early spring.

SPECIES

- *Ruddy Shelduck* Can number more than 1000 in early spring.
- *Calandra Lark, Woodlark and Rock Sparrow* Occur around the lake.

ACCESS

Yarişli Gölü lies north of the Burdur–Yeşilova road. Turn north at Kocapınar on the road signposted to Sazak and Harmanlı. After *c.* 1 km take the first track off to the right and follow this to its end (1.1 km) where there is a good view of the whole lake. More distant views are possible from the road on the western and northern sides.

Karataş Gölü

37°23N 29°58E

South-west of Burdur on the Burdur–Tefenni road. A relatively small and shallow fresh-water lake with areas of reed along the western and southern shores, surrounded by open arable and steppe with few trees.

TIMING

The lake is best known for its wintering waterfowl.

SPECIES

- *White-fronted and Greylag Geese* Both occur in winter
- *Short-toed and Golden Eagles, Long-legged Buzzard and Lesser Kestrel* Are among the many birds of prey which hunt around the lake.
- *Great Bustard* May still occur in the area.
- *Calandra Lark* Common around the lake.

ACCESS

The lake is perhaps most easily worked from the south, if the roads are dry. From Karamanlı drive north towards Burdur and after 6.7 km turn right to Kılavuzlar. Continue along here for 4.4 km to where dirt tracks go off to the left at some farm buildings, leading down to the lake for views of the northern and central areas. For the southern end continue along the road to the brow of the hill (another 1.1 km) and turn left down a made-up track towards the lake.

The northern edge of the lake can be reached either on foot from the pumping station (in the south-east corner), or by returning to the main road and continuing towards Burdur to the next road junction, a crossroads with a garage. Turn right and drive as far as you can, walking the last section to the lake.

Greater Flamingo

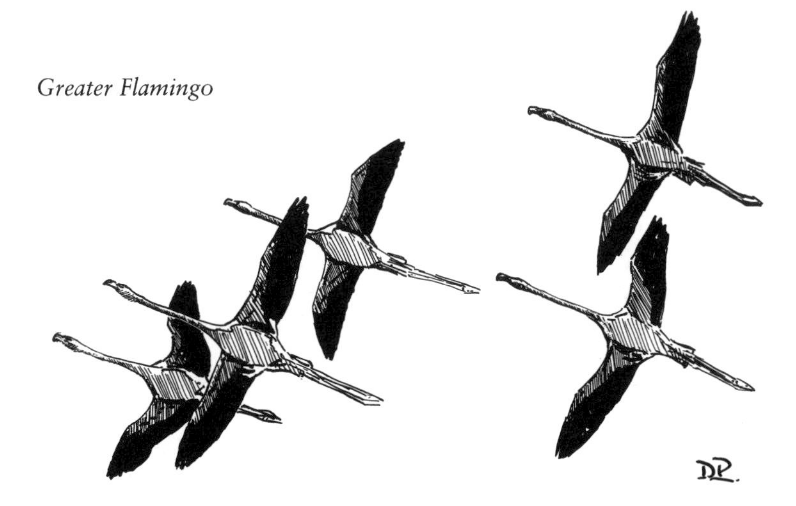

Gölhisar Gölü

37°08N 29°37E

A small lake and seasonal wetland in the south-west of Turkey's lake district, a few kilometres east of Gölhisar. Mountains and farmland surround the lake and drainage pipes dot the landscape. There is virtually no fringing vegetation. Avoid weekends if possible.

TIMING

This is another little-known site that may be good for migrants, particularly in spring. Visit in the morning for the best light.

SPECIES

- *Night Heron and Spoonbill* On migration.
- *Ruddy Shelduck and Spur-winged Plover* Breed.
- *Hen Harrier and Merlin* in winter and Osprey on passage.
- Migrating passerines, particularly pipits, wagtails and chats seem to be drawn to the hüyük, and Rock Nuthatch is resident here.

ACCESS

Turn south off the Çavdır–Gölhisar road at Yamadı and follow this road through the village and round the edge of the hills, bearing right when faced with a choice. After 3 km a rough track goes off to the right to a hüyük giving excellent views over the lake.

Eğirdir Gölü

38°00N 30°54E

This is the second largest fresh-water lake in south-western Anatolia, with astonishingly blue-green water, and steep rocky shores rising to mountains, 35 km north of Isparta. It is figure-of-eight shaped, with the area north of the central bottle-neck of greatest interest, with marshes and reedbeds. Seasonally flooded fields in the north-east can be good in late winter and early spring for waders and, if you are lucky, Great Bustards.

Mountain birds, including Shore Lark, White-throated Robin and Red-fronted Serin can be seen on the mountains nearby to the north-west.

TIMING

In winter the lake is used by good numbers of waterbirds with Tufted Duck and Coot in their thousands. For the greatest variety of birds, particularly passerines, visit in late spring/early summer (May–July).

SPECIES

- *Squacco Heron and Little Egret* In the reedbeds and marshes.
- *Egyptian and Griffon Vultures, Short-toed and Golden Eagles* Over the mountains around the lake.
- *Whiskered Tern* Over the marshes in spring.
- *Shrikes* Many nest in the old trees along the road near Ortayazı.

ACCESS

The lake is easily observed from the road along the northern and western shores. In the north-east a road to the right signposted to Aşağı Tırtar goes across an area of marsh which can be full of migrating Ruff in spring.

Mountain birds can be seen along the ridge at the pass over Karakus Dağ, on the road to Şuhut in the north-west.

Kovada Gölü

37°38N 30°53E

A seldom-visited national park a few kilometres south of Eğirdir Gölü. The water is deep with steeply shelving shores, surrounded by mature mixed forests with juniper and box trees. A small area of shallow water with emergent vegetation at the northern end of the lake.

TIMING

This site is so little known that a visit at almost any time of year could find something new. A visit in spring would be best for the forest birds.

SPECIES

- *Griffon Vulture and Golden Eagle* Over the surrounding mountains.
- *Middle Spotted Woodpecker and Bonelli's Warbler* In the forest areas.

ACCESS

East of Eğirdir, take the turning to Kovada from the Eğirdir–Konya road. The park entrance is signposted with standard brown-and-yellow national park signs 1 km after Kırıntı. A surfaced track around the western and southern lake shores passes through mature forest and provides good views of the lake. The northern end may only be accessible on foot.

Beyşehir Gölü

37°45N 31°36E

Beyşehir is the largest fresh-water lake in Turkey, lying 90 km west of Konya, and is unusual in having several large islands. This is a beautiful lake with mountains in the west rising from the lake to give steep rocky shores covered by forests, scrub and arable land. In the south-west corner around Yeşildağ sizable marshes and reedbeds hold such species as Great Reed Warbler and Penduline Tit. These marshes are very little known and would be worth exploring.

SPECIES

◆ *Black-necked Grebe* Common on migration in early spring.

◆ *White Stork* A common nesting bird in Yeşildağ, with 25 nests in 1994.

◆ *White-tailed Eagle* Used to nest but is now seen mainly in winter.

◆ *Woodlark and Tawny Pipit* Nest on the sparsely vegetated slopes.

ACCESS

The best area for birdwatching is the west side of the lake. Approaching from the north via Şarkikaraağaç, take the turning signposted to Yenişar Bademli. This follows the water's edge and here you can scan the sheltered waters between the shore and the islands. At Yenişar Bademli the road turns away from the lake for a short distance. To return to the lake shore and reach the marshes at the southern end, make sure you pass the Jandarma (police station) in Yenis,ar Bademli and then follow the signs to Kurucuova; after this Beyşehir is signposted.

The marshes in the south-west corner can be observed from the main road on the east side of Yeşildağ, and from the hills to the east and west. A track from the cemetery in Yeşildağ leads into the marshes.

KARAMIKBATAKLIĞI

38°26N 30°50E

A fresh-water swamp in a wide valley between two mountains, 20–30 km south-west of Çay. The marsh is mainly reedbed with some areas of open water, surrounded by wet-meadows and farmland. When the southern end of the marshes is dry, large areas of reed are cut and temporarily grazed. Typical birds include Little Bittern and Bearded Tit in the reedbeds, Black-winged Stilt and Whiskered Tern on the marshes, and Black-necked Grebe and Ferruginous Duck on the marshy pools. Rocky steppe along the lower slopes of the mountains brings mountain species such as Golden Eagle, White-throated Robin and Chough close to the marsh on the southern and eastern sides.

TIMING

When water levels are high birdwatching can be good at any time of year.

SPECIES

◆ *Purple Heron* In good numbers on migration.

◆ *Lesser Kestrel* Nest in the surrounding villages, particularly Akkonak and Karamıkkaracaören, north of Orhaniye.

◆ *White-tailed, Spotted and Imperial Eagles* Occur in winter.

ACCESS

The surfaced track around the southern and eastern sides gives the best overview of the marsh and is also good for mountain birds. The north-west corner, between Devederesi and the lake, is tightly grazed and usually wet making it good for waders; both Broad-billed and Marsh Sandpipers are seen on migration. From Çay, take the Afyon road and turn left onto the minor road to Dinar. Take the next left to Akkonak, Orhaniye and Karamık for the eastern side of the marsh; continue straight on for the western side.

EBER GÖLÜ AND AKŞEHIR GÖLÜ

38°38N 31°10E AND 38°30N 31°28E

Two huge reedbeds between Çay and Akşehir. Both are important areas for birds with more than 275 species recorded, but birdwatching is extremely difficult because of the immensely tall (5–6 m) and dense reed. The greatest birdwatching attraction lies in the surrounding orchards and farmland which can hold thousands of migrating passerines in spring.

SPECIES

- *Dalmatian Pelican* May breed in small numbers at Akşehir.
- *Pygmy Cormorant* Flies between the two reedbeds at dawn and dusk.
- *Lesser Kestrel* Nests in several villages around the reedbeds.
- *White-throated Robin, Barred Warbler and Crimson-winged Finch* Breed on the scrubby hillsides to south.
- *Citrine Wagtail and River Warbler* Two less common spring migrants.

ACCESS

To watch birds over the reedbeds find somewhere with a view from the edges as the lake itself is inaccessible. Along the southern edge of Eber and western edge of Akşehir are orchards and farmland. These provide varied birdwatching – common migrants here include Nightingale, Redstart, Whinchat and Tree Pipit – and higher ground with many tracks from which to scan the reedbeds. Birds fly between Eber and Akşehir at dawn and dusk, the canal that links them, near the village of Taşköprü, can be a good vantage point for seeing Pygmy Cormorants, herons and egrets. The eastern edge of Akşehir, between Karabulut and Ortaköy, can be good for waders in spring.

ÇAVUŞÇU GÖLÜ

38°21N 31°53E

A shallow fresh-water lake north of Ilgın, between Konya and Afyon. The lake is long and thin from north to south with very little emergent vegetation, making birdwatching very easy. Arid, sparsely vegetated hills surround it on all sides except the south where there is some farming.

TIMING

There are small numbers of breeding birds, but the lake is at its best in winter and during the migration periods.

SPECIES

- *Glossy Ibis, Spoonbill and Little Stint* Can be numerous on migration in early autumn.
- *White-fronted Goose* In mild winters more than a thousand birds may use the lake.
- *Wood and Marsh Sandpipers* Regular and sometimes numerous migrants in spring.

ACCESS

The whole lake can be seen from the road which circuits the site. An area in the north-east can be good for waders when water levels are right.

Balik Dami

39°14N 31°38E

An area of marshes on the river Sakarya, 130 km south-west of Ankara. Somewhat off the beaten track, this small wetland is compact, varied and easy to work. The areas of open, shallow water and reedbeds are surrounded by low, uncultivated hills, with those to the south and east providing good vantage points. The rest of the river valley to the west and east may also be worth exploring.

TIMING

Birds can be seen here at all times of year, with open water even in the height of summer. During early spring migration thousands of White Storks, Garganeys and Ruffs may be seen, and Spotted Crake is common in autumn.

SPECIES

- *Pygmy Cormorant* Probably resident.
- *Bittern* This is one of the few sites in Turkey where they may breed.
- *Night Heron* Roosts in bushes along the river and probably breeds here.
- *Great White Egret* Regularly seen in winter.
- *Montagu's Harrier* Breeds around the edge of the wetland.
- *Bearded and Penduline Tits* Both can be seen here.
- *Great Bustard* Could still occur in the surrounding steppe.

ACCESS

The marshes lie 30 km south of the main Eskişehir–Ankara road. At Sivrihisar, take the minor road south marked with yellow signs to 'Ballıhisar (Pessinus)', this is the first turn immediately east of the E-96 to Afyon. At Ballıhisar bear right past the village, and continue for several more kilometres until the road forks. The marshes lie in the fork with Ahıler to the right for views of the western side, and İlyaspaşa to the left for views from the hills on the eastern side.

Pygmy Cormorant

Gölbaşi Gölü (Mogan Gölü, Mugan Gölü)

39°47N 32°50E

A small fresh-water lake immediately south of Ankara. Although not as scenic as most other wetlands in Turkey, it can be *covered* with birds. The lake is long and thin from north to south with some reed along the northern shore, and cultivated steppe on the surrounding hills. Various building developments are beginning to threaten the area.

TIMING

Large numbers of birds use the lake in autumn and early winter.

SPECIES

- *Ferruginous Duck* Common in the post-breeding period with a flock of 200 in September 1994.
- *Little Crake* An autumn migrant.
- *Whiskered and White-winged Black Terns* On migration.

ACCESS

West of the main Konya road, just south of Gölbaşı. The lake can be worked from tracks on the east and west sides according to the light. The tracks off the main Ankara–Konya road are difficult to spot, so drive slowly. On the west side there are more tracks to choose from.

Çöl Gölü

39°20N 32 55E

A large plain set among by hills, between the Karaca and Teke mountains, 80 km south of Ankara. Çöl Gölü is a shallow saltlake which varies in size and shape according to the amount of rainfall. It generally covers *c.* 600 ha and is surrounded by saltplain, grazed steppe and farmland.

In the hills above the plain are two small, fresh-water areas, Uyuz Gölü (in the south) and Yağliören Pool (in the north-west). Uyuz is usually the best of the two for birds; with permanent open water and large clumps of reed it is excellent for White-headed Duck.

TIMING

Important for waders and waterfowl in spring and autumn.

SPECIES

- *White-fronted Goose* Thousands spend the winter here.
- *White-headed Duck* Excellent views of birds on Uyuz Gölü throughout the year.
- *Lesser Kestrel* Breeds in Kömişi (near Uyuz Gölü) and Gölbak.
- *Greater Sand Plover* Breeds.
- *Red-necked Phalarope* A late spring migrant in good numbers.
- *Asian Short-toed Lark* A common resident breeding bird.

ACCESS

From the south, take the turning signposted to Altınçanak, 34 km north of Kulu (mile marker 045). As the road descends from the hills there is a good overview of the whole Çöl Gölü plain with all the main water areas visible. Çöl is a difficult site to work without causing a lot of disturbance because of its large size and the flat landscape. Unless water levels are very low it can be best to birdwatch from the road (which circuits the whole area). This is particularly advisable in the winter when the large numbers of geese present are already regularly disturbed by hunters.

In the south-west of the plain, just before Gökler, a track goes off to the left and winds up the hillside to Uyuz Gölü, Kömişini and ultimately back to the main road.

For Yağlıören Pool turn off at Gölbek in the north-west. Keep bearing left at major junctions until you reach the shallow marshy area of the pool a few kilometres south-west of Gölbek.

Kozanli Saz Gölü and Samsam Gölü

39°08N 32°50E

A small wetland *c.* 20 km west of Kulu. For its size this site supports a remarkable variety of waterbirds. It is set in an open landscape of low hills with a mixture of arable land and steppe, and a marsh at the north-western end where water flows into the lake from Samsam Gölü. Samsam lies 12 km to the north and was finally drained in 1994, but if the winter is wet Samsam may reflood and be worth a look, particularly if the water stays into the spring.

TIMING

Despite its small size Kozanlı Saz Gölü stays wet throughout the year so there are always birds to see. However, it is possible that the drainage of Samsam may have an adverse effect on Kozanlı Saz Gölü.

SPECIES

- *Black and White Storks* Can be common among during migration periods.
- *White-headed Duck* Breeds.
- *Black-winged Stilt, Avocet, Ruff, Black-tailed Godwit, Marsh and Wood Sandpipers* Some of the wide range of waders that can be seen here in spring.

ACCESS

From Kulu turn left to Kozanlı at the southern traffic lights on the main Konya–Ankara road. **Kozanlı Saz Gölü:** In Kozanlı turn left at the round-about and follow this road to the village of Saz. At the village, a track off to the left (4.8 km from the roundabout) goes along the lake's southern shore and gives good views of the water if levels are high. **Samsam Gölü:** At the Kozanlı roundabout go straight on and turn right after 100 m. Follow this road for 8 km to Sarıyayla from where there is a good overview of the lake basin. If there is extensive water, back-track towards Kozanlı and turn sharp right 400–500 m before the roundabout. This track takes you alongside the drainage canal, crosses it and comes out at a village on the southern shore from where you can walk and birdwatch along the lake's western edge.

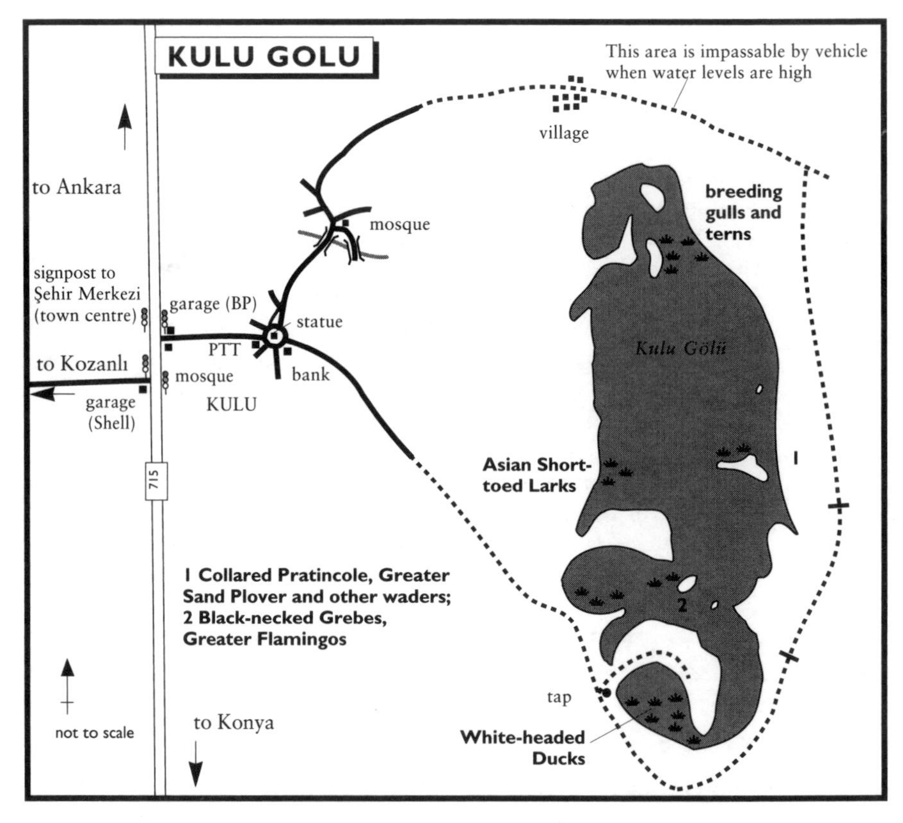

KULU GÖLÜ (DÜDEN GÖLÜ)

39°05N 33°09E

Kulu lies in a rolling, treeless landscape 100 km south of Ankara and west of Tuz Gölü. This is an excellent lake for birds with Mediterranean and Slender-billed Gulls, and Gull-billed Terns among the birds breeding on its islands. At the southern end a small pool fringed by reeds supports a wide variety of species and is the area favoured by White-headed Ducks.

TIMING

Access is easiest and the birds at their best from spring to autumn. In winter the lake often freezes, and when wet the dirt tracks are impassable.

SPECIES

- *Black-necked Grebe* Several hundred pairs breed.
- *White-fronted Goose* Sometimes summers in large groups.
- *Ruddy Shelduck* A few pairs breed with the largest numbers (sometimes several thousands) in the post-breeding period.
- *Marbled Duck* Odd birds seen regularly in spring.
- *Great Bustard* Occasionally seen in the surrounding farmland and steppe where Black-bellied Sandgrouse also breeds.
- *Little Crake* Regularly seen on migration and may also breed.

- *Red-throated Pipit* A very common migrant, alongside small numbers of Citrine Wagtails.

ACCESS

For access to the lake from Kulu *see* map. It is recommended to start from the reed-fringed pool in the south-west corner and work north. At times of high water levels – often in spring – it may not be possible to drive right around the lake, in which case the eastern shore is best reached by returning to Kulu and approaching the lake from the north. The east side is the best area for waders with highlights including Collared Pratincole, Greater Sand Plover, and Broad-billed, Marsh and Terek Sandpipers.

Bulak Gölü, Ağabeyli and Tersakan Gölü

38°32N 32°56E

West of Tuz Gölü and south of Cihanbeyli are some spring-fed wetlands; they are easier to work than the vast, inaccessible Tuz and yet benefit from the focus that it provides for migrating birds; flocks of storks, cranes and waders are regular in this area in spring and autumn.

TIMING

Bulak and Tersakan are both best viewed from the west so the best light is in the afternoon. Both lakes are likely to be largely inaccessible after rain.

SPECIES

- *Greater Flamingo* Regularly breeds on Tuz Gölü and can frequently be seen on these smaller wetlands.
- *White-fronted Goose and Teal* Are the two commonest wildfowl in winter with thousands of each recorded.

Gull-billed Tern

- *Montagu's Harrier* A typical bird of the area.
- *White Stork, Common Crane, Dotterel, Golden Plover, Ruff and Little Stint* All occur in large numbers on migration.
- *Spoonbill, Slender-billed Gull, Caspian Tern and Collared Pratincole* All breed.

ACCESS

Ağabeyli Immediately north of Ağabeyli, fresh-water marshes develop in winter and can hold storks, dabbling ducks and waders in spring. They are crossed by the main Konya–Cihanbeyli road so they are easily checked in passing. Grazing and arable land surrounds the area. Various farm tracks give access.

Bulak Gölü The lake shore is easiest to find at its northern end, at a point 8.2 km south of Cihanbeyli. Approaching from the south look for a quarry-scarred hill on your right. The main road goes up a hill as it approaches the quarry, and just over the brow an unsurfaced road goes off to the right signposted to Köy Hizmetleri and Konkasar Santiyesi. Take this, bearing right when you have a choice, eventually crossing a bridge near the saltworks and following the track along the lake's edge. Check the lake and islands from this track. When you reach the saltpans at the southern end of the lake, cross a bridge and follow this track back to the road.

Tersakan The largest of the three sites and very difficult to work because of this, but it can hold thousands of flamingos and waders. There are various possible routes marked on maps, but probably the easiest to find is via Bulak Gölü. Instead of baring right as you near the saltworks at Bulak Gölü, take the left turn which is again signposted to Köy Hizmetleri and Konkasar Santiyesi. Pass the saltworks and follow this track alongside a channel all the way to Tersakan.

Eşmekaya

38°15N 33°30E

At the southern end of Tuz Gölü, Eşmekaya is an excellent landfall for migrating species such as storks, cranes and raptors and, when water levels are right is an important breeding area for Common Cranes. It consists of a shallow, salt-water lake in the south and a larger fresh-water one with reedbeds in the north, with an area of marsh lying between the two. The site is crossed by the Konya–Aksaray road and lies 44 km west of Aksaray.

TIMING

The marshes are likely to be at their best when wet, in winter and spring, but the area is insufficiently known and virtually unvisited in autumn.

SPECIES

- *Greater Flamingo* Can be seen on the saltlake in winter.
- *Honey Buzzard and Red-footed Falcon.* Among the raptors seen on migration.
- *Lesser Kestrel* Nests in Eşmekaya.

ACCESS

For the northern lake, take the main road north from Eşmekaya, signposted to Eskil and Cihanbeyli, and follow the western shore. There are marshes and reedbeds in the south and deep water in the north. For an overview of this area from the east side, cross the marshes on the main Konya–Aksaray road and turn left on the first likely-looking farm track. Explore on foot or by car. For the central marshes and saltlake take the Karapınar turn south off the Konya–Aksaray road at Eşmekaya. Follow this for 11.1 km to the outskirts of Çağlak and turn left opposite the cemetery to cross the marsh. At the bottom of the hills on the far side turn left and drive for *c.* 2 km until you are at the top of a hill with views of the central marshes. Retrace your route and this time follow the side of the hill south for views of the saltlake. Continue south, following and visible tracks, to rejoin the Karapınar road.

Hotamış Sazlığı and Suleymanhaci Gölü

37°35N 33°03E

These once-extensive and bird-filled marshes which 10 years ago from covered 200 km^2 are still marked on many maps. Greater Sand Plover and White-tailed Plover were then regular, and large colonies of herons and egrets nested on floating reed islands. Today most of the marshes have been drained and, although there is still a large wetland in the west, the erratic annual rainfall, together with pressure from too many people and their livestock have resulted in severe degradation of what remains.

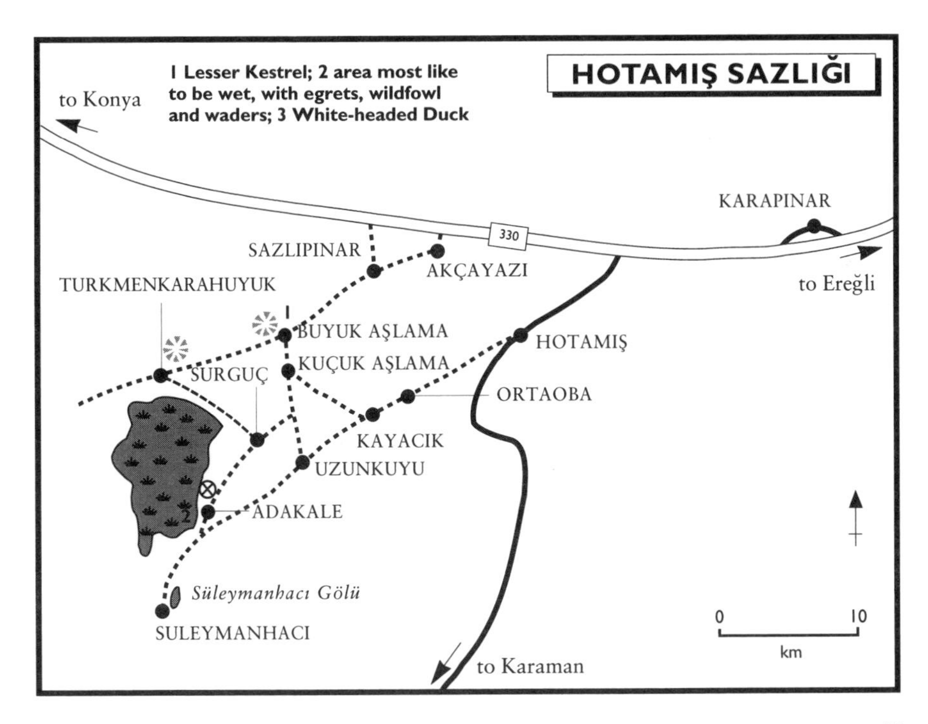

However, the situation on Turkish wetlands can change dramatically given good winter rains, and hopefully the small lake in the south at Süleymanhacı will remain whatever the state of the marshes.

TIMING

The are is likely to be most productive when water levels are at their highest, March–early June, but during autumn migration (late August–early October) there should also be birds to see here.

SPECIES

More than 190 species have been recorded.

- *Pygmy Cormorant* Large numbers once bred.
- *White Pelican* Passage migrant, in large numbers in the past.
- *White-fronted Goose* Several thousand birds use the marshes in winter.
- *Marbled Duck* Breeds (10–15 pairs in 1991) and winters.
- *White-headed Duck* a population of up to 40 pairs once bred in the marshes and birds are regularly seen on Süleymanhacı Gölü, sometimes in groups of several hundred.
- *Lesser Kestrel* A small colony breeds in Büyük Aşlama.
- *Little Crake* On passage and may also breed.
- *Black-bellied Sandgrouse* Resident with largest numbers seen in autumn and winter.
- *Bimaculated Lark* A summer visitor, breeding in small numbers.
- *Asian Short-toed Lark* Abundant throughout the area.

ACCESS

On the Konya–Ereğli road take the turning to Hotamıs 11 km west of Karapınar. In Hotamıs, turn right where the main road swings left at the small village square and on leaving the village, bear left onto the road to Ortaoba. For an overview of the lowest-lying area, try an escarpment next to the Sürgüç/Adakale road, 2–3 km north of Adakale – the light is excellent here in the mornings. If the marshes are wet other possibilities for further exploration are the Küçük Aşlama/Büyük Aşlama road where roadside fields have held geese in winter and migrants in spring. Hüyüks west of Büyük Aşlama and east of Turkmenkarahüyük provide opportunities to view the northern side of the area. From the marshes continue south from Adakale to Süleymanhacı where a reed-fringed lake just north of the village can provide some excellent birdwatching.

EREĞLI SAZLIĞI

37°30N 33°44E

During the last Ice Age a vast fresh-water sea covered the basin on the Konya and Ereğli plains. Sadly, the great marshes which were left behind when the sea retreated have now all but gone, and although the area at Ereğli is much reduced from that shown on road maps, it can still be extensive in wet years, centred around the area of water called Akgöl. Scattered reedbeds, open water and low islands can hold a variety of herons, egrets and ducks, with wading birds on the extensive muddy fringes, including Collared Pratincoles, Greater Sand Plovers, Marsh

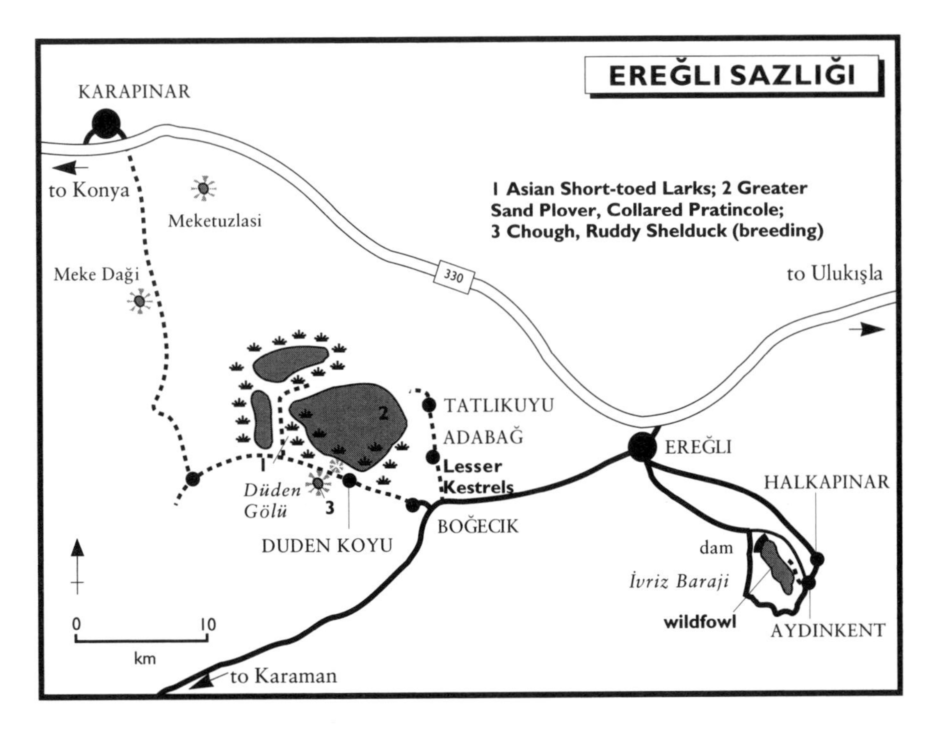

Sandpipers and, if you are very lucky, White-tailed Plovers. In the south rocky hills are used by nesting Ruddy Shelducks, Egyptian Vultures, Finsch's Wheatears and Rock Nuthatches.

TIMING

Spring and early summer are usually best as water levels tend to be high and the birds are easier to see. Hunters can be particularly numerous at weekends in the shooting season.

SPECIES

- *Red-necked Grebe, Pygmy Cormorant, Dalmatian Pelican, Spoonbill, Marbled and White-headed Ducks, Common Crane, Stone-curlew and Gull-billed Tern* all breed.
- *White-fronted Goose and Ruddy Shelduck* Can occur in their thousands in winter.
- *White-headed Duck* Most numerous on spring passage and in summer.
- *Lesser Kestrel* A small but well-protected colony nests in piles of rocks in the school playground in Adabağ.
- *Demoiselle Crane* Seen here on passage in May and August.

ACCESS

From Ereğli take the Karaman road. After *c.* 18 km turn right into Böğecik, and right again at the mosque. This track follows the edge of the hills along the south side of the marsh and after 7.5 km arrives at the hüyük of Düden Köyü; from here there are raised views of the marshes. Continue along the track, birdwatching as you go; 1.4 km beyond the hüyük some rocky outcrops give an overview of the whole area – these outcrops also enclose a crater lake, with Choughs nesting in the crevices. The final opportunity to scan the lake is 3 km farther west where a well-marked track goes out into the marsh. The northern side is more difficult: you may need to walk across large areas of wet mud, particularly in autumn when water levels are low, but it can be best for good views of a variety of waders. Return to the main Karaman road and drive east towards Ereğli. After 2 km turn left after a quarry; this track leads to Adabağ (3 km – look for Lesser Kestrels) and Tatlıkuyu (9 km). In Tatlıkuyu turn left at the mosque and then take tracks which lead west-south-west, past a large water pump and towards the lake shore.

İvriz Barajı lies *c.*18 km south-east of Ereğli and can hold good numbers of wildfowl, particularly during the passage periods. Follow the signs to İvriz and when the road forks take the left to Dereyüzü. This road winds through farmland which is worth checking for migrants. At Halkapınar take the right turn to İvriz, and at the mosque turn right again down a track to the reservoir. This follows the north-east edge of the water and provides good views.

Seyfe Gölü

39°12N 34°25E

This is a typical attractive Central Anatolian lake, with shallow, brackish water and surrounded by steppe and farmland rising to low hills. The main centres of interest are the hüyüks and areas of mixed cultivation in the south-west – and the marshes in the east.

TIMING

As long as there is water there are birds here, except when it freezes in winter. Water levels are highest from March–early June, and lowest from August–December when it can be limited to the west or dry out altogether. The shallow water attracts a good variety of waders, especially on passage.

SPECIES

- *White Pelican* Has bred in recent years.
- *Greater Flamingo* Several thousand are present for much of the year.
- *White-fronted Goose* Several thousand in November and December.
- *Lesser Kestrel* Breeds in the villages round the lake.
- *Great Bustard* May still occur in the steppe to the north-west.
- *Collared Pratincole and Greater Sand Plover* Breed.
- *Slender-billed Gull and Gull-billed Tern* Breed with more than 1000 pairs of each in the past.

ACCESS

The lake is signposted north from the Kırşehir–Kayseri road at Mucur. A full day is needed to do this site justice. Start in the west at the hüyük at Seyfe (the track to the hüyük starting opposite the cemetery has the best surface). A good range of habitats surrounds the hüyük with marshes, the lake, farmland, and willow and poplar plantations providing varied bird-

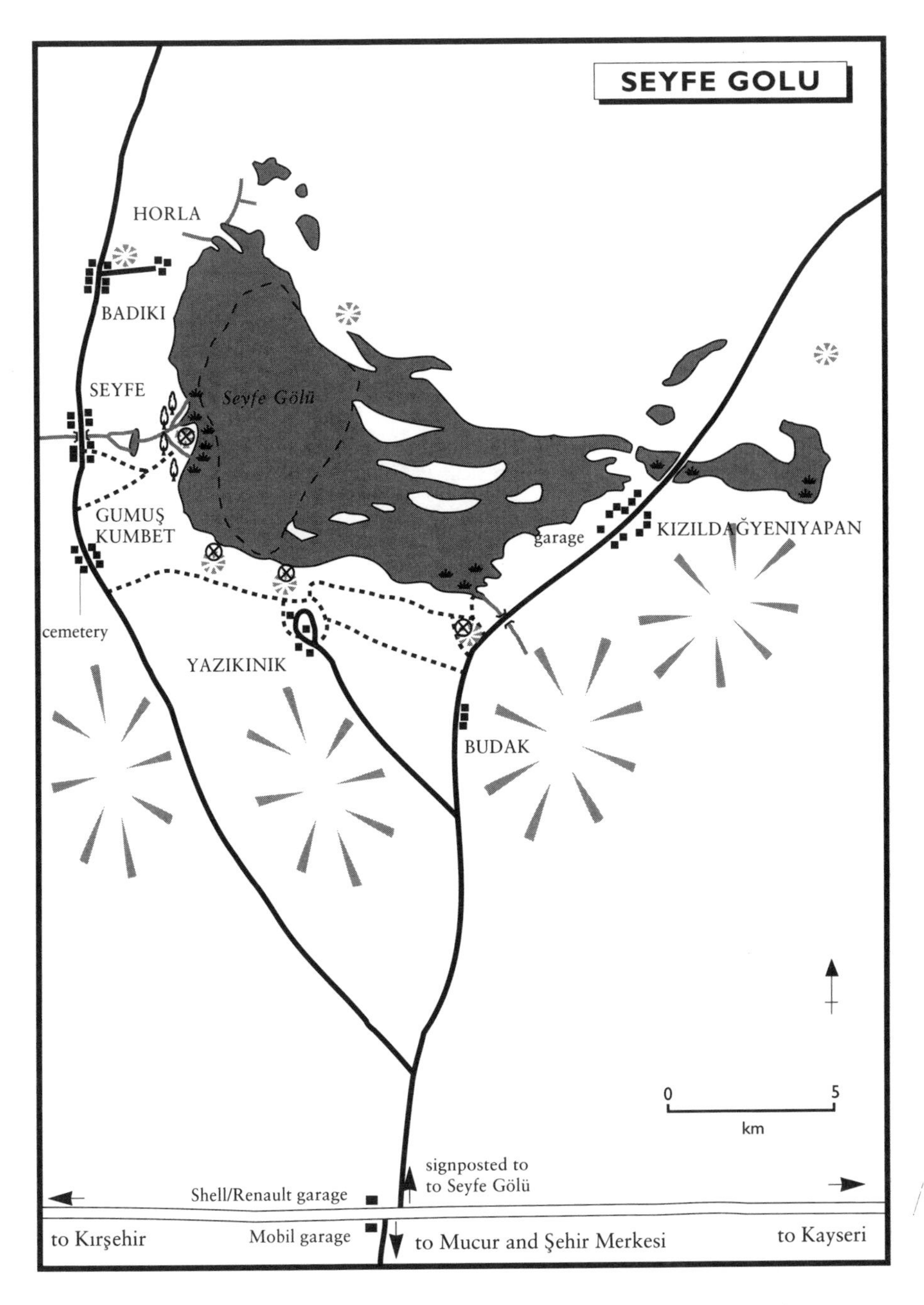

watching. The three hüyüks on the lake's southern edge generally provide rather distant views of the lake and the birds, but the best spot will always depend on water levels. In the east the road cuts across an area of shallow water and marsh – this can be an excellent area and is worth a look, particularly in spring before water levels drop.

TUZLA GÖLÜ (PALAS GÖLÜ)

39°01N 35°49E

This small saline steppe lake lies close to the Kızılırmak river, 45 km north-east of Kayseri. In the west a low range of mountains separate the lake from the river, and their steep slopes descend almost to the lake shore. On the other sides the lake is surrounded by salt steppe with some fresh-water marsh where streams run into the lake, most of the area is heavily grazed. The lake has no outlet, but the water level – at its highest in April/May – soon drops during dry weather. Tuzla attracts many migrants, but the combination of low water and the loss of important areas of habitat in recent years may have reduced the area's attraction for birds.

TIMING

Spring passage of waders was studied here in 1988 and species such as Little Stint and Ruff were recorded in their thousands along with smaller numbers of Greater Sand Plover and Broad-billed Sandpiper.

SPECIES

- *Glossy Ibis and Purple Heron* Can be numerous on spring passage.
- *Garganey* Hundreds in late March/early April.
- *Common Crane* Occurs in large numbers on passage.
- *Citrine Wagtail* Bred here in 1988.

ACCESS

From the Kayseri–Sivas road turn left turn through Burhaniye to reach the west and north shores of the lake. From the west, this turning is easy to miss, so look for the Petrol Ofisi garage in the north-west corner of the junction. Follow this road – dusty, pot-holed tarmac – and, after crossing the railway, fork right to Karahidir. When the lake comes into view look for a dirt track leading towards the lake's southern shore for views of the muddy fringes.

The road along the western shore does go close to the water but the shores here are steep and birds usually few. Continue to the northern end of the lake, beyond Ömerhacılı, and turn right onto a wide surfaced track which skirts the foot of the mountains with a wide band of steppe between the road and the lake. After 6 km more turn right again; this road crosses the shallow northern arm of the lake. Stop along this road wherever there are birds. Continue along the road to Palas and in the village take any likely-looking track which leads towards the lake. Immediately west of Palas several fresh-water streams discharge into the lake creating an extensive area of open mud which can hold many waders, although birdwatching is difficult. From Palas a well-defined dirt track goes south across the saltmarsh, some distance from the eastern shore of the lake – stop wherever birdwatching looks interesting. The last possibility is likely to be near a hüyük, gradually being quarried away, where more fresh-water streams enter the lake and marshes form when water levels are high. From the hüyük a made-up track leads back to the main road near Tuzhisar.

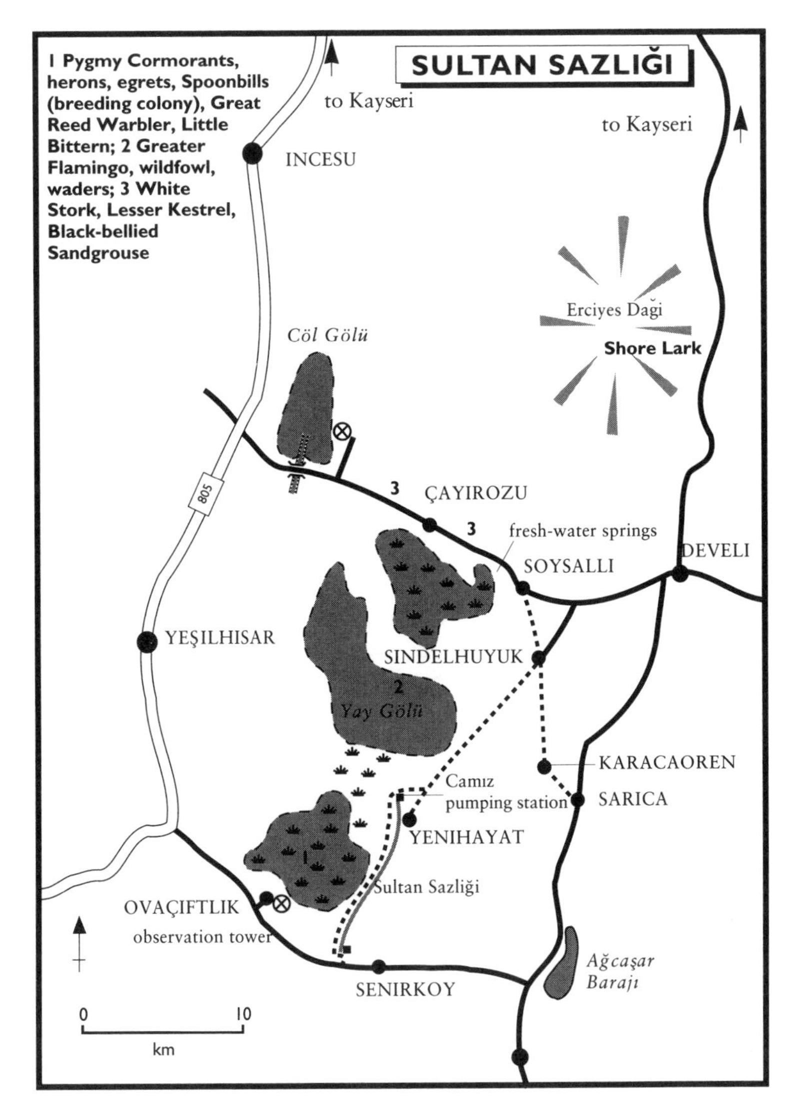

Sultan Sazliği

38°20N 35°15E

South of Kayseri a 1000-km^2 basin enclosed by mountains contains the Sultan Marshes complex. Composed of fresh-water marshes to north and south, a shallow brackish lake (Yay Gölü), a saltlake (Çöl Gölü), and large areas of mudflats and salt steppe, this wetland is huge. The marshes are renowned as one of Turkey's premier wetlands – more than 250 species of bird have been recorded, of which *c.* 120 breed.

In the south the Sultan Sazlığı is large fresh-water reedbed with floating reed islands and small lakes. Here there are nesting Pygmy Cormorants, Night and Squacco Herons, Little Egrets, Glossy Ibises and Spoonbills, and on the islands a few Red-necked Grebes and White-headed Ducks along with a variety of diving ducks.

Yay Gölü is often covered with birds – a haze of Greater Flamingos (more than 10,000 in autumn), waders feeding round its shallow shores (more than 2000 Ruff in early spring), and thousands of ducks. In winter, if the water does not freeze, there can be hundreds of thousands of waterbirds – more than 3000 White-fronted Geese, 21,000 Greylag Geese, 11,000 Ruddy Shelducks, 9000 Shovelers and 2000 Common Cranes.

Warm fresh-water springs at Soysallı feed the northern marsh and can hold birds, especially in winter. Further west lies Çöl Gölü. This saltlake dries out in summer and holds few birds but it is accessible and can be worth a look. The lakes and marshes are surrounded by huge expanses of mudflats and salt steppe which are crossed by the Soysallı–Çöl road. Collared Pratincoles, Spur-winged Plovers, Slender-billed Gulls, Gull-billed Terns and sometimes Greater Sand Plovers nest here in the wetter areas, and true steppe birds such as Black-bellied Sandgrouse nest where it is dry. However, much of the steppe has been converted to agriculture, and thousands of sheep and cattle graze large areas of the plains.

TIMING

There is a magnificent birdwatching spectacle here all year round but the area is probably at its very best from April to June. At this time of year the days can be warm and sunny but, due to the high altitude (1070 m), the nights are cold. It is often windy.

SPECIES

- *White Pelican* Occurs on migration and is present all summer.
- *Little Bittern* Numerous breeding in the fresh-water marshes with *c.* 300 pairs.
- *Marbled Duck* Present in small numbers and probably breed.
- *Whiskered Tern* Common on migration with some staying to breed.
- *Great Reed Warbler* Very common in the reedbeds along with Savi's and Moustached Warblers.
- *Bearded Tit* Nests and is probably resident in the reedbeds.

ACCESS

Warning Only the main roads which circuit the marsh are tarmac and passable in wet weather. In bad weather it is therefore only possible to view the area from the edges.

If approaching from the north, take the road from Kayseri which passes over Erciyes Dağ – mountain species may be seen en route (Shore Lark is guaranteed) and the views of the marshes are spectacular. At Develi take the road to Yahyalı and stop at Ağcaşar reservoir; this is easy to work from the road and can hold a variety of ducks.

For a first look at the marshes visit Ovaçiftlik. Here an observation tower overlooks the reedbeds and some pools – except when water levels are very low. Access to the tower is free. Boat trips into the marshes provide a valuable source of income for the locals, but I doubt whether these trips are good for the birds or birdwatching. Scarce species such as Red-necked

Grebe and White-headed Duck spend all their time in the reedbed pools so are only likely to be seen from a boat, but they are only seen flying off by the first boat of the day. If you are keen on a boat trip and you have a choice, go out with Ahran. He runs one of the Çay houses in the village and works closely with DHKD; he is easily recognized as he has no legs.

From Ovaçiftlik turn left (south-east) onto the main road and drive 6.5 km to where a track goes off to the left by a pumping station, and then follow a canal into the marshes. Follow the west side of the canal and stop frequently to birdwatch over the marshes. From the pumping station the vast expanse of Yay Gölü can be seen. Birdwatching over the lake to the north, on the Sultan Marshes to the south, and the intervening steppe is best done on foot. Various banks provide slightly elevated viewing. Further views of Yay Gölü can also be had from the car by driving north out of the marshes via Sindelhüyük.

The northern part of the marshes is best viewed from the road. The chief areas are the springs near Soysallı, the steppe along the roadsides, and Çöl Gölü. The latter can be viewed from a road on the hillside to the east or from the banks that go into the centre of the lake.

DEMIRKAZIK

37°50N 35°10E

Demirkazık lies in the Ala Dağ range of the Taurus mountains roughly midway between Kayseri and Adana. Amongst birdwatchers this is the best known site for seeing Caspian Snowcock in Turkey, but they are often not easy here (they are much easier and more accessible in the Sivrikaya area) and those who come here only interested in seeing the Snowcock will miss a great deal. This is a five-star site with incredibly dramatic scenery and a wonderful range of technicolour mountain birds – it deserves at least a day to enjoy what there is to see.

Around the Ski Centre the meadows hold species such as Black Redstart, Rock, Ortolan and Black-headed Buntings, whilst Red-fronted Serin and Crimson-winged Finch can often be seen at this altitude, at the bottom of the gorge, near the road. The sparsely vegetated mountain sides abound with Snow Finches, Shore Larks and Finsch's Wheatears, whilst White-throated Robins and Rock Thrushes occur in smaller numbers. Caspian Snowcocks may be found on the plateau if there is snow on the ground, and Radde's Accentor frequents the juniper scrub at the top of the gorge. In the gorge itself Blue Rock Thrush, Rock Nuthatch and Rock Sparrow are common. Finally, the skies overhead should be watched for raptors – including Lammergeier and Golden Eagle – as well as Alpine Swift, Crag Martin, Alpine Chough and Chough.

TIMING

The Caspian Snowcocks are probably easiest to see in April and May when there is still some snow on the ground and they have not retreated far up the mountain, but they have been seen as late as September. Visits in June are likely to find the greatest variety of species.

Snow Finch

SPECIES

◆ *Alpine Accentor* the race which occurs here is *subalpina.*

ACCESS

Travelling on the Tarsus/Ankara highway (E90), take the turning to Çamardı north of Pozantı. Follow this road north past Çamardı and after Çukurbağ look for signs to the Demirkazık Mountain and Ski Centre. The Centre, lying above Demirkazık village, can offer accommodation and when full it is possible to camp. Food can be a problem here so, to be safe buy food in Çamardı, the nearest place with shops.

Caspian Snowcocks prefer to feed around the snow-line and retreat high into the rocky crags as it gets light. The birds call frequently in the spring (sounding similar to Curlew) and with patience can be found by searching for the source of the sound with binoculars. This method causes far less disturbance to the birds than 'thrashing' the mountainside for them before dawn and, although views may not be so close, means you can start up the mountainside in daylight when it is safer and you can enjoy the birds on the way up!

The initial aim is to reach the plateau 500 m or so above the Ski Centre. A track continues beyond the centre and, if you are so inclined, it is possible drive part of the way up. However, you will see more birds by walking, and a climb straight up the mountain is shorter and not too strenuous if taken at a gentle pace. A relatively easy route lies a short distance beyond the Centre where a gully cuts the mountainside; walk up the ridge to the right (south) of this gully, following any path upwards which may be visible. This route takes 1½–2 hours. At the top you will find a wide, sparsely vegetated plateau and the rocky peaks of the mountain beyond. Continue towards the peaks, bearing left, and pick up a well-defined track which continues up the mountain. Caspian Snowcocks are usually found around the rocky crags.

The most interesting route down is a steep and narrow rocky gorge, reached via a grassy hollow at the north end of the plateau. The gorge is a bit of a scramble in places , but not too difficult or dangerous if you take care. The gorge is very spectacular. Stop regularly to birdwatch, scanning the rock faces for Wallcreepers and roosting Scops Owls. At the bottom the path comes out on the road to the north of the Ski Centre.

SOUTH-EAST

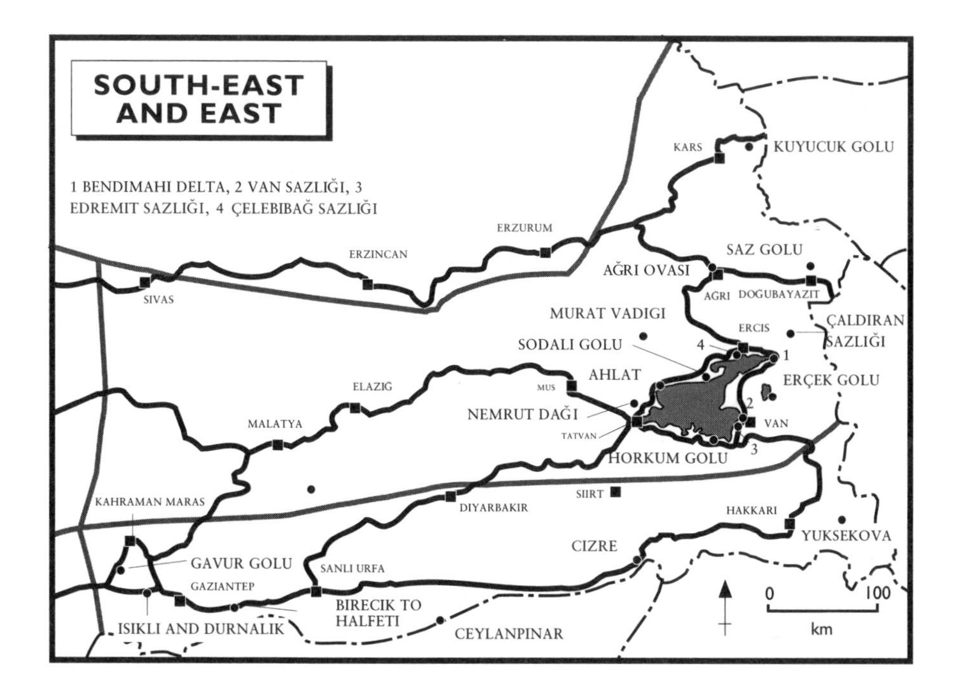

East of Gaziantep one enters an area of Turkey with a true flavour of the Middle East. The Tigris and Euphrates bring water and thus cultivation to what is otherwise a dry, desert region with an unbearable summer heat. Travelling eastwards, roads noticeably deteriorate and hotel facilities become more primitive as the landscape becomes steadily more rugged. The extreme south-east is possibly the most physically forbidding area of Turkey, and has been largely impossible (and inadvisable) to visit for some time due to the major military presence here. Rugged inaccessible mountains and small isolated settlements, roads badly potholed and heavily guarded – it was to these harsh mountains that many thousands of Iraqis fled after the Gulf War in 1991.

The Turkish government's South-eastern Anatolian Project (GAP) aims to raise the local economy above its current subsistence levels by providing water to facilitate cultivation. A series of dams are thus being built along the Euphrates (the massive Atatürk dam is the largest) – and will result in major changes to the region's hydrology.

Continuing military activities mean that the birds of this area of Turkey are little known, although we do know that there is a large diversity of species despite the lack of significant wetlands. The Euphrates provides a connection with birds of the Syrian desert, and the Tigris with Iraq – species such as Striated Scops Owl and Dead Sea Sparrow are at the northern limit of their ranges here. Other edge-of-range species include See-see,

Cream-coloured Courser, Red-wattled Plover, Little Swift, Blue-cheeked Bee-eater, Desert Lark, Desert and Red-tailed Wheatears, Ménétries' Warbler, Great Rock Nuthatch, Dead Sea and Pale Rock and Yellow-throated Sparrows, Desert Finch and Grey-necked Bunting.

Upcher's Warbler and Cinereous Bunting are characteristic birds of this region, and Birecik remains the only place in Turkey where Bald Ibis can be seen, although there are probably now no truly wild birds remaining.

Species which occur just to the south and could well be present include Bar-tailed Desert and Thick-billed Larks, Red-rumped Wheatear (already claimed on a number of occasions) and Mourning Wheatear.

Gavur Gölü

37°20N 36°50E

Lying south of Kahraman Maraş, Gavur Gölü is an area of reedbed, seasonally flooded wetlands and cultivation – mostly rice and cotton. Although little known, this is likely to be an excellent site for seeing migrants, for the Rift Valley reaches its end here. Once there were three Rift Valley wetlands within Turkey's borders, of which the most famous was the fabulous Amik Gölü, east of İskenderun. Covering some 350 km^2, Amik held Turkey's only breeding Darters, and was a stop-off point for thousands of migrants, including many rarities such as Turkey's first recorded Yellow-billed Stork. It was finally drained in the early 1970s.

How many migrants Gavur Gölü can still attract remains to be seen – the site has only recently been rediscovered and as yet has been little visited by birdwatchers – but species of interest seen on just two visits in early spring have included Little Crake, Greater Sand Plover, Marsh Sandpiper, Red-necked Phalarope, Citrine Wagtail and Bluethroat.

TIMING

Visits during the migration periods are likely to be most rewarding.

SPECIES

◆ *Pygmy Cormorant* Regularly seen in spring.
◆ *Great White Egret* Winters in good numbers.
◆ *White Stork* Seen in migrating flocks in spring.
◆ *Harriers* All four species have been recorded.
◆ *Graceful Warbler I*in the scrubby vegetation around the wetland edges.

ACCESS

Lies next to the 825 road from Kahraman Maraş, just south of Türkoğlu. 1.1 km after leaving the town a track to the left crosses the railway line (which runs parallel to the road), the turning is marked by two white buildings. The track leads onto a raised bank which gives good views over the flooded areas. The most productive route is generally the main track towards Minehöyük (9 km from the main road) – Citrine Wagtails seem to like the shallow flooded fields close to the village in March and April. The track down the centre of the wetland may be worth investigating but is very rough and impassable when the weather has been wet. This area can also be much disturbed by hunters.

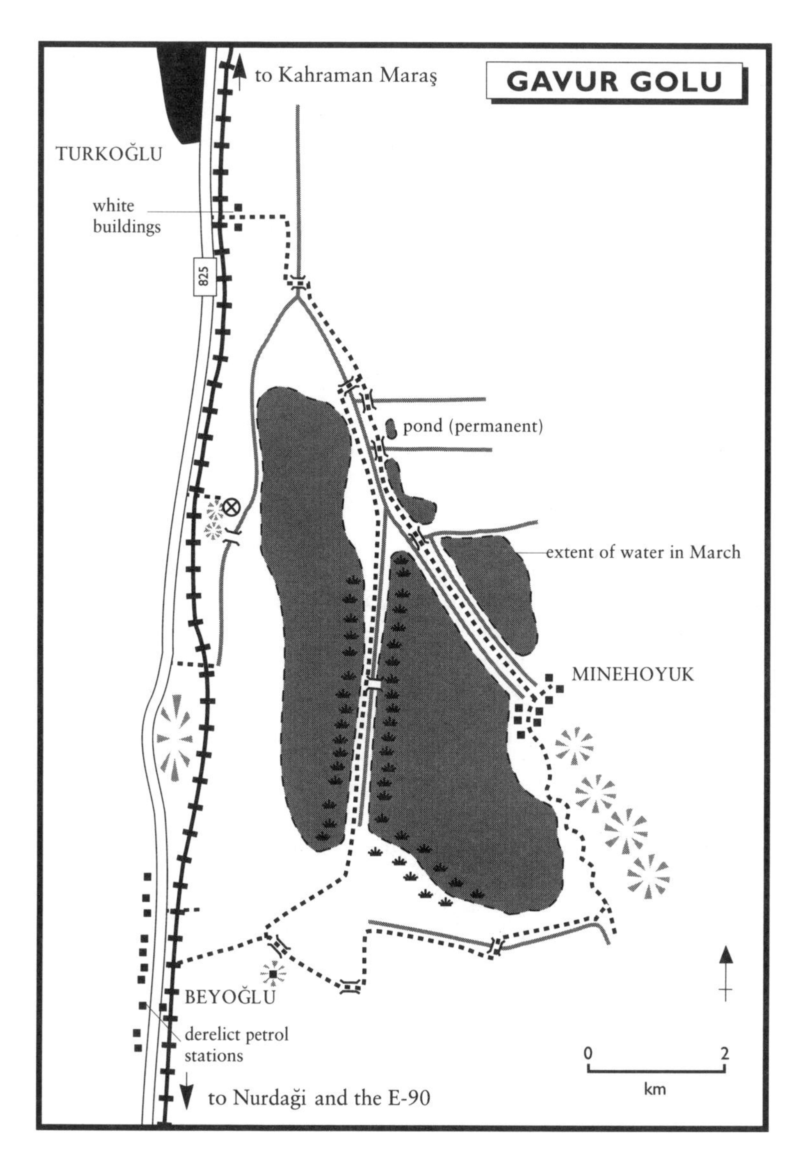

Another productive area is the hüyüks next to the main road in the west. Those to the north give a good panoramic view over the whole wetland and parts of the western side of the wetland can be investigated from here: the drain running past the hüyük provides cover for migrants.

Işikli and Durnalik

37°12N 37°08E

The Karasu river valley lies at the northern end of the Rift Valley and acts as an amazingly clear east/west divide for many bird species. East of the line Red-tailed Wheatear, Ménétries' Warbler, Great Rock Nuthatch and Pale Rock Sparrow first appear, whilst western species such as Olive-tree Warbler and Cretzschmar's Bunting reach the eastern limit of their ranges here.

From the west, the first opportunity to see these 'new' eastern species comes in the hills west of Gaziantep, where a group of villages provides the right combination of altitude, cultivation, scrub and rocky hillsides for several specialized species to occur side by side.

TIMING

It is best to visit in the early morning when the birds are most active, it is not too hot and there are less people (particularly children) about. Red-tailed Wheatear is probably the most elusive of the specialities to be seen here, they seem to move out immediately after the breeding season and, although they have been seen in August, May and June are the easiest months.

As well as the wheatear this is an especially good site for seeing species which are difficult to find elsewhere such as White-throated Robin, Upcher's Warbler, Great Rock Nuthatch (which can be compared with Rock Nuthatch), Pale Rock Sparrow (April–August), Desert Finch and Cinereous Bunting (present from the second half of April).

SPECIES

- *Chukar* Regularly seen here.
- *See-see* Seen occasionally and must breed in the area.
- *Pallid Swift* Frequently seen and may breed in the area.
- *Syrian Woodpecker, Rufous Bush Robin, Yellow-vented Bulbul and Scarlet Rosefinch* All occur in the orchards.
- *Radde's Accentor* In the scrub on the rocky hillsides in winter.
- *Trumpeter Finch* Rare in Turkey, bred here in 1977.

ACCESS

The two villages most regularly visited by birdwatchers, Işıklı and Durnalık, lie just over 20 km west of Gaziantep, between Yamaçoba and Yesilce.

Durnalık The road which leads to the village lies 9 km east of Yamaçoba; *c.* 600 m west of the turn is a BP petrol station on the right, and opposite the junction is a lime kiln (a large, rectangular chimney-like structure built of stone). Park close to the junction and walk the 1 km from the main road to the village – birdwatching can be good along the road and there will be few people to disturb you. Just before the village the valley opens out in front of you with a well marked track leading down to the orchards; from here paths go into the rocky side valleys.

Işıklı 1.2 km east of Durnalık and just west of Yesilce is the turning to Işıklı. The village lies 4.3 km from the main road. 200 m into the village take the first left and park just beyond a small bridge over a stream (likely to be dry in summer). A track follows the stream and crosses the farmland to enter a relatively narrow pass below two crags, opening out into a bare rocky area beyond.

In both villages the orchards and cultivation are the places to look for White-throated Robin and Upcher's Warbler, whilst the rocky hillsides and scree slopes are favoured by Red-tailed Wheatear, Great Rock Nuthatch,

Pale Rock Sparrow and Cinereous Bunting; Orphean and Barred Warblers inhabit the scrub. The cultivated valley and surrounding scrub are also good for migrants with both Semi-collared and Collared Flycatchers in spring.

Birecik to Halfeti, the Firat (Euphrates) Vadigi

37°02N 38°00E

Birecik lies on the western edge of south-eastern Turkey and provides an accessible taste of Middle Eastern birds. The area is a mecca for bird-watchers for the many new birds to be seen here, and especially for several difficult species – such as Pale Rock Sparrow – which can be seen here relatively easily. The river valley is heavily cultivated, and on the surrounding hills are groves of the delicious Gaziantep pistachios; where the rolling limestone hills are cut by wadis (seasonal watercourses), they create impressive blinding white gorges in the hot summer sun. The river is wide and swiftly flowing, and sand and gravel banks, many thickly covered with tamarisk, provide a haven for species such as Night Heron, Stone-curlew, Spur-winged Plover, Gull-billed and Little Terns and Cetti's Warbler. Further north, at Halfeti, the landscape changes dramatically and the river runs through a deeply cut ravine with steep cliffs and breeding Egyptian Vultures and Bonelli's Eagles.

The river and its rich variety of habitats provides a focus for many species which are on the edge of their range here. Many belong to the Syrian/Arabic region, or even farther east, and include – See-see, Cream-coloured Courser, Little Swift, Blue-cheeked Bee-eater, Red-tailed Wheatear, Ménétries' Warbler, Great Rock Nuthatch, Dead Sea, Pale Rock and Yellow-throated Sparrows and Desert Finch. The Bald Ibis ('Kelaynak' in Turkish) which once nested in the chalk cliffs above the town and for which Birecik became famous, is now extinct as a wild breeding bird in Turkey (the free-flying birds at the breeding station do not migrate and cannot be considered 'wild').

Edge-of-range species continue to be found and in the 1980s three new breeding species were added – Striated Scops Owl, Desert Lark and Desert Wheatear – whilst rare migrants in recent years have included Sooty and Barbary Falcons, White-tailed Plover, Spotted Sandgrouse and Isabelline Shrike. Without doubt there is still much to be discovered here.

TIMING

To see all of the species for which Birecik is famous it is necessary to visit in May, although the heat will restrict birdwatching to the beginning and end of the day. Visits in April may miss some of the later arrivals but temperatures are pleasanter, many migrants can be seen – the Euphrates is an important migration route – and the wild flowers wonderful.

Black-bellied and Pin-tailed Sandgrouse come in their hundreds to drink at the river from around 7.30 am, landing on the sand bars in the river; they can be seen well from near of the Bald Ibis station.

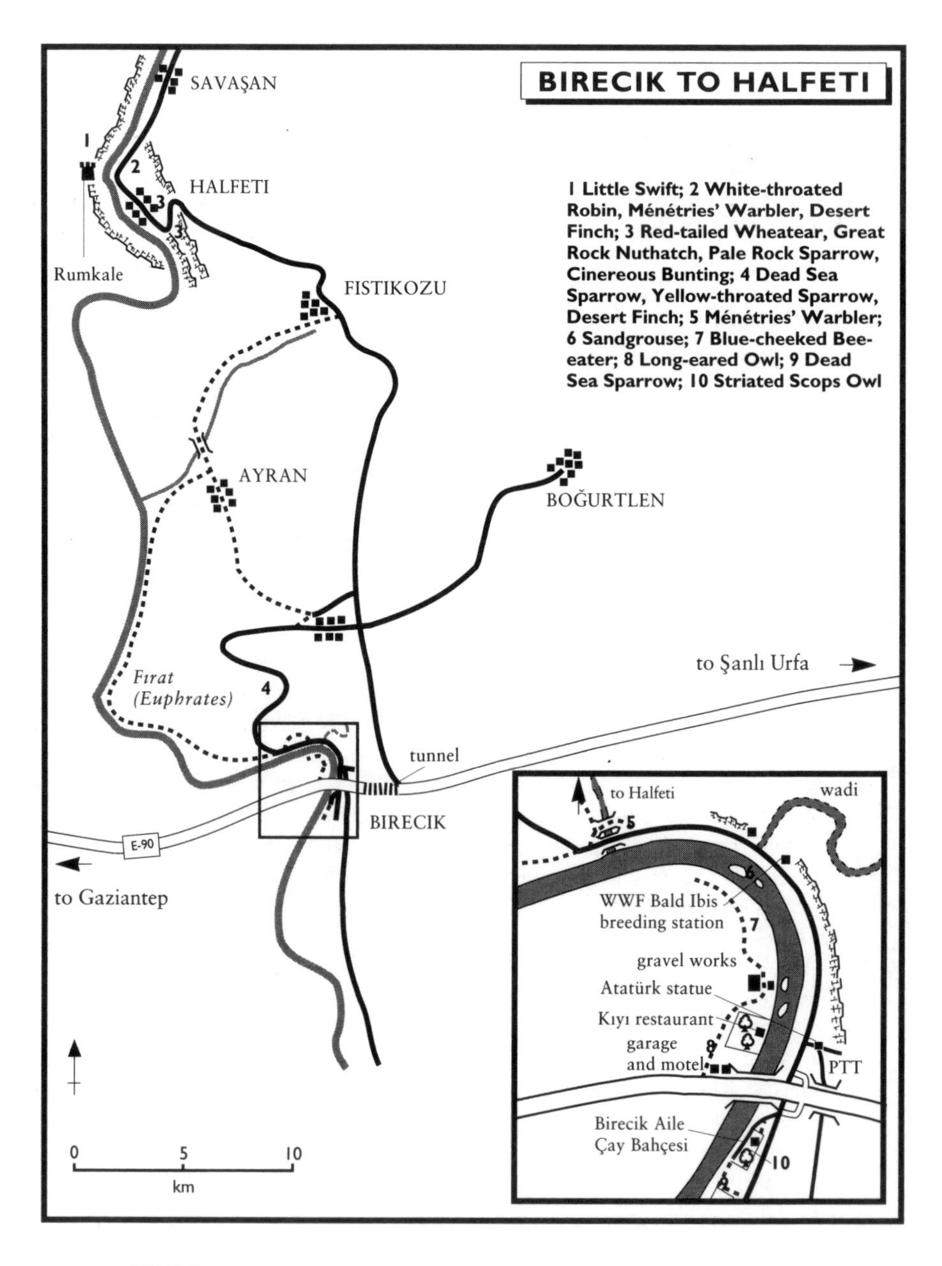

SPECIES

- *Cream-coloured Courser* Can occur in small flocks in autumn.
- *Little Swift* Odd birds may be seen in House Martin colonies along the river, but they are commoner at Halfeti and Rumkale.
- *Pied Kingfisher* Commonly seen over the river, often hovering.
- *Bee-eater and Blue-cheeked Bee-eater* Nest along the Euphrates.
- *Radde's Accentor and Wallcreeper* Both occur here in winter.

ACCESS

Birecik west bank the stone track down the side of the motel is regularly used by lorries from the gravel works and is noisy and dusty, but beyond the works it is quieter – an area of pools and shingle can hold waders, terns and Blue-cheeked Bee-eaters. Look for Long-eared Owls, common breeding birds around Birecik, in the trees near the Kıyı restaurant.

Birecik east bank South of the bridge, in the bizarre setting of an open-air Çay house – with loud music, television, neon lights and crowds of people – Striated Scops Owl can be seen hunting for insects and perched in the trees overhead. If asked the owners are often able to find the birds for you – night and day; do pay them if they provide a good service. This species has also been seen in orchards and suitable clumps of mature trees elsewhere in the valley. Scops Owl also breeds at the Çay house, and Tawny and Long-eared Owls have been seen. At the end of the road beyond the Çay house is a tree nursery which can be a good area for seeing Dead Sea Sparrows (look for their large round nests in the tamarisk clumps) and Ménétries' Warblers.

Following the riverside road north, 3.6 km from the bridge is the Bald Ibis station. You can visit the station to see the ibises, and free-flying birds can be seen outside the enclosure up and down the river nearby. The wadi next to the station, and the rocky plateau above it are worth exploring for Chukar, See-see, Eagle Owl, Desert Lark, Desert Wheatear, Pale Rock Sparrow and the ubiquitous Rock Sparrow.

1.5 km farther on, the road crosses a wadi in a deep gully, and a minor road to the right takes you through some orchards – these can hold Upcher's Warbler, Dead Sea Sparrow, Yellow-throated Sparrow (May to July) and Desert Finch, with Ménétries' Warbler (rarely with the pink breast shown in the field guides) in the scrub.

Beyond the gully the road forks. Both routes pass through areas of cultivation with further possibilities to search for species such as Yellow-throated Sparrow – try in the early morning when they are singing – and Desert Finch – which can occur in large flocks. The left turn, signposted to Birecik Barajı, follows the river valley and goes through some excellent areas of riverside woodland and scrub – this area does not appear to have been much visited by birdwatchers although it would be worth exploring in spring for migrants. The track is not marked on road maps – shown on the map here is the section I have driven, it may continue farther north.

Halfeti 39 km north of Birecik, Halfeti is set in the bottom of a deep gorge. Where the road descends the gorge to the village, Red-tailed Wheatear, Great Rock Nuthatch, Pale Rock Sparrow and Cinereous Bunting can be found on the rocky slopes.

Beyond Halfeti up to Savaşan are areas of pistachio groves and farmland with White-throated Robin, Ménétries' Warbler, Woodchat Shrike and Desert Finch; on the opposite side of the river is the impressive castle of Rumkale. This may be reached by rather basic ferry from Halfeti or Savaşan, although with a telescope it is possible to pick out Little Swifts from the east side of the river!

✖ CEYLANPINAR

36°51N 40°03E

Ceylanpınar is on the border with Syria, in a vast flat plain on the edge of the desert. Originally the habitat here would have been steppe/semi-desert, but a state farm covers 1700 km^2 of the area and much of the land is now farmed, mainly for wheat; there may still be small areas of remnant habitat in a few places. On the desert edge species such as See-see and Pale Rock Sparrow can be seen.

Around the state farm many trees have been planted, and there are trees and scrub along the Al Khabour River, which runs into the desert carrying water in winter and spring but largely drying up in summer. This area of cultivation on the edge of the desert attracts many migrating and breeding birds. Along the river species include Little Bittern, Purple Heron, Crane and Dead Sea Sparrow.

Ceylanpınar is important for the large population of Great Bustards it supports. A survey of bustards throughout Turkey in 1981 found this to be the most productive site for them with 45 seen during a brief 100 km drive. There were reports of 800–1000 birds in winter.

TIMING

The heat is intense here during the day so visit in early morning, and ideally in spring when there is still water in the river and migrants are passing through.

SPECIES

- *Pallid and Montagu's Harriers* Both occur along the river during the breeding season.
- *Little Bustard* Two males were seen here in 1981. This is one of the few sites in Turkey where this species may still occur.
- *Pin-tailed Sandgrouse* A typical breeding species; more than 500 have been seen at drinking places.

ACCESS

Because of its sensitive position on the Syrian border, this site has not been visited by birdwatchers since 1981.

✖ CİZRE

37°20N 42°11E

This dismal frontier town stands in a stark rocky landscape on the banks of the Tigris. A major military presence dominates the area which makes the town uncomfortable to stay in for long, and it is so close to the border that Syrian watch-towers can be seen; in addition the Iraqi border is less than 30 km away. In fact the only attraction is Red-wattled Plover – a short section of river valley from the border northwards is the only place in Turkey where they occur, although visits are generally only made by the impetuously keen! The birds were first discovered displaying here in 1983 and, although the whole area is very disturbed, they are still seen, nesting on gravel islands in the river with as many as 10 adults and 3 chicks reported. Other birds seen here regularly include Black Francolin (in the scrub between the river and the Silopi road), Black-bellied and Pin-tailed Sandgrouse, and Pied Kingfisher.

TIMING

Most visits have been made between May and July; the plovers could well be resident.

SPECIES

- *Eleonora's Falcon* Several records in recent years.
- *Saker* Seen occasionally.
- *Brown-necked Raven* A group of 7 seen on a rubbish tip here in July 1985 was the first (and only) record for Turkey.
- *Yellow-throated Sparrow* Has been recorded on a few occasions.

ACCESS

Before birdwatching in Cizre you must obtain permission from the police (the police station is on the south-west side of the bridge). A curfew is frequently in operation and this will restrict both *where* you can birdwatch and *when*. Even with permission you may still be arrested (a group was in 1994) so proceed with caution and do not leave the road. The Red-wattled Plovers can either be seen from outside the police station, or from the garage on the east side of the bridge. Scan the area of shingle with scrub and pools to the south.

Alternatively, take the Şirnak road out of town for about 5 km. Here there are large shingle banks in the river where Red-wattled Plover has also been seen regularly. Although the army are still much in evidence, this area is further from the border so is likely to be less sensitive.

✖ YÜKSEKOVA

37°33N 44°15E

Approximately 200 km south-east of Van, Yüksekova lies on a large plain at about 2000 m. The Nehil river winds across the plain and has extensive, botanically-rich marshes and wet meadows along its bends, and the whole area is still largely traditionally managed. Montagu's Harrier and Redshank are common breeding birds and a good variety of birds of prey occur in the surrounding mountains including Levant Sparrowhawk and Lesser Spotted Eagle.

TIMING

The most recent known visit to the area was in June 1989 when Spotted Crake and Caspian Snowcock were recorded for the first time, both are assumed to breed.

SPECIES

- *Great Bustard* Occurs in small numbers and may breed.

ACCESS

Yüksekova lies in an inhospitable and politically unstable corner of Turkey which currently makes it impossible to reach. This general area was host to thousands of Iraqis after the Gulf War in 1991 and their presence could have had some effect on this site

EASTERN TURKEY

Eastern Turkey is dominated by Van Gölü, a vast inland sea covering almost 4000 km^2, created thousands of years ago when lava flows blocked its outlet. The terrain is rugged and mountainous – Van Gölü stands at 1750 m – and culminates in Turkey's highest mountain, the 5137-m peak of Büyükağrı Dağ (Ararat) on the border with Iran. The landscape has much in common with Iran and the Pontic range connects with the Elburz mountains farther east. The natural vegetation is steppe or alpine, and the river valleys are characterized by cultivated areas with virtually the only trees of the region the poplars and willows round the villages. The climate is severe too – the summers, from May to September, are hot (although nights are cold) and winters freezing and snowbound. Spring and autumn are wet with many of the roads turning to mud.

Despite the foregoing the east has much to attract birdwatchers, which makes the recent trend for kidnapping tourists and subsequent inadvisability of visiting the area at present frustrating. Numerous and typical birds of the region include Red-necked Phalarope (on spring migration), Rose-coloured Starling, Bimaculated and Lesser Short-toed Larks, Finsch's Wheatear, Roller, Rock Sparrow, White-winged Black Tern (common migrant through wetlands in spring) and Crimson-winged Finch. Some of those which give a more eastern flavour to the birdlife, include distinctive eastern races of familiar western species such as Black Redstart, Stonechat and Penduline Tit along with the more exotic – Demoiselle Crane, Black-winged Pratincole (a scarce breeding bird and probably not uncommon passage migrant), Sociable Plover (passes through in September, a flock of 79 was seen in 1991 near Ağrı), Armenian Gull, Citrine Wagtail (breeding), Pied Wheatear (localized breeder), Paddyfield Warbler, Great Rock Nuthatch, Mongolian Trumpeter Finch and Grey-necked Bunting.

✖ Kuyucuk Gölü

40°45N 43°27E

Kuyucuk Gölü, approximately 40 km east of Kars and 30 km from the Georgian border, is a 219-ha fresh-water lake surrounded by grazed steppe and grassland. Parts of the lake are covered with reed and Flowering Rush, especially in the shallow bays where there are inflowing streams. These bays also contain small islands of vegetation favoured by breeding grebes, the most notable being Black-necked Grebe with several hundred pairs.

TIMING

Summer and early autumn (May–September), with late June to early July the best period. In May migrating Red-necked Phalaropes can be numerous (150 in 1965). Red-necked Grebes and White-headed Ducks breed in small numbers.

ACCESS
The lake lies south of the Kars–Akyaka road beyond Küçük Çatma.

✖ Ağrı Ovası

39°45N 43°00E

A huge plain covering 1250 km^2 and containing many villages around the town of Ağrı. The upper Murat river, which passes Ağrı, is fed by numerous rivers and streams, the majority still bordered by more or less original grassland which is regularly flooded in spring.

TIMING
Common and Demoiselle Cranes both breed here.

ACCESS
On the eastern edge of Turkey, between Van Gölü and Kars.

✖ Iğdır Ovası

40°00N 44°05E

The Iğdır plain lies in the Aras valley, north of Büyükağrı Dağ (Ararat). The valley is much lower than most of eastern Turkey, and this is reflected in the birdlife, with Pygmy Cormorant and Blue-cheeked Bee-eater both possible breeding species.

SPECIES
- *Cattle Egret* Likely to be a summer visitor.
- *Ménétries' Warbler* Breeds in waterside tamarisks.
- *Mongolian Trumpeter Finch* Can be seen in the surrounding foothills; Trumpeter Finch has also been seen in the area.

ACCESS
This is a sensitive border area – the Aras forms the international frontier between Turkey, Georgia and Iran, and Jerevan is visible on the north side of the plain – gun emplacements dot the landscape.

✖ Saz Gölü

39°45N 44°03E

A huge area of marshes enclosed by mountains at the foot of Büyükağrı Dağ. The area consists of wet grazing marsh, with large stands of short reed and rushes, some areas of open water, and small islands which are often used for livestock grazing. The marshes can be very wet in May and hold a good range of breeding herons, ducks and waders, including Ferruginous Duck; Moustached Warblers are abundant in the reedbeds. Other breeding birds include Montagu's Harrier and Bee-eater.

Saz Gölü lies only a few kilometres north of Doğubayazıt, the 'tourist centre' of the area where the İshak Paşa Sarayı palace is a major archaeological attraction. Mongolian Trumpeter Finch is regularly seen around the café near the palace. The mountain road between Doğubayazıt and Muradiye goes over the highest pass accessible by road in Turkey at Tendürek Dağı and many mountain species are regularly seen along here.

These include Golden Eagle, Shore Lark, Black Redstart, Rock Thrush, Snow, Crimson-winged and Mongolian Trumpeter Finches.

TIMING

The marshes often dry up in summer and are best visited when the area is wet during the breeding season, in May/June.

SPECIES

- *Demoiselle Crane* Bred here in 1971 but has not been found since.
- *White-winged Black Tern* Good numbers in spring and may breed.
- *Citrine Wagtail* Probably breeds.
- *Alpine Accentor and Grey-necked Bunting* In the surrounding hills.
- *Paddyfield Warbler* This is one of the few places away from Van marshes where this species has been recorded.

ACCESS

Saz Gölü is mostly easily reached on the road from Ağrı, east of the Doğubayazıt/İğdır road. From Van the most direct route is the minor road via Muradiye. This road is badly maintained, heavily used and controlled by the army, passes close to the Iranian border and is currently closed after 5 p.m. but, if you are allowed to stop (and it is wise to make it clear to any check-point that you would like to), is an excellent area for birdwatching! This sensitive area lies close to the Turkey/Iran/Georgia border, only 30 km south-west of Jerevan.

✖ Murat Vadigi, north of Bulanik

39°10N 42°19E

This section of the Murat River lies north of Van Gölü, and the Muş–Patnos road. Here the river has a wide floodplain which is part cultivated and part wet grasslandwith a gorge at the western end. Winding irrigation channels criss-cross the cultivated steppe to the south of the river.

Black-winged Stilt

On the floodplain Montagu's Harrier, Quail and Black-bellied Sandgrouse are common and Short-eared Owl possibly breeds. Great Bustards are regularly recorded, and 26 Little Bustards were seen in September 1989. In the river are islands and gravel spits where Spoonbill, Common Crane and Gull-billed Tern nest, but the star bird is Demoiselle Crane. Eastern Turkey is the only place in the Western Palearctic where Demoiselle Crane can be seen on its breeding-grounds, but they can be difficult to find in the long grass. Black-winged Pratincole has also bred here and can be common on passage in September.

Nearby Haçlı Gölü is also worth visiting. The lake is shallow with muddy fringes and the surrounding wet grassland can be full of birds, particularly during passage periods.

TIMING

Visit from May to August to see the Demoiselle Cranes. Caspian Plover has been seen in August, and Great Snipe is regular in May and June.

SPECIES

- *Pygmy Cormorant* This is one of only a few places in eastern Turkey where this species may be encountered.
- *Cattle Egret* There have been several records here since the mid-1980s.
- *Spotted Crake* Has been heard calling in the breeding season.
- *Marsh Warbler* Regularly seen and probably breeds.
- *Paddyfield Warbler* Recorded here in late May 1993.

ACCESS

The most interesting area for birds is the river floodplain. There are various tracks that cross the farmland, although their accessibility will depend on the weather. About 8 km west of Bulanık, Yoncalı lies north of the main road. Turn into the village and the road follows a ridge above the floodplain giving panoramic views; various tracks off this road go towards the river.

The access most frequently used by birdwatchers lies beyond Yoncalı and leads to some gravel islands in the river farther west. Where the main road to Mus, swings south-west, turn off following the road straight on to Varto until, after about 1 km, you reach Balutu. A track to the left goes into the village and opposite a rough dirt track leads almost to the river (3–4 km) although it may not be accessible to vehicles for its entire length. The Demoiselle Cranes are usually to be found on the gravel islands in the river. Alternative look on the islands at the end of the track from Yoncalı. It is also worth scanning from this track for feeding birds.

Haçlı Gölü lies about 12 km south of Bulanık on the Ovakışla road.

✖ Nemrut Daği

38°37N 42°13E

It was the lava flows from Nemrut Dağı volcano which blocked the outflow from Van Gölü and created the waterbody which exists today. The volcano has not been active since the 1440s but there are still signs of

Shore Lark

geological activity with hot springs, sulphurous gases and rumblings from rock crevices! The main crater-lake is one of the largest in the world, measuring 5 x 2.5 km and is 150 m deep; there are also smaller pools with hot springs and reedbeds. The inside of the crater is vegetated with low scrub that gives way to barren rock at higher altitudes. Rocky cliffs form the 3000-m high crater walls.

The crater-lake is best known as one of only a handful of sites in Turkey with a relict population of breeding Velvet Scoter. Common birds inside the crater include Woodlark, Shore Lark, Tawny Pipit, Alpine Accentor, White-throated Robin, Rock Thrush, Ring Ouzel, Red-fronted Serin and Desert Finch.

TIMING

The climate is hard with long, cold winters and hot, dry summers. The best time to visit – and probably the only time when the crater is accessible – is late May–July/August.

SPECIES

- *Eagle Owl* Nests and roosts in crevices in the sheer crater walls.
- *Radde's Accentor* Can be unobtrusive and difficult to find amongst poplar and birch thickets in higher rocky areas.
- *Trumpeter Finch* Has been seen here once, in August 1987.
- *Cinereous Bunting* Has been recorded here a few times and probably breeds in small numbers.

ACCESS

Take the Ahlat road north out of Tatvan along the north-west shore of Van Gölü and turn left at the Türkpetrol garage on the edge of town. From here it is about 15 km along an unsurfaced road to the crater rim, and a further 3 km from the rim down to the edge of the main lake. The track into the crater is badly eroded each winter by snow-melt and has to be re-made each year; it is therefore usually impassable and dangerous until mid-June. This is not a good place to get stuck!

✖ SODALI GÖLÜ (ARIN GÖLÜ)

38°49N 42°59E

Sodalı Gölü lies between Ahlat and Ercis. To the south lies the northern shore of Van Gölü, and to the north Turkey's second highest mountain, Süphan Dağı. The lake is saline and on the whole is surrounded by arable land. To the east, between the lake and Göldüzü village, is a small but rich area of marshes and wet meadows. Common breeding birds include Black-necked Grebes, Black-winged Stilts and Redshanks with a few pairs of White-headed Ducks and Caspian Terns. In autumn waders are numerous and amongst the hundreds of Little Stints are smaller numbers of species such as Broad-billed and Marsh Sandpipers.

TIMING

The lake's greatest importance is as a moulting and passage site from July to September, with more than 4000 Black-necked Grebes, 6000 Ruddy Shelduck and 750 White-headed Ducks. A wide variety of birds breed in the marshes, so visits in May and June should be rewarding. Avoid late evening when the sun is dazzling.

SPECIES

- *Lammergeier, Golden Eagle and Saker* All are seen and probably breed.
- *Great Bustard* May still breed in the area.
- *White-winged Black Tern* large numbers can be seen in summer and some may breed along with a few pairs of Whiskered Terns.

ACCESS

From the main road take the road to Gölduzu and then the first track to the right as you enter the village. From the end of this track walk out to a small hillock which provides a good view of the lake and marshes. You can also birdwatch over the marshes from the village, but you may find yourself followed by interested locals!

✖ ÇALDIRAN SAZLIĞI

39°09N 43°56E

The Bendimahi river, although only 50 km long is a powerful watercourse, fed by springs at the base of Tendürek Dağı and flowing through a rugged jumble of black lava into the north-eastern corner of Van Gölü. Much of the river valley is deeply cut, but to the north of Çaldıran it widens to an area of wet meadows and marshes. These are inundated for several months by the river and cut for hay by hand – and this tradition has resulted in marshes rich in flowers and birds. Species which occur and may breed here include some seldom seen this far east such as Pygmy Cormorant and Bittern, along with Common Crane and Montagu's Harrier.

The valley provides a migration flyway for many birds, with a small but visible movement of birds of prey overhead in autumn, and any stands of poplars and willows used by migrating passerines, especially warblers and flycatchers. Breeding birds include White-throated Robin, Black Redstart and Rock Thrush on the rocky slopes, with Bimaculated Lark and Crimson-winged Finch on the plateaux.

TIMING

May/June for the breeding birds and mid-August to the end of September for migration. Search for passerines in the early morning.

SPECIES

- *Saker* Seen regularly in this area.
- *Eagle Owl* Occurs in narrow rocky gorges along the river valley.
- *Snow Finch and Twite* Common on the higher slopes of Tendürek Dağı.
- *Armenian Gull* Regularly seen along the river.

ACCESS

The Muradiye–Doğubayazıt road follows the river valley and provides a good view of the marshes. However, the road runs close to the Iranian border. All vehicles are checked by the army, so explain that you are birdwatching and ask if there are any objections to you stopping along the road. This road is usually closed after 5 p.m.

✖ Erçek Gölü

38°39N 43°33E

Erçek Gölü lies east of Van, divided from Van Gölü by an ancient lava stream. The lake is brackish with with gently shelving shores to the south and east; here saltflats border the lake and provide excellent feeding areas for migrant waders with Marsh, Terek and Broad-billed Sandpipers regular in autumn. There is little fringing vegetation except in the east where there is a small area of damp meadows and reedbeds. Common nesting birds include Black-necked Grebe, Ruddy Shelduck, Shelduck and Redshank, but the lake's greatest importance is probably as a post-breeding area. In July/August thousands of Ruddy Shelducks and Shelducks come here to roost, and families of newly fledged Greater Flamingos, probably birds from Lake Irmia, Iran in can be seen.

Çenge Gölü, a small lake off the south-west tip of Erçek and largely overgrown by reed, is also worth a visit. Red-necked Grebes breed here, crakes can be numerous and Paddyfield Warbler can be easy to find with as many as 10 birds seen on one visit.

TIMING

In late May Red-necked Phalarope passes through in large numbers (as many as 900 recorded). The post-breeding flocks of birds in autumn include concentrations of up to 3000 Black-necked Grebes.

SPECIES

- *Goldeneye* There have been several recent summer records.
- *Saker* Several records.
- *Great Bustard* may breed in the surrounding area in small numbers.
- *Caspian Plover, Great Snipe and Desert Wheatear* Among the rare migrants recorded here.
- *Crimson-winged Finch* Regularly recorded and probably breeds.

ACCESS

Erçek Gölü lies north of the Van–Özalp road. Much of the lake can be viewed from the road. The shallow east side is best for birds.

Çenge Gölü next to the road south-west of Erçek. Best viewed by walking around the perimeter; this takes about one hour.

Travelling to Erçek from Van the road passes a reservoir and rubbish tip (a regular spot for Armenian Gull). 7 km farther on the rocky hillsides between the reservoir and a deep railway cutting to the right of the road are good for Grey-necked Bunting; Eagle Owl is often seen in the cutting itself.

✖ Van Wetlands

Despite its size little lives in Van Gölü and birds are seldom seen upon it because of its high mineral content.

By contrast, where fresh water enters the lake small deltas form, and the floodplains of these streams and rivers can be rich in wet-meadows, reedbeds and saltmarshes, providing valuable habitat for breeding and migrating waterbirds and passerines. There are at least 30 such water-courses draining into Van Gölü, but only five of them are IBAs.

Since about 1985 water levels in Van Gölü have been rising (the reason for this is unclear), and in 1995 were 2.5 m above previous 'normal' levels. This has lead to the loss, probably permanent, of 3 of the IBAs, with 3 more seriously threatened. It is possible that when levels stabilize once more new wetlands will form upstream at some sites, so for now, the 6 sites adjacent to Van Gölü and affected by the water level rise are listed together below.

TIMING

May to September with the migration periods providing some exciting birds and birdwatching.

SPECIES

- *White Pelican* Can be numerous although probably does not breed.
- *Red-necked Grebe, Squacco and Purple Herons, Marbled, Ferruginous and White-headed Ducks* All characteristic breeding species.
- *Black-winged Pratincole, Broad-billed and Terek Sandpipers and Great Snipe* Regular migrants in small numbers.
- *Red-necked Phalarope* Good numbers on migration in spring.
- *Armenian Gull* Can be seen at all sites and may be numerous.

✖ Ahlat

38°45N 42°26E

On the north-west shores of Van Gölü, a short distance south-west of Ahlat, lies an area of open water, reedbed and wet grassland. Although disturbed by locals and their livestock, this area can provide some excellent and easy birdwatching with an excellent range of wetland species and migrant passerines. Rising water levels in Van Gölü have affected this site.

ACCESS

The site is bordered to the south-east by the raised Tatvan–Erciş road, and this divides the wetland from Van Gölü. Birdwatching is best from the north-westerly side where there is a steep slope which provides good raised views. The shoreline of Van Gölü is the best area for waders.

✖ ÇELEBIBAĞ SAZLIĞI

38°58N 43°20E

The Ilıca river enters Van Gölü south-west of Ercis, and has created an area of saltmarshes with some reedbeds at fresh-water inflows. Inundated in 1995 and now probably lost.

✖ BENDIMAHI DELTA

38°56N 43°39E

In contrast to the deep-cut gorges below Çaldıran, this powerful river is slow and winding in its lower reaches, and wet meadows with rush and reedbeds 10–20 m wide lie along its bends. Citrine Wagtail breeds in this habitat. The land is still managed traditionally with the meadows cut once a year by hand, large areas grazed by cattle, and arable land on the higher ground where Montagu's Harrier, Quail and Crimson-winged Finch can be found. The rushes and reeds provide valuable cover for nesting and roosting birds, whilst the river with its dense growth of submerged vegetation provides good feeding for wildfowl.

At the Bendimahi's outlet to the lake a delta has formed and the water is shallow with mud banks and sand bars. These are excellent feeding and roosting places for waders, gulls and terns, whilst muddy inlets and extensive reedbeds provide shelter and feeding areas used by wildfowl and Red-necked Phalaropes.

Once one of the most important wetland areas in eastern Turkey, the delta is now largely under water but it is possible that replacement habitat will gradually develop upstream.

ACCESS

View from road and various tracks through and around the village on the north side of the river.

White-winged Black Tern

✖ VAN SAZLIĞI

38°29N 43°19E

The Van marshes consist of several hundred hectares of wet-meadows and small lagoons between Van town and the lake – separated from the latter by a narrow strip of sand – and divided in two by the railway and the road to the ferryport. The northern marshes are rather open, heavily disturbed by people and probably not worth visiting, although there are birds there. The marshes to the south consist mainly of reed- and sedgebeds – where Savi's Warbler and Bearded Tit occur in small numbers – with wet grazing marsh and pools along the lake shore. Van Kalesi (an ancient fortress standing on a huge rock) provides wonderful views over the southern marshes and the lake, and species such as Lesser Kestrel, Eagle Owl, Alpine Swift, Bee-eater and Rock Thrush can be seen here, most of them breeding. Around Van town Scarlet Rosefinch occurs in poplars and Yellow-throated Sparrow has recently been found.

The marshes support a wide range of breeding birds – Caspian Terns are seen here regularly and may breed locally. During the migration periods in May and September almost anything could turn up. Paddyfield Warbler was first found here in 1986 and has been seen every year since. A few pairs probably breed but the birds can be extremely difficult to find.

These marshes were still largely intact in summer 1995 but are likely to disappear if the water level continues to rise.

ACCESS

View the marshes from the castle (which looks west) in the morning, and from the sandbar (which looks east) in the afternoon. To reach the sandbar take the road from Van to the ferryport; turn left just before the port down a small track which leads to a restaurant on the shore. From here it should be possible to wade across to the sandbar, which stretches for about 2 km along the edge of the marsh, to the airport in the south.

The marshes cannot be reached from the castle because of a series of large dykes separating the meadows from the marshes.

✖ EDREMIT SAZLIĞI

38°24N 43°18E

A small shallow lake about 10 km south of Van, separated from Van Gölü by a narrow sandy ridge. A 5-m wide strip of reed stretches along part of the inland shore. Inundated in July 1995.

✖ HORKUM GÖLÜ

38°20N 42°56E

A small lagoon just east of Göründü, south of Van and separated from the lake by a narrow strip of gravel and sand. The lagoon has relatively large reed- and sedgebeds, and there are wet-meadows and pastures to the south and south-west. Inundated in July 1995.

GREECE

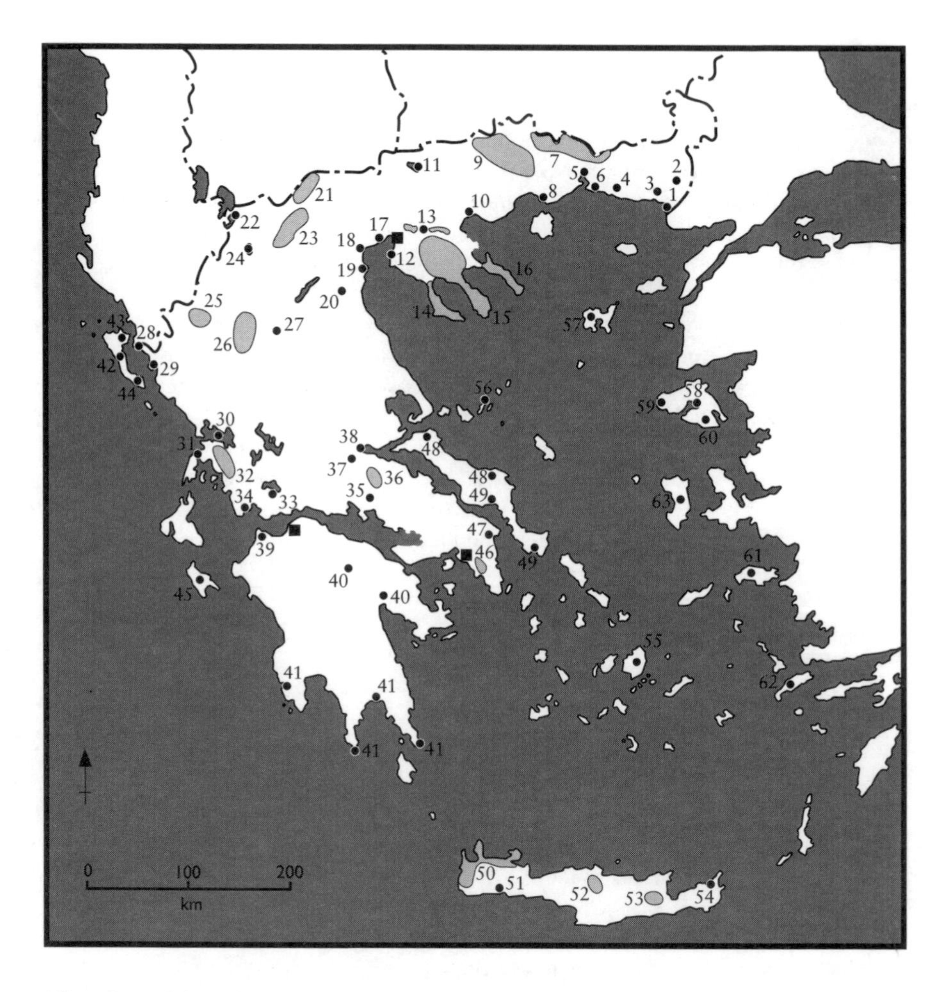

1 Evros Delta, 2 Dadia-Soufli forest, 3 Avas Gorge, 4 Lake Mitrikou (Lake Ismardia), 5 Porto Lagos, 6 Thracian Lagoons, 7 Eastern Rodopi, 8 Nestos Delta, 9 Nestos Valley and the central Rodopi, 10 Strymon delta, 11 Lake Kerkini, 12 Angelochori and Epanomi Lagoons, 13 Lakes Volvi and Koronia, 14 Kassandra Peninsula, 15 Cholomontas Mountains and Sithonia Peninsula, 16 Mount Athos Peninsula, 17 Axios Delta, 18 Aliakmon delta, 19 Alyki Kitros lagoon, 20 Mount Olympus, 21 Voras Mountains, 22 Prespa Lakes, Lakes Petron, Vegoritis, Cheimaditis and Zazaris, 24 Lake Kastoria, 25 Vikos-Aoos national park, 26 Pindos Mountains, 27 Metóra, 28 Kalamas delta and Gorge, 29 Acherondas Gorge and Souliou mountains, 30 Amrvrakikos gulf, 31 Lefkas and Lake Voulkorio, 32 Akarnian mountains, 33 Klissoura Gorge, 34 Mesolongi wetlands, 35 Delphi, 36 Mount Parnassos, 37 Mount Iti, 38 Sperchios Delta, 39 Cape Araxos, 40 Mykenai and Lake Stymfalia, 41 Southern Pelopponese, 42 Central Corfu, 43 Northern Corfu, 44 Southern Corfu, 45 Zakynthos and the Strofades, 46 Athens City, 47 Marathon marshes, 48 Northern Evvia 49 Southern Evvia, 50 West Crete (Chania), 51 Samaria Gorge, 52 Central Crete, 53 Lesithi Plateau, 54 Crete: offshore isalnds and headlands, 55 Naxos, 56 Northern Sporades, 57 Limnos, 58 Lesbos: Kallonis Bay, 59 West Lesbos, 60 Agiassos, 61 Samos and Fourni, 62 Kos, 63 Chios

Greece is a diverse country, covering about 132,000 square kilometres, made up of a mountainous peninsula and thousands of islands. The far north-west is almost continental in character, despite the proximity of the Mediterranean, and the interior is mainly mountainous. There are only three really large cities (Athens, Thessaloniki and Patras) sharing about half of the country's human population of 10,000,000. Agriculture and tourism are the most important sources of income. In the east, the plain of Thessaly, the so-called bread-basket of Greece, is the centre of an extensive grain, cotton and tobacco industry. Elsewhere, the rural landscape is one of olive groves and smallholdings of figs, peaches and almonds, or extensive citrus groves (especially in the wetter west). Goat and sheep grazing, along with forestry, dominate the uplands.

Greece is an exciting place for the naturalist: there are about 5000 species of wild plants, of which 742 are endemic. Thousands more endemic subspecies are found on isolated mountains and islands.

Crete is the largest and the most southerly of the islands, and its mountainous interior lends to it an almost continental character. I have grouped the other islands into various sets. Of the Ionian, Corfu (Kérkira) is the most northerly. The Dodecanese hug the Turkish coastline and share with their continental neighbour many migrants and a few speciality residents. The Cyclades are strung across the Aegean as if thrown there, their many secret inlets and inaccessible cliffs the haunt of Audouin's Gulls and Eleonora's Falcons.

Importance for birds

Conservationists classify birds according to their status, those which are threatened with extinction at world level being the highest priority. Of 24 European species which fall into this category, Greece is important for eight: Dalmatian Pelican, Ferruginous Duck, White-headed Duck, Spotted and Imperial Eagles, Lesser Kestrel, Slender-billed Curlew and Audouin's Gull. A further three species occur in small numbers or irregularly: Lesser White-fronted and Red-breasted Geese and Aquatic Warbler.

Several species with very restricted ranges, are found in Greece: Levant Sparrowhawk, Rock Partridge, Olive-tree and Rüppell's Warblers, Semi-collared Flycatcher, Masked Shrike, Sombre Tit, Krüper's and Rock Nuthatches and Cinereous, Black-headed and Cretzschmar's Buntings.

Other species sought after by visiting birdwatchers include Black Vulture, Lammergeier, Lesser Spotted Eagle and Eleonora's Falcon (of which Greece has the largest population in the world).

Getting there and getting around

Most of the cheaper flights from Britain and northern Europe are charters. These mostly go to the more popular islands (Crete, Corfu, Kos, Lesbos, Rhodes, Samos, Skiathos and Zákynthos). Scheduled flights go to some of these, Athens, where there are numerous connections, and Thessaloniki.

Some of the less popular islands can be reached by air from Athens, and all but the very smallest and uninhabited islands have a regular ferry service connecting with a larger neighbour. In the Dodecanese, Sporades and Cyclades these voyages can be good for Cory's Shearwaters, Eleonora's Falcons and occasionally British Storm Petrels and Audouin's Gulls. Greece is also connected by sea-crossings to various ports in Turkey and Italy.

Crossing to and from Turkey is no problem (although if you fly to and from Greece on a charter flight, but also stay overnight in Turkey during that time, your return ticket is invalidated, apparently). The border with Bulgaria is open, and the only hassle may be long queues. It is with the Former Yugoslav Republic of Macedonia (known to Greeks as Skopje) and Albania that relations with Greece are sufficiently volatile to warrant checking and re-checking the latest frontier situation. Some of the best birdwatching is to be had in this border region (for example at the wonderful Prespa lakes), but binoculars may be treated with suspicion away from known birdwatching areas. However, courtesy and patience with military personnel are usually enough to prevent serious difficulties.

Once in Greece, a car is practically essential. The international companies tend to be expensive, but are linked with various breakdown services. I have to say that even the international firms have let me down with alarming regularity and I have never hired a problem-free car from Thessaloniki airport. However, unless you have a reliable recommendation, or are a mechanical whizz-kid, I would advise avoiding local firms.

Public transport is among the most comprehensive in Europe, so there are few places which are truly inaccessible to non-drivers. However, the big wetlands and montane forests are best explored by car as you need to cover the sort of distances which cannot be contemplated on foot.

A note on place-names: firstly, some towns, lakes, rivers and islands are known by two or more names locally and in some cases, such as Corfu, have alternative names used only by foreigners. Spellings for any given place-name are not always uniform in the Greek script, and when transliterated often spawn a plethora of variants. The two most confusing letters are *gamma* and *chi*. Iannades, Yannades, Giannades would all refer to the same village in Kérkira (that is, Corfu). Here I use the Latin G throughout. Similarly, Chíos and Chalkidiki (my preferred spellings) are often Híos and Halkidiki, and sometimes Khíos, etc: the *Ch* is pronounced as in the Scottish *loch*. Other common variants include oi = i, ph = f (Delfi/Delfoi/Delphi), k = c (Kyklades/Cyclades), nd = nt (Rendina/Rentina), d = dh (reflecting the soft pronunciation of *delta* as in *this*), gg = ng (Mesologgi/Mesolongi).

Conservation

Greece was one of the first countries to sign the Ramsar convention on the conservation of wetlands and has designated 11 wetlands as Ramsar sites. However, until recently none of them were delineated and they all await agreed management plans. This is evident in the frequent conflicts over resource use, not helped by the fact that no fewer than seven ministries have some claim on the use and management of water resources. Thus over the last two decades the loss and degradation of Greek wetlands has been appalling. Sadly, this loss has continued to increase since Greece joined the European Union. EU funds are being spent at such a pace, and with so little practical safeguard, that habitat damage occurs almost before anyone knows what is going on.

The Hellenic Ornithological Society, the BirdLife Partner in Greece, along with bodies such as WWF-Greece, are fighting such threats and gradually getting the message home. Public interest is slowly warming to their cause.

Habitats

Agriculture accounts for much of Greece's land-cover, and traditional land-uses such as olive groves and livestock-raising are important for birds. Local specialities, including the rarer shrikes, buntings and warblers, are dependent on the small-scale, mixed or non-intensive agriculture typical of much of the country. Forestry is also important, but now only 6 per cent of the country is covered by broadleaved woodland.

Greece has some of the largest and – historically at least – most important wetlands in the Mediterranean. For the reasons outlined above, this is changing, but there are still several outstanding examples.

Montane habitats – high alpine moor, forest and pasture – are important features of much of the land-mass of continental Greece. Species such as Shore Lark and Alpine Accentor feature in the highest parts, and the more intact forests are important for raptors, owls and woodpeckers. In the Peloponnese and many islands, the hills are drier and covered in maquis or garrigue, good for Cretzschmar's Buntings, Rüppell's Warblers and, on limestone, Rock Nuthatches.

The country has an immensely long coastline, much of it rocky. Many of the islands remain undeveloped despite the march of mass tourism and are important for Eleonora's Falcons and Audouin's Gulls.

Seasons

Greece enjoys a typical eastern Mediterranean climate, tempered only by altitude. Spring and autumn can be wonderful but unreliable seasons. March can be glorious and the following May awful, or vice versa. Spring migrants start to arrive in early March, and for many species there are still birds on the move in May, especially Arctic-nesting waders. Summers are hot with temperatures often reaching 35 °C and more. At this time, many of the wetlands will be dry and summer migrants are thinking of leaving. By August, migration is well under way for many breeding species and positively steaming along in September and early October. In the mountains spring is a good month later and winter a month earlier. Winter can be stormy, but with fine, sometimes warm, days.

BIRDWATCHING SITES

EVROS DELTA

40°52N 26°00E

Long-standing Hellenophile birdwatchers try to avoid comparing the Evros delta of the 1960s with that of today. The Evros, which forms the border with Turkey where it is called the Meriç has been canalized, so that many of its lagoons rely more on ground-water and rain than on seasonal flooding. The great Drana lagoon was illegally drained in the tragically mistaken belief that it caused soil salinity in the surrounding farmland.

On the other hand, those who did not know the area before the dreadful drainage schemes can enjoy what is still an interesting wetland, without realising how great the loss has been. The Evros delta lies on one of the great migration highways of the world. Thus during April, May, August and September spectacular congregations of waders and waterfowl can be seen, and rarities such as Sociable, Greater Sand and White-tailed Plovers and Great Black-headed Gulls are regular, with odd records of Caspian Plover; Broad-billed and Terek Sandpipers are annual, and Slender-billed Curlews are more likely here than anywhere else in Europe.

The passage of White and Black Storks and White Pelicans can be spectacular, especially in August, while spring sees a regular influx of Red-footed Falcons (sometimes in their hundreds), dozens of Pallid Harriers, and the arrival of an impressive list of breeding birds. These include Spur-winged Plovers, Ruddy Shelduck and Gull-billed Terns, but no longer many of the egrets and ibises which form so indelible a memory for the old Evros hands.

Winter wildfowl numbers can fluctuate, but there are usually internationally important numbers of the usual northern ducks, which are joined by Pygmy Cormorants, Dalmatian Pelicans and small numbers of Spotted and White-tailed Eagles. Many raptors forage in the area throughout the year, from the forests and hills to the north described in the next entry.

TIMING

Good all the time, but nothing compares to spring passage in late April and early May.

SPECIES

- *Lesser White-fronted Goose* Seems to occur when winter is mild in Greece and severe elsewhere, in the saltmarsh around Drana.
- *Slender-billed Curlew* Most often recorded in the saltmarsh area immediately south of the Drana lagoon.
- *White-tailed Eagle* Often seen sitting around what remains of the Drana lagoon from late summer onwards.

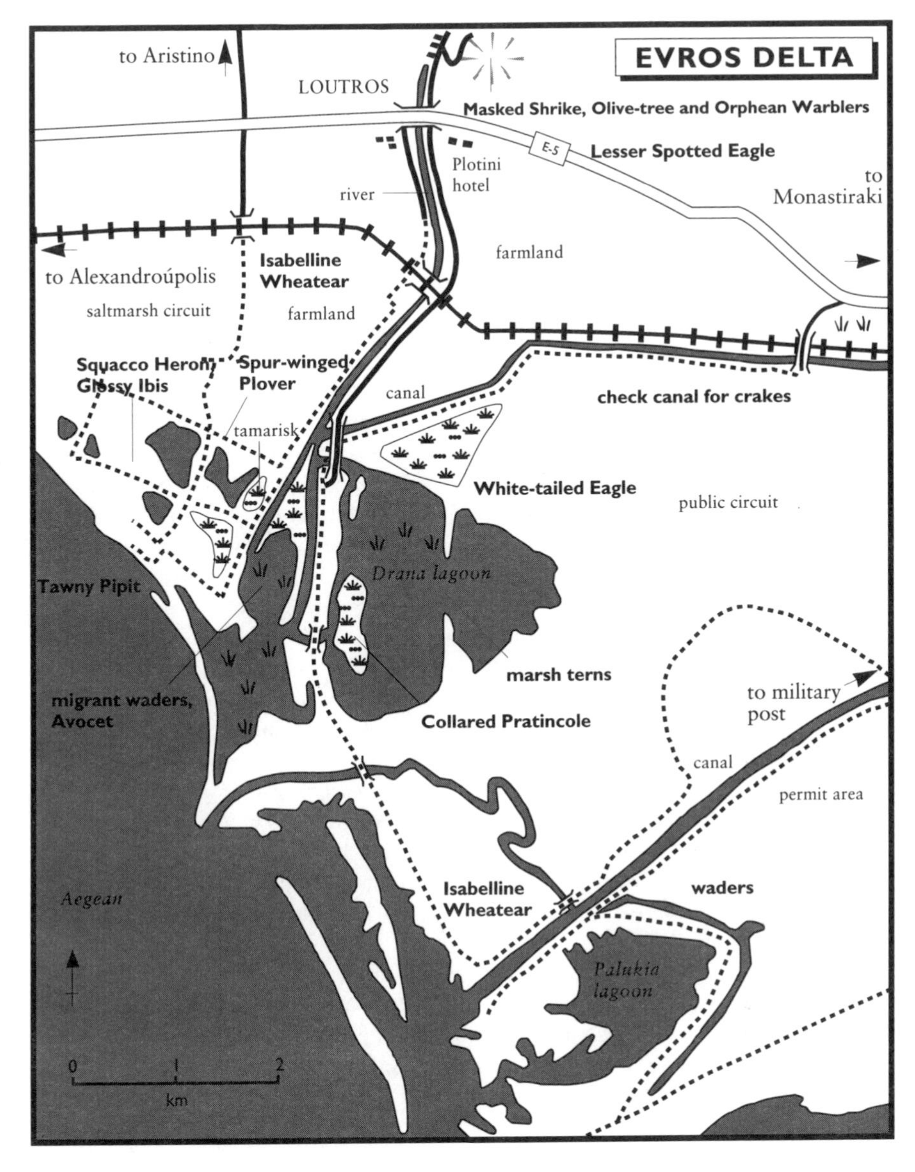

- ◆ *Isabelline Wheatear* Among the species at the western limit of their range, breeding alongside all the dirt roads in the area.
- ◆ *Masked Shrike and Olive-tree Warbler* Nest on the scrubby hillside at Loutros.

ACCESS

There is an area of open access in the delta, and an adjacent area for which a military permit is required. This is not difficult to obtain with proper pre-planning, but practically impossible on spec. In any case there will be some delay, since the permit will need stamping by both the police and the army:

this can take 24 hours (or only a few minutes) *after* arrival in the area. The military area can be excellent and can add value to the trip, or it can be no better than the public area. The only way to be certain of not missing anything is to cover both. For a permit is it best to contact Gareth Trewartha, who runs a Thessaloniki-based agency, Charioteer Ltd by fax (31 228968) allowing eight weeks. A fee (£20 in 1995 – which may include more than one person) is payable. A proportion of this goes into a conservation fund. You then receive your permit from the Security Police in Alexandroúpolis (opposite the theatre), which you take to the white army building a few blocks to the west. It may also be possible to have the permit ready stamped and delivered to an Alexandroúpolis hotel, courtesy of Charioteer.

The E-5 road from Alexandroúpolis passes Loutros on its way to Monastiraki. These two villages roughly mark the limits of the accessible area. South of the road is a railway line and beyond this is the public area, surrounded by a track. There are two access points to this circular track: a turning south of Loutros by the Hotel Plotini, or about 8 km farther along the E-5. This circular route takes in, anticlockwise from Loutros, the Drana lagoon (now much rehabilitated, and becoming quite good), and some estuarine habitat before running east alongside an arm of the Evros. Turn left at the military post and left again along a drainage canal (look for crakes) back to Drana and the Loutros track. If you have a permit, you can cross at the military post onto another circuit which includes the excellent Palukia lagoon and Lake Nymfon.

A little-known area is the seaward saltmarsh south-west of Loutros, and across the main channel from the Drana lagoon. A track leads from the *west* (Alexandroúpolis) side of Loutros bridge along the bank. Zero the kilometre counter at the bridge: to cross the railway it is necessary to come off the bank at km 1.3 and rejoin it at km 2.5. From here on there is good marsh alongside the bank and at km 5.4 a grid of tracks leaves to the right, as detailed on the map, affording access to areas with varying degrees of salinity and water levels.

Accommodation is available at the Plotini hotel and other places in the area. Alexandroúpolis is served by flights from Athens, but not, frustratingly, from Thessaloniki. Thessaloniki-hired cars can be dropped at Alexandroúpolis airport for a big one-way hire fee (around £70 in 1995). The distance between these two cities is some 335 km via several of the sites covered in the next few pages. Recently Budget and Europcar have established services out of Alexandroúpolis airport.

DADIÁ-SOUFLI FOREST

41°00N 26°00E

So far no one has found a better place in Europe for birds of prey than this forest in the Evros mountains, and there probably isn't one. Of 32 (yes, thirty-two) raptor species regularly recorded here at least 20 breed in this Evros valley forest. This is not including seven types of owls, six of which breed here. Until recently, this magnificent area was severely threatened by overexploitation of the forest, which does still happen.

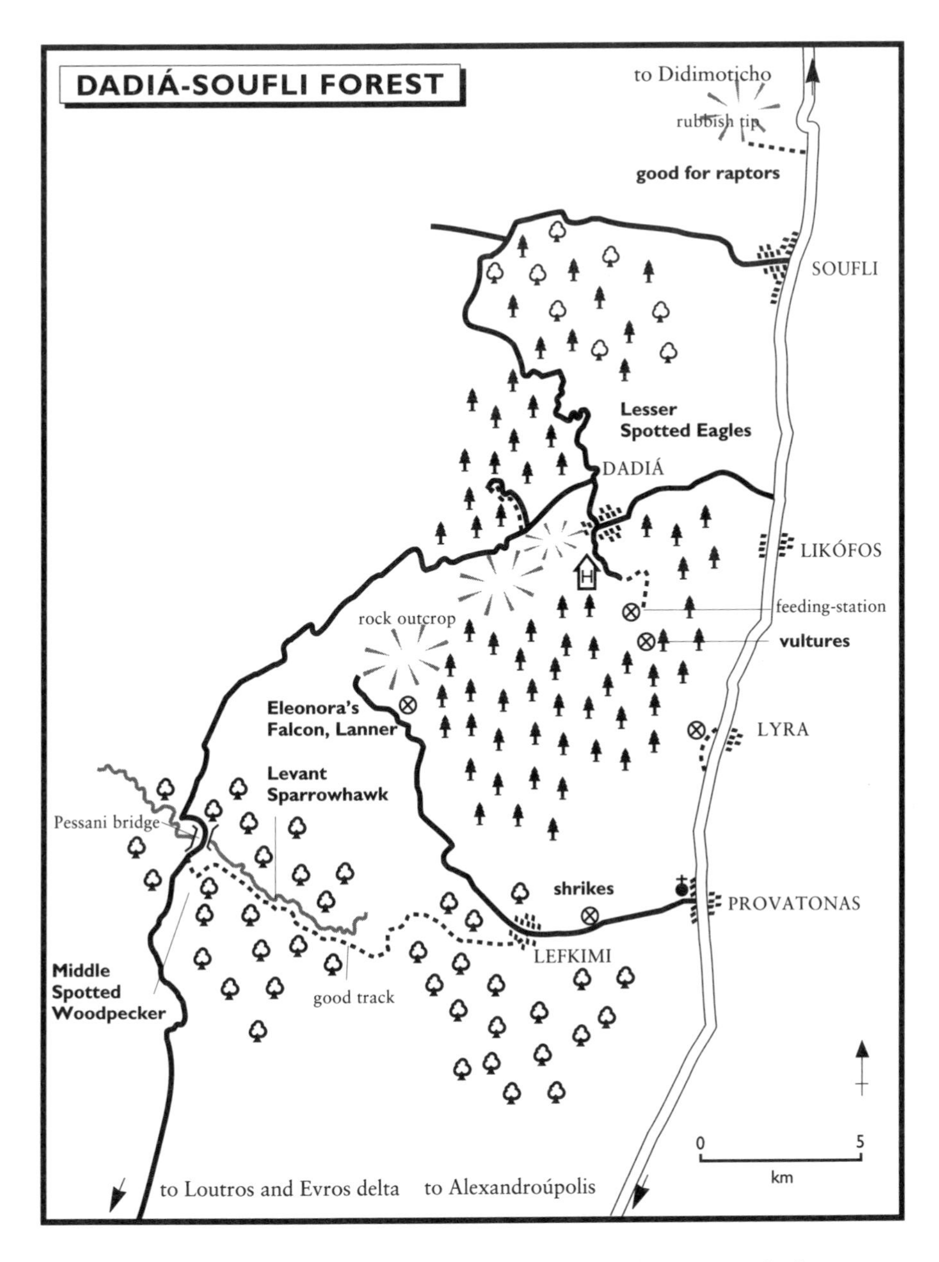

However, the area is now a reserve and WWF are running a raptor-feeding station which attracts hundreds of visitors, in a deliberate attempt to boost the local economy through wildlife tourism. So please use the facilities and spend lots of money in the surrounding area!

Already the benefits of this work are beginning to show. Black Vulture numbers have climbed to well over 100 and these, along with Griffons and Egyptians, come to the feeding station in front of the hide at Dadiá.

A lone Lammergeier awaits the chance arrival of a mate to complete the vulture set. Of the eagles Imperial, sadly, is in decline, and White-tailed continues to struggle, but the other five are doing well (12 pairs of Lesser Spotted, 3–4 of Golden...), as are the three *Accipiters*. White-tailed and Imperial Eagles are more common in winter, when they are joined by Spotted Eagles, Merlins and, occasionally, Sakers. Rarer visitors include Red Kites sporadically and Steppe Eagles on passage. Eleonora's Falcons, which breed late at the coast, spend the first half of the summer hawking insects over the numerous rocky outcrops.

To this mouth-watering menu can be added the 12 pairs of Black Storks, numerous Rollers and three north-eastern Greece specialities: Semi-collared Flycatcher, Masked Shrike and Olive-tree Warbler.

TIMING

Early spring sees most raptors take to the air in display, and they are at their most visible. Reptile and flower enthusiasts should wait until mid-May.

SPECIES

- *Imperial Eagle* Occasionally visits the feeding-stations and is still seen around Lefkimi village from time to time.
- *Lesser Spotted Eagle* Can nearly always be seen hunting over the farmland below Dadiá village.
- *Lanner* Often seen at the rock pinnacle above Lefkimi, where it may nest alongside the Griffon and Egyptian Vultures.
- *Masked Shrike and Orphean and Olive-tree Warblers* Inhabit scrubbier farmed or grazed areas above Lefkimi.

ACCESS

The road from Alexandroúpolis runs east past the Evros delta, then north to the borders with Turkey and Bulgaria. Some 67 km from Alexandroúpolis is Soufli, at the north-eastern corner of this superb area. Dadiá is reached by turning left just past Likófos. In the village signs (depicting eagles) lead you south to the information centre and on to the hide. The main road continues through Dadiá into excellent forest areas.

There are several other vantage points, shown on the map. Several kilometres beyond Lefkimi the road is closed and here there is a vantage point across to a rocky outcrop which attracts raptors and Black Storks.

A slower but highly profitable way into Dadiá village is to take the road north through Loutros (*see* Evros delta). After 49 km there is a right turn (not signposted) to Dadiá, a couple of kilometres farther on. At Pessani bridge, two-thirds of the way along this back road, is a good area for watching for raptors, woodpeckers and warblers. There is a comfortable small hotel at the information centre. For the information centre tel (0)554 52360.

AVAS GORGE

40°55N 25°45E

A mere 10 km north of Alexandroúpolis is the Avas valley, effectively the south-western extreme of a wonderful forest ecosystem stretching to Dadiá at the opposite corner. Well known to birdwatchers because of its ease of access, it is genuinely important for breeding raptors and as a migration bottleneck (a single wave of 1100 Levant Sparrowhawks in late April, for example...) as well as for sought-after species such as Masked Shrike. The gorge is essentially an area of high, steep rocks rather than cliffs. On the rocks and in the riverine woodland are Sombre Tits, Bonelli's Warblers, Rock Nuthatches and Rollers. South of Avas the area around a ruined castle is good for Masked Shrikes, Rufous Bush Robins and Orphean Warblers.

Raptors are the main interest, and Honey Buzzards, Black Kites, Egyptian, Black and Griffon Vultures, Short-toed, Imperial, Golden and Booted Eagles, Lesser Kestrels, Lanners and Peregrines all put in regular appearances.

TIMING

The last week in April is peak passage time for Levant Sparrowhawk and many passerines which use the valley. The area is little known outside the spring 'high season' for birdwatchers; all information welcome.

SPECIES

- *Eagle Owl* Calls at night, and is occasionally seen flying in the gloom above the gorge.
- *Isabelline Wheatear* Has been seen at the railway line west of the ruins.

ACCESS

In Alexandroúpolis, cross the railway line and head north towards Avandas (the signpost from the main road is in Greek only – Αβανδας). After about 8 km there is a track off left to the railway station past the ruined castle. The main road continues through Avandas and on, after a kilometre or so, through the gorge. There is a track to the right which makes a pleasant and profitable walk up the hill. There is plenty of accommodation in Alexandroúpolis and along the coast.

Lake Mitrikou (Lake Ismarida)

40°59N 25°19E

In summer, the white water lilies covering this fresh-water lake are its most important feature, for it is here that Black and Whiskered Terns balance their nests and Squacco Herons stalk their prey. The salinity of the lake is increasing because of excessive abstraction of fresh water, and the lilies may disappear. There are now fewer herons than once there were.

However, Squacco, Purple, Night and Grey Herons still breed here, and in some years they are joined by Glossy Ibises. There are always a few pairs of Spoonbills, Ruddy Shelducks and Ferruginous Ducks add to the interest, and Red-necked Grebes have been seen nest-building.

Three of the most interesting species occur in winter. Dalmatian Pelican, White-headed Duck and Lesser White-fronted Goose are classed as globally threatened, and the goose has become somewhat irregular in Greece. They occur in small numbers: around 30 White-headeds and as many as 70 Lesser White-fronts; up to 50 Dalmatian Pelicans are regularly seen.

TIMING

A relatively quiet period is during the late winter and early spring period before the bulk of migrants have arrived, but after most overwintering birds have left. From mid-April things really get going.

SPECIES

- *Lesser White-fronted Goose* Should be sought among the many wintering Greylags which feed in the fields around the lake.
- *Roller and Bee-eater* Often on the roadside wires south of Pagouria.
- *Penduline Tit* Occurs in the wooded area to the north of the lake.

ACCESS

Lake Mitrikou is east of the more famous Porto Lagos wetland complex and south of Komotiní. From the village of Pagouria a road runs south towards Molivoti beach. A right fork leads down the west side of the lake (a signpost gives its alternative name of Ismarida) and on towards the beach. There are few tracks off to the left from which to gain access to the rather distant shore, but low hills by the road offer a useful view over the whole area.

Alternatively, instead of taking the right fork, continue over the river to take a rough track which leads to an area of willows to the north of the lake, and on to the east shore via some excellent wader pools. This track is not, however, for the faint-hearted, so alternatively, ignore it and continue through Schinia towards the south-east corner of the lake and some good wader pools. The village of Fanari is a good base for Mitrikou, the Thracian lagoons and Porto Lagos.

Porto Lagos

40°59N 25°00E

The huge Lake Vistonis dominates the coast east of Xánthi, but it is the complex of lagoons, saltpans and intertidal shore which fringes the lake to the south which attracts our attention. Not that Vistonis itself is without interest: there must be thousands of Black-necked Grebes there in winter and spring, surely one of the most important assemblages of this species in Europe.

In the lagoons breeding birds include Pygmy Cormorants, all the herons and Ferruginous Ducks, as well as small numbers of the much sought-after Spur-winged Plover. Greater Flamingos are now resident and increasing, and show every sign of one day settling down as a regular breeding species.

During spring migration, the lagoons can be outstanding for waders, and there is always the chance of the occasional rarity. The prize bird is Slender-billed Curlew, and Porto Lagos accounts for more records of the species than any site in Greece apart from the Evros delta. Passerine migrants are also worth checking out, for example in the tamarisk scrub which fringes the lagoons. River Warblers and Thrush Nightingales are found in early autumn. Late summer sees the arrival of Dalmatian Pelicans, which stay for the winter when White-headed Ducks usually also turn up. On two occasions, more than 400 White-headed Ducks have appeared at Lake Vistonis, and the best recent count was 338.

The coast here is tidal, unusually for the Mediterranean, and attracts waders, gulls and terns. The state of the tide affects the numbers of birds on the adjacent lagoons as well. In April 1995, I watched about 1000 Yelkouan Shearwaters feeding close enough to the shore to hear their constant calling. There are two patches of woodland at the coast which attract falls of migrants.

TIMING

Outstanding throughout the year. Some of the lagoons (such as water tower lagoon) may dry out completely in summer. Some recently published information wrongly suggests that the lagoons are now permanently dry.

SPECIES

- *Dalmatian Pelican and Greater Flamingo* Frequent the large lagoon at the junction with the Fanari road.
- *Spur-winged Plover* Found around the sandy margins of the water tower lagoon.
- *Slender-billed Curlew* Has been recorded mostly in September, with several May and August records and a few at other times. The grassy area east of the water tower lagoon is the place to look.
- *Lesser Grey Shrike* Inhabits the farmland around the saltworks.

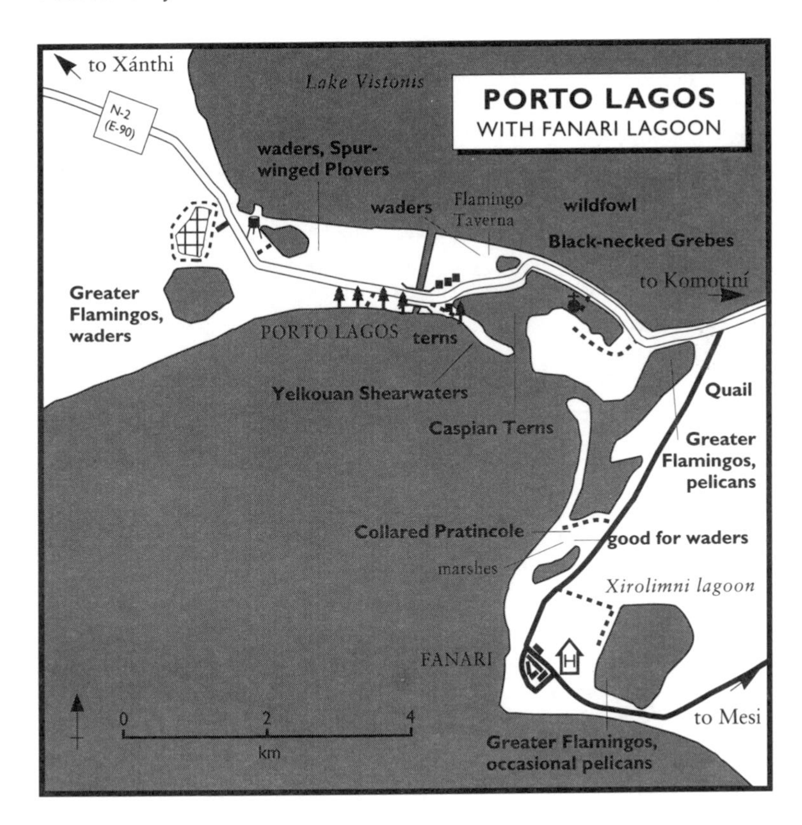

ACCESS

The whole area is strung out along the main coast road between Xánthi and Komotiní. Coming from the west, the saltworks are the first stop, reached by turning right down a track signposted 'Ellenikes Alykes'. Soon afterwards Lake Vistonis comes into view on the left, and a water tower marks the first lagoon. There is a path around the lagoon and interesting small pools which separate it from the lake.

Just before Porto Lagos village are two small areas of woodland, with short tracks through them leading to the shore. Within the village itself there are interesting saltings, and at the eastern end a taverna, named after the Greater Flamingos which occasionally visit the pool which it overlooks. This is perhaps the easiest lagoon to work; herons, ibises and waders can all be seen from the restaurant itself. There are rooms here, of a somewhat basic standard. Nearby Fanari offers more variety of accommodation.

This village is reached by turning right after the Flamingo Taverna but before this turn there is the large 'pelican-flamingo' lagoon and some interesting saltings to explore. These surround a Byzantine church which is built on a jetty into the pool (this is the second of two signposted Byzantine churches). A track beyond the church is barred to vehicles, but can be followed on foot between the church pool and the pelican-flamingo lagoon. There are also tracks off the Fanari road to the eastern shore of this lagoon.

Thracian lagoons

40°45N 25°10E

Situated between the excellent wetland areas of Porto Lagos and Lake Mitrikou, this chain of coastal lagoons – from east to west Elos, Ptilia, Alykí (or Mesi), Arogí (or Karatza) and Fanáriou (or Xirolimni) – add further spice to a two- or three-day exploration of the Thracian coast. Their high salinity makes them perfect for Avocets, which are rather uncommon breeders in Greece, as well as the more usual Black-winged Stilts, Stone-curlews and Collared Pratincoles. A few pairs of Spur-winged Plovers breed.

The eastern lagoons are usually good, the western pair sometimes disappointing. There are often Greater Flamingos around, and they seem to favour Ptilia and Alykí lagoons in particular. The former is also the haunt of Dalmatian Pelicans in the post-breeding period, with up to 150 recorded. Smaller numbers of immatures may stay there all year round.

The lagoons are also important for passage birds of all kinds, ranging from Ospreys through waders to passerines such as Red-throated Pipits and a variety of races of Yellow Wagtails.

TIMING

There is considerable pressure in summer from local tourists using the beaches, and late winter/early spring may be quiet for birds, but the area is good at other times.

SPECIES

- *Greater Flamingo* Appears to be on the increase in the area, and has attempted to breed.

Black-headed
Wagtail
Red-throated
Pipit
Citrine
Wagtail
Cyprus Pied
Wheatear
Cyprus
Warbler
Rock
Partridge
Mediterranean
Gull
Chukar
Audouin's
Gull
Slender-billed Gull

Crimson-
winged
Finch
Caspian Snowcock
Radde's
Accentor
Caucasian
Black Grouse
Red-fronted Serin
Krüper's
Nuthatch
Rose-
coloured
Starling
Great
Bustard
Cinereous
Bunting
Palm Dove

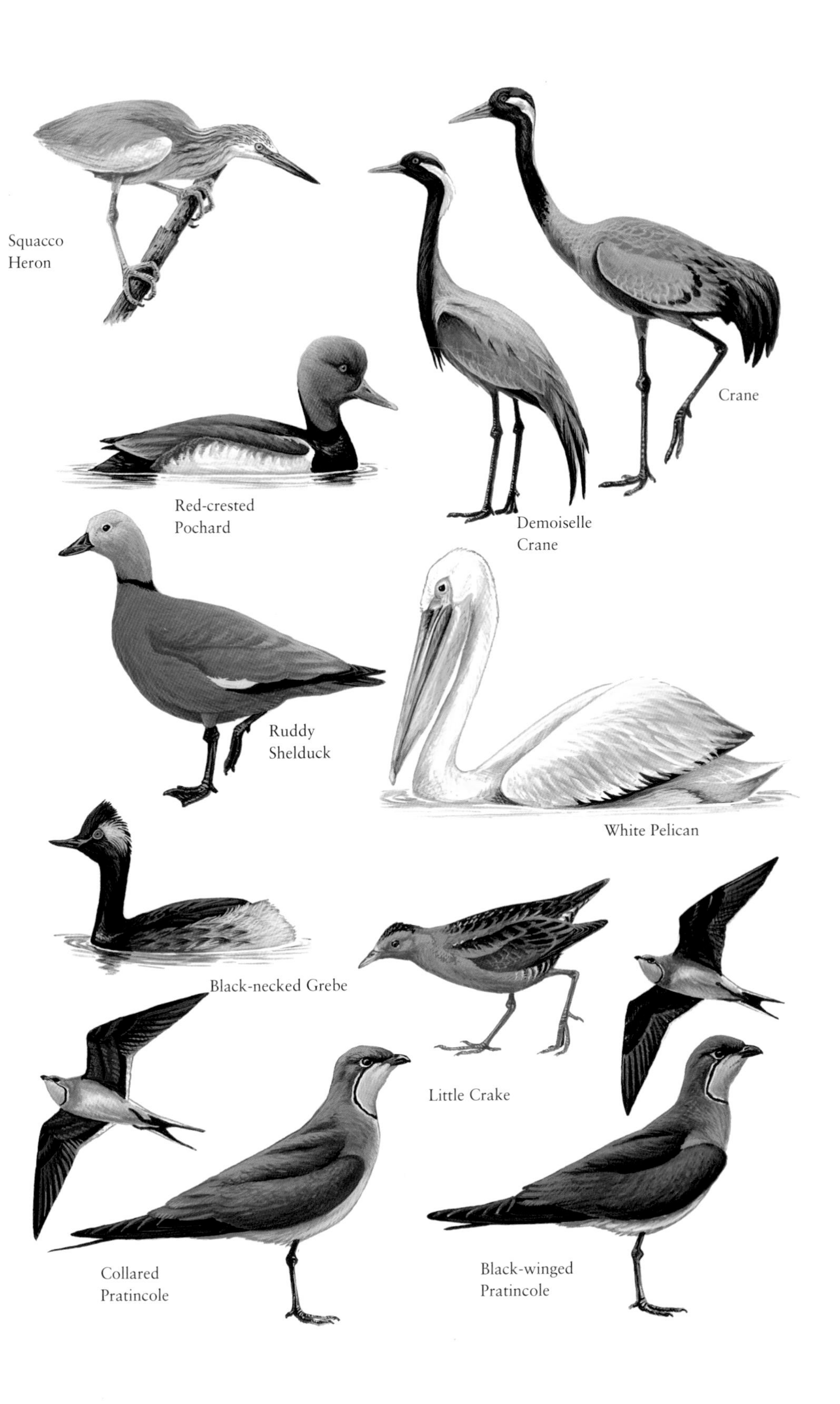
Squacco Heron
Crane
Red-crested Pochard
Demoiselle Crane
Ruddy Shelduck
White Pelican
Black-necked Grebe
Little Crake
Collared Pratincole
Black-winged Pratincole

Bald Ibis
Blue-cheeked
Bee-eater
See-see
Striated Scops
Owl
Black-bellied
Sandgrouse
White-throated
Robin
Red-tailed
Wheatear
Little Swift
Dead Sea
Sparrow
Desert Finch

Thrush Nightingale
Calandra Lark
Rufous Bush Robin
Olive-tree Warbler
Olivaceous Warbler
Rüppell's Warbler
Subalpine Warbler
Rock Bunting
Cretzschmar's Bunting
Black-headed Bunting

Marbled Duck
Dalmatian Pelican
White-headed Duck
Purple Gallinule
Black Francolin
Graceful Warbler
Pied Kingfisher
Greater Sand Plover
White-breasted Kingfisher
Yellow-vented Bulbul

Long-legged
Buzzard
Pallid Harrier
Lammergeier
Levant Sparrowhawk
Red-footed
Falcon
Eleonora's
Falcon
Lesser
Kestrel
Lanner
Masked
Shrike
Lesser Grey
Shrike

Roller
Bee-eater
Blue Rock Thrush
Rock Thrush
Rock Nuthatch
Black-eared Wheatear
Syrian Woodpecker
Finsch's Wheatear
White-backed Woodpecker
Isabelline Wheatear

- *Short-toed and Calandra Larks* Inhabit the fields east of Alykí lagoon, with other grassland species such as Quail and Montagu's Harriers.

ACCESS

The Fanariou (Xirolimni) lagoon is within sight of the village of Fanari to the west, and is on the edge of the Porto Lagos complex (*see* map on page 111). Continuing east, the road bears left to Mesi. A right turn (to the south) in this village leads between Alykí (Mesi) and Arogí (Karatza) lagoons.

Eastern Rodopi

41°10N 25°07E

The Rodopi Mountains stretch the entire length of the border with Bulgaria and are among the most sparsely populated areas of the country. This section concerns the area between the Filiouri and Kompsatos valleys, including Iasmos gorge.

The area is rich in birds of prey, with all four vultures feeding in the area, and Griffons and Egyptians breeding as well. Lesser Spotted Eagles nest in the denser forests and Golden Eagles on the crags. Levant Sparrowhawks and Black Storks breed in the riverine forests.

The Iasmos gorge is just east of the town of the same name, and forms part of the valley of the river Kourou, which flows into Lake Vistonis. Egyptian Vultures and Peregrines regularly perform for visitors here and Rock Nuthatches and Blue Rock Thrushes are confiding. Levant Sparrowhawks can usually be found, with patience.

TIMING

As with all such sites, late April to late June is best, but do not expect too much in the higher hills before mid-May.

SPECIES

- *Levant Sparrowhawk* Migrates through the valleys in late April and early May, and breeds in denser stretches of riverine forest.
- *Red-backed Shrike* Frequents bushier areas, especially around the numerous farmsteads.
- *Ortolan Bunting* Can be common on higher ground, for example, above Iasmos.

ACCESS

Iasmos is half-way along the old Xánthi–Komotiní road. East of the village a new bridge crosses the Kourou river. Take the old road from here to where it, too, crosses the river where there is space to park by the road. From here, a track heads north along the east side of the river past a still earlier (Ottoman) bridge where the rocks and forest are particularly worth scanning.

Nestos delta

40°56N 24°30E

The Nestos delta remains an interesting and accessible wetland despite having suffered the same problems of reclamation and neglect which have afflicted most of the Greek river deltas. Most birdwatchers are

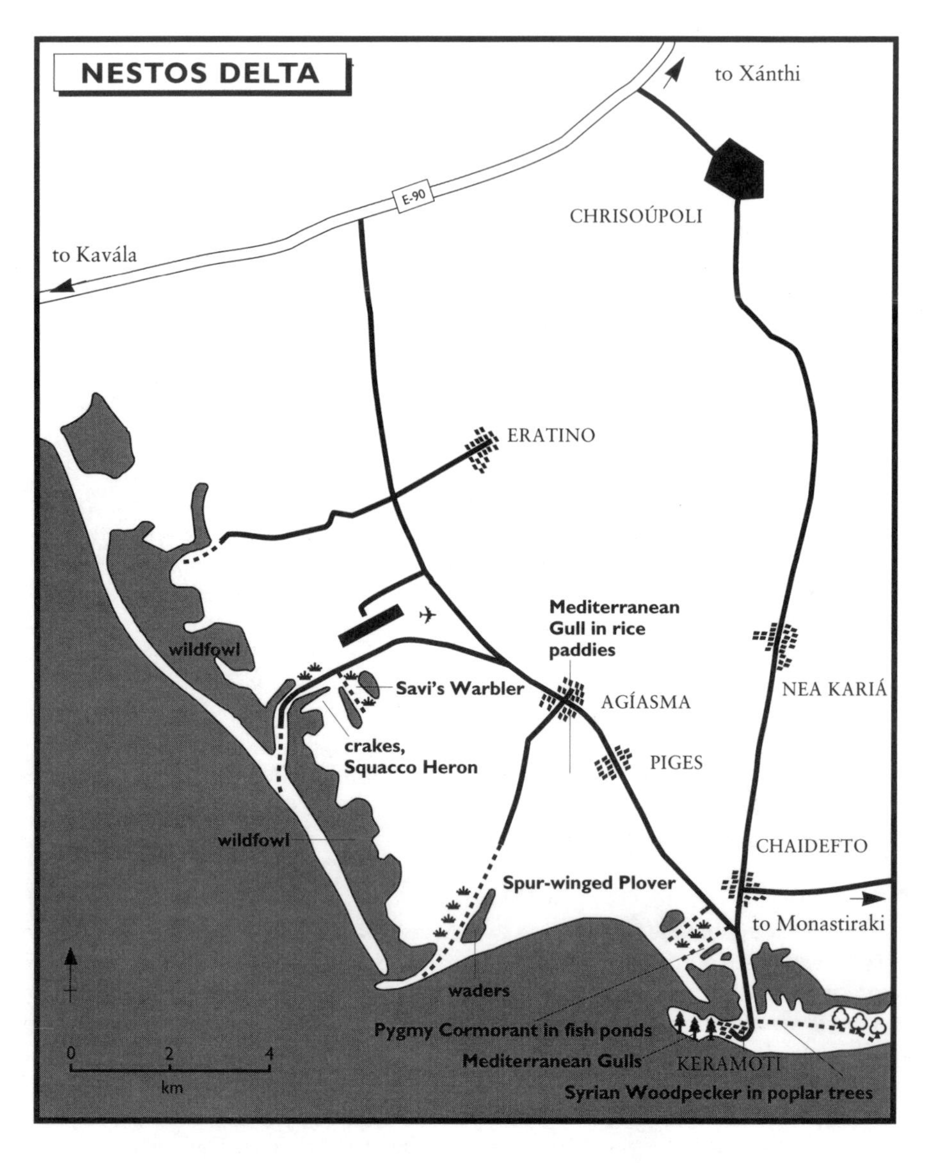

attracted by Spur-winged Plovers in the most important of their few Greek breeding-grounds, but there is much more besides. More than 300 species have been recorded.

The main habitat of interest is now the belt of coastal lagoons stretching for almost 50 km east and west of the river mouth. Much of the brackish marshland has been drained and a once vast forest has largely disappeared, but the delta still retains the largest riparian softwood forest in Greece.

In the lagoons there are around 30 pairs of Avocets, 40 pairs of Collared Pratincoles and the usual Black-winged Stilts, Stone-curlews, Kentish Plovers, Greater Flamingos, Purple Herons and Little Bitterns.

Ruddy Shelducks are often around. Little and Common Terns nest on the sand bars along with two recent colonists: Mediterranean Gull and Sandwich Tern. In winter Pygmy Cormorants and Dalmatian Pelicans are common, and White-tailed and Spotted Eagles are usually somewhere to be seen. Waterfowl numbers reach 50,000, including occasional Lesser White-fronted and Red-breasted Geese.

During spring and autumn passage there is a good variety of waders, with the usual Wood Sandpipers and Little Stints often joined by Marsh Sandpipers and Temminck's Stints and sometimes less common species such as Broad-billed Sandpipers. Glossy Ibises are often to be seen.

The remaining forest areas hold Lesser Spotted Eagles and Levant Sparrowhawks. Eleonora's Falcons breed offshore and are often seen, especially in the evening, hunting along the shoreline.

TIMING

Only in very early spring and again in mid-summer is the delta relatively quiet for birds. Summers are hot and dry, winters cold, wet and windy.

SPECIES

- ◆ *Spur-winged Plover* Sometimes found around the shallow pools to the west of Keramotí village, and particularly at the Agíasma lagoons.
- ◆ *Little Crake* Can be found, often over a dozen at a time, in April in the canal and lagoons behind the airport.

ACCESS

The main areas are the lagoons near Keramotí, which comprise the most accessible part of the area, and the western lagoons along the shore of the Gulf of Kavála. From Kavála the E-5 runs east towards Xánthi. After 27 km there is a right turn to Chrisoúpoli, where there is an information centre, the Nestos Museum of Nature at 117 Venizelou St (tel 0591 24 289, fax 0591 24 236: English spoken). This is on the right before the small roundabout in the town.

Beyond Chrisoúpoli the road leads towards Keramotí. Before you get there, there is a left turn to Monastiraki at Chaidefto. Beyond the village a track leads along an irrigation canal to the coast and some lagoons. Turning inland along this track, and heading east at every turn, leads eventually to a poplar plantation and the remaining, securely fenced-off, gallery forest.

The road crosses some deep lagoons which can be good for pelicans, but there are better areas to the west, which are reached from the airport road just before the village. Farther along the airport road is Agíasma. A left turn in the village leads along a long unpaved but good track to some more lagoons, where Spur-winged Plovers are found. One of the best areas is reached by continuing towards the airport. One km beyond Agíasma, a left turn along the best stretch of tarmac in the delta, leads behind (not *to*) the airport. When the ricefields are wet they can be excellent for terns and herons. On the left of the road are reedbeds which are good for warblers and Bearded Tits: these are followed by a long, narrow lagoon which widens out at the end of the road. This is good for

Little Crakes and the surrounding *Scirpus* marsh good for Squacco Herons. The tarmac runs out at the coast, where a left turn leads to another large lagoon.

Another area worth mentioning is known as the seven lakes, actually a series of small pools, and the Nestos forest. They are along the Xánthi road beyond the turn to Chrisoúpoli. A kilometre or so past the junction there is a BP garage, and a right turn here leads along a track to the seven lakes. These are worth a check during spring passage and winter. Ferruginous Ducks breed. After a further 12 km the road crosses the Nestos river. Before the bridge there is a track leading to some remnant gallery forest which is good for migrant flycatchers and warblers, Hawfinches and raptors, including Levant Sparrowhawks, and, from the forested hills across the river, Booted and Lesser Spotted Eagles.

There are hotels in Chrisoúpoli and Keramotí where in summer there is also a camp-site.

NESTOS VALLEY AND THE CENTRAL RODOPI

41°20N 24°45E

This area comprises three IBAs: the Central Rodopi, the Nestos Gorge and Mount Kroussia. It is an exceptionally rich area with breeding Black Storks, Egyptian Vultures and Short-toed, Golden, Booted and Bonelli's Eagles. In the Nestos gorge these species are joined by Levant Sparrowhawks and Lesser Spotted Eagles. Here the hillside scrub rings with the songs of Nightingales and Subalpine and Orphean Warblers, and in April 1995 I was amazed at the number of Collared Flycatchers passing through.

The northern forests have Hazel Grouse and Capercaillie, two birds with extremely restricted ranges in Greece. Woodpeckers are a particular feature, with Grey-headed, Black, Middle Spotted, White-backed and Three-toed all believed to nest. Tengmalm's Owls take over disused Black Woodpecker holes in the beechwoods. In 1985 Red-breasted Flycatchers were recorded breeding for the first time. The area is a stronghold of the Brown Bear, and there are several rare and endemic plants.

TIMING

In May, the flowers on the lower slopes are at their best, the birds are all breeding and the weather is fairly reliable. The higher slopes are often inaccessible until June.

SPECIES

- *Imperial Eagle* Has been recorded in the Nestos valley north of Drama and on Mount Mavro Mouni (Mount Kroussia), an IBA above Agios Vrondoú.
- *Capercaillie* Inhabits the sphagnum bog on mount Lailiás north of Serres.
- *Hazel Grouse* In the border forest north of the Nestos valley.
- *Grey-headed Woodpecker* Is present on the southern slopes of Mavri Petra, east of Dipotamo.

- *Pygmy Owl* Has been recorded in the Koúla range.
- *Rock Thrush* Can be seen by the roadside along the ridges of the Falakró massif.

ACCESS

You can reach the gorge's northern end by walking alongside the railway tracks from Stavroúpoli. However, it is easier to walk along an excellent footpath which begins in the village of Galani, near Toxoti on the Kavála–Xánthi road. There are signposts (not easy to follow – keep left and head for the railway line) for the 'Aesthetic Forest' leading to a car park. This is an interesting half-day trip from the delta.

The best-preserved areas of woodland are north-west of Paranetsi and Sidirónero. Much of this area is accessible only via forest tracks or on foot and is not recommended for those without escorts, maps or at least a well-developed spirit of adventure. However, the roads out of Sidirónero through Skalatí; from Paranesti north-east to Dipotamo; and from Echinóu (north of Xántri) to Kotili and Dimari will get you into the right general area.

There are good, accessible areas in the Falakro massif to the north-west of Drama, in the region of Kato Nevrokopi. These include the mountain roads north of Vólakas and west of Kato Vrondoú to Agios Vrondoú, or from here southwards to Serres. There is said to be a minefield along the road west of Kato Nevrokopi, towards Katáfito, so take care! Drama is a good base for the northern part of this area, and has several hotels.

Strymon delta

40°47N 23°49E

By the time the Strymon reaches the sea, having nourished the wonderful wetland at Lake Kerkini and irrigated thousands of hectares of its once extensive floodplain, it does not amount to much. However, at its mouth are some lagoons which amply justify a few hours' exploration *en route* along the coast between Thessaloniki and the Nestos. Most of the usual migrant waterbirds and waders can be seen here, and some – Collared Pratincoles, stilts, Stone-curlews and Little Terns – stay to breed.

TIMING

A combination of visitor-pressure and seasonal dryness makes mid-summer disappointing, but spring and late summer are good.

SPECIES

- *Yelkouan Shearwater* Often attracted to the waters around the river mouth, and can be seen close to the shore.
- *Rufous Bush Robin and Orphean Warbler* Breeds in the remaining undisturbed scrub on the hillsides between the delta and Asprovalta to the west.

ACCESS

There are two areas to explore: the river mouth and a small lagoon on the west bank are reached by taking the road signposted Ichthyoskala (in Greek only – Ιχθυοσκαλα) in Nea Kerdilia. The main road to Kavála crosses the river and a turning signposted to Limín leads back to the east bank, a port and another lagoon. A few kilometres to the east the Kavála road passes a large lagoon which often looks devoid of birdlife from the road, but is connected to a smaller lagoon at its seaward end which is vey interesting. The surrounding almond groves are good for shrikes and passage songbirds. A track leads through the olive and almond trees to the shore of this lagoon and its smaller neighbour, and from there along the shore to the river mouth and back to Limín.

Lake Kerkini

41°12N 23°09E

Originally an ox-bow lake in the floodplain of the river Strymon, Lake Kerkini was dammed in the 1930s. The resulting reservoir has, unusually, become an outstanding wetland. At present it is one of the best places in Greece for waterbirds, and very easy to work.

Breeding birds include Ferruginous Ducks, around 50 pairs of Pygmy Cormorants and an outstanding heronry. This is situated in a flooded forest in the north-east of the lake and includes 100 pairs of Night Herons and almost as many Squacco, with Grey and Purple Herons, Little Egrets, Glossy Ibises and Spoonbills all well represented. Even more impressive is its colony of Cormorants, with at least 700 nests and over 3000 individuals. There are extensive patches of water lilies which attract breeding Whiskered and Black Terns, and reedbeds with breeding Little Bitterns.

Kerkini is the most important wintering site for Dalmatian Pelicans in Greece, with around 6 per cent of the world population present. Immature birds are present all year, and there are signs that they may one day breed here. Kerkini is also the most important White Pelican stopover site in Greece. In April and again in late summer, up to 300 may be present.

The surrounding mountains are important for raptors including Golden, Lesser Spotted, Booted and Short-toed Eagles; there is a pair of White-tailed Eagles, and Levant Sparrowhawks breed in the Strymon valley upstream. Nearby Mount Beles, on the border, is also important for raptors as well as Black Storks, which come to feed at the Strymon where it enters the lake.

TIMING

Lake Kerkini is excellent all year round. In recent years, a few White-headed Ducks have appeared in January.

SPECIES

- *White Pelican* Usually around in April and August, Dalmatian with year. Best seen in the north-east corner of the lake near Vironeia.
- *Squacco Heron* Feeds on the lily pads at the western edge of the lake and roosts in the bushes below the north-eastern embankment.
- *Glossy Ibis* Congregates below the dam near the village of Lithótopos.
- *Nightjar* Hunts after dark along the track west of Lithótopos along the southern shore.

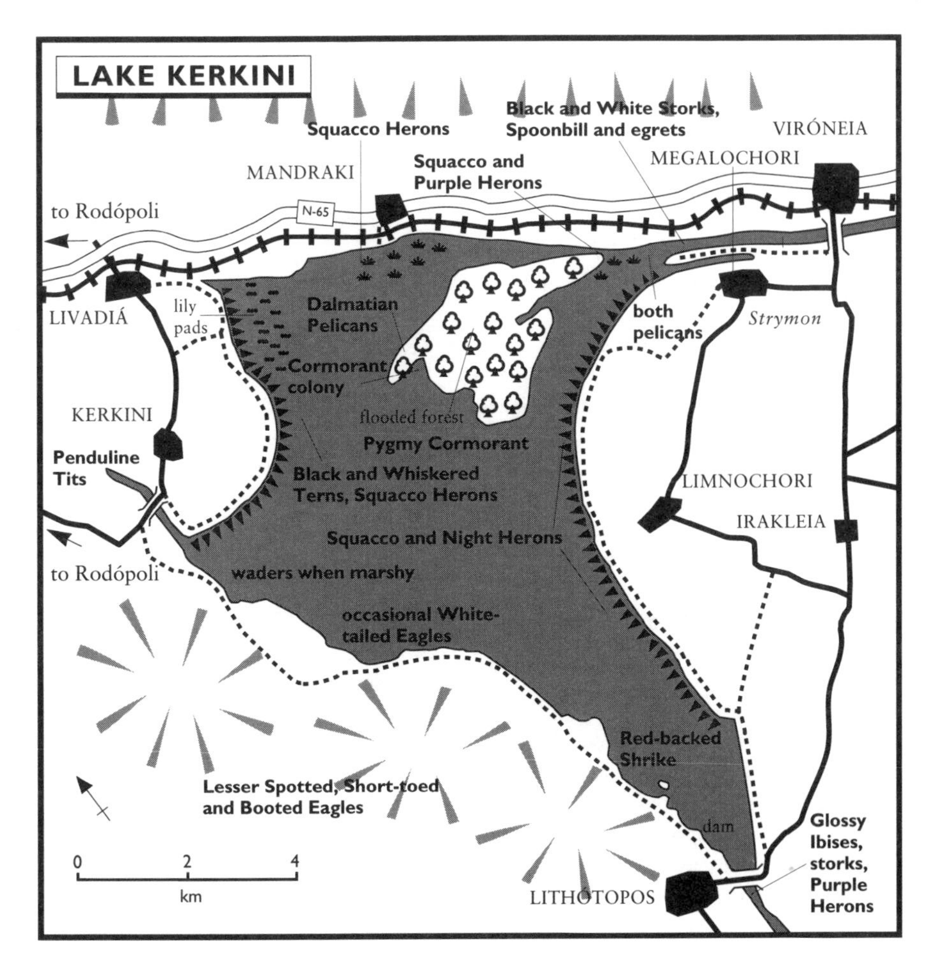

ACCESS

The N-12 heads north from Thessaloniki, towards Serres, and to reach the lake turn left after about 61 km, just before it crosses the Strymon. After a further 14 km, you reach the village of Lithótopos on the south-eastern corner of the lake. Here the area below the dam is marshy and usually has large numbers of waterbirds within easy view.

The southern and western shores can be explored via a track running west from the dam at Lithótopos. This track also borders the hills and can be very good for raptors. After 17 km, the track meets the road into Kerkini village, crossing a small river inlet. Immediately over this small bridge (looking out for Penduline Tits which nest in the poplars here) turn right along the embankment. This leads past the most extensive area of lily pads and on to Livadiá.

Another excellent area is south of Mandraki on the northern shore, where a road leads across the railway line to an area which is good for (fairly distant) views across to the cormorant colony.

The spectacular north-east corner is reached via an embanked track which runs from the minor road south of Viróneia. From Viróneia, cross the river towards Irakleia. Over the bridge, turn right down a track which leads to the embankment. This first track follows the river, one of the most interesting feeding areas for pelicans, egrets, storks and Spoonbills. There is a second embankment reached by returning to the road and turning right to Megalochori, following the signs to the lake. This eventually leads back to Lithótopos and the dam. Sidirókastro has several hotels, and there are rooms in some of the larger villages.

Angelochori and Epanomi lagoons

40°29N 22°49E

Only a few kilometres from Thessaloniki airport, this complex of saltpans and reedy marshes, sand dunes and heath is primarily of interest for passage waders and terns, it nevertheless boasts a good selection of breeding birds.

Angelochori is at the westernmost tip of the three-fingered Chalkidiki peninsula and the mouth of the Gulf of Thessaloniki. Wader passage is interesting for its diversity if not abundance, and often less common species such as Red-necked Phalarope, Temminck's Stint and Terek Sandpiper are encountered. A lucky few have seen Slender-billed Curlew here in recent years. Collared Pratincoles breed along with Black-winged Stilts, whilst Glossy Ibises and Spoonbills are regular on passage.

Gulls and terns are well represented, with breeding Little Terns, regular Gull-billed and Caspian Terns, and both Slender-billed and Mediterranean Gulls throughout the year.

The sand dunes hold Short-toed and Calandra Larks and Tawny Pipits, while the scrubbier areas can be good for passage shrikes, flycatchers and warblers and breeding Black-headed Buntings. In the pinewoods around the resort areas there are both Syrian and Middle Spotted Woodpeckers.

Farther south the small coastal lagoon near Epanomi, now subject to considerable human pressure, has similar species. Red-breasted Geese occasionally appear in winter, while Rufous Bush Robins and Stone-curlews inhabit the drier areas in summer.

TIMING

These sites are of interest throughout the year, but late April to early May and again in mid- to late September are best.

SPECIES

- *Slender-billed Curlew* Has been recorded twice in early May.
- *Rufous Bush Robin* Regularly seen around the entrance to the Epanomi camp-site.

ACCESS

From the main Thessaloniki airport road, beyond the resort area of Agia Triás, a minor road runs west to Angelochori, eventually leading to the saltworks and lagoons. Epanomi lagoon is reached by taking the road which leads to the EOT camp-site between Nea Michonia and Epanomi. Walk the few hundred metres from the camp-site to the lagoon.

Lakes Volvi and Koronia

40°41N 23°20E

Within a short drive of Thessaloniki, Lake Koronia (also known as Lake Langada or Lake Vassilios), and beyond it Lake Volvi, isolate the Chalkidiki peninsula from the rest of Greece. These are fresh-water lakes which are connected to each other when their water levels are high in winter.

They have important populations of breeding herons, including Night, Squacco and Purple, Little Bitterns and Little Egrets, as well as breeding Ruddy Shelducks. Outside the breeding season both pelicans are found, with up to 550 White and 50 Dalmatian. Large numbers of ducks and grebes occur in winter, including the occasional White-headed Duck. The reedbeds of Lake Koronia attract roosting finches and hirundines and are good for warblers and Penduline Tits.

The surrounding hills and remnant gallery forests are good for Levant Sparrowhawks, Long-legged Buzzards and at least one pair of Lesser Spotted Eagles. The riverine forest of Apollonia, though subject to uncontrolled cutting, is important for herons, White Storks and raptors.

At the eastern end of Lake Volvi is the Rendina gorge (more a rugged valley than a gorge) which is important for raptors. These include Short-toed, Golden and Booted Eagles, Eagle Owls and possibly Egyptian Vultures. Black Storks and Olive-tree Warblers are also present.

TIMING

During the winter Lake Koronia usually freezes over for two or three weeks, but Lake Volvi has never been known to freeze.

SPECIES

- *White Pelican* Common in April and August on passage. Dalmatian Pelican from September to March.
- *Olive-tree Warbler* Can be seen in the trees in a marshy area between Langadika and Scholari.
- *Penduline Tit* Also nests in this area, among the willows.
- *Spanish Sparrow* Frequent lodger in the nests of herons and storks.

ACCESS

Lake Koronia is about 25 km east of Thessaloniki along the E-5 Kavála road. Lake Volvi is 20 km or so farther on. For Koronia, depending on the water levels, there are several good vantage points. The shoreline immediately south-east of Langadas has excellent reedbeds: for these turn right at the traffic lights in the town. There are several viewpoints from where the main E-5, and much of the excellent south-west shore can be covered on foot. In Agios Vassilios there is a picnic area on the shore which is a good vantage point.

Lake Volvi is deeper and less easy to work, but at the western end there is a track through a small pine wood to the shore. The north-west corner is reed fringed and there are tracks off the road east of Nimfóletra with occasional views through, or over, the reeds. Ruddy Shelducks are often seen here. The lakeside forest at Apollonia is best reached by walking or driving alongside the river, or along the (often dry) river bed.

Rendina Gorge starts at the eastern end of Lake Volvi. The road to Kavála runs along the valley and there are several places where it is possible to pull over and scan the hills and forest. There are hotels and guest houses in Langadikia, Apollonia and Nea Apollonia.

Kassandra peninsula

40°14N 23°20E

The Chalkidiki (often spelt Halkidiki) peninsula is like a three-fingered hand jutting into the northern Aegean east of Thessaloniki. The westernmost finger is the Kassandra peninsula, rugged and pine clad but with small holiday resorts around its coast. As the first landfall after a long Aegean crossing, it is a natural funnel for concentrating northbound migrants.

Thus almost anything can turn up here in April and early May, and Lesser Grey, Red-backed and Woodchat Shrikes, Collared and Semi-collared Flycatchers (the former are exclusively passage birds, the latter probably breeders), Tawny and Red-throated Pipits, Ortolan, Black-headed and Cretzschmar's Buntings and almost any warbler can be expected.

Larger land birds at this time include Red-footed and Eleonora's Falcons, Hobbies, Bee-eaters and Rollers. There are several small marshes where Squacco and Purple Herons, Glossy Ibises and the full range of waders and terns are often found. Just north of the neck of the peninsula is an important marsh area, at Agios Mamantos. This has up to 100 pairs of Collared Pratincoles, three times as many Black-winged Stilts, and several pairs of Stone-curlews, Kentish Plovers and Avocets breeding.

TIMING

The period late April to early May sees the area at its best by far.

SPECIES

- *Cory's and Yelkouan Shearwaters* Frequent offshore all round the peninsula.
- *Nightjar and Scops Owl* Breed in the pinewoods along the coast, such as at the Sani beach resort area.
- *Olive-tree Warbler* Found, unsurprisingly, in the olive groves and occasionally other woodland areas.

ACCESS

The whole peninsula is circumnavigated by a 76-km long road which allows access to the main sites. The area immediately north of the peninsula has several marshy areas, and the coastal strip near Nea Moudania is particularly good.

Cholomontas mountains and Sithonia peninsula

40°08N 23°50E

The central finger of Chalkidiki is the Sithonia peninsula, while the 'palm' of the Chalkidiki land mass is dominated by a chain of mountains running east-west.

Spanish Sparrow

Petralona is at the western end of the Cholomontas mountains, and is famous for its caves. These foothills are good for Subalpine Warblers, Cretzschmar's Buntings, Rock Nuthatches and Rock Partridges. The Cholomontas mountains run east and north from here, reaching a height of 1165 m. They are clad in mixed broadleaved woods which are punctuated by rocky outcrops and steep gullies. Honey Buzzards, Golden, Booted and Short-toed Eagles breed and Black Woodpeckers call loudly from the forest. Black Storks and Lesser Spotted Eagles have been recorded and may breed. Eleonora's Falcons are often seen in early to mid-summer, playing the updrafts prior to settling down at the coast to breed in late summer.

On the Sithonia peninsula is another mountain range with similar species breeding and all the migrant raptors passing through, often in good numbers. Mount Itamos is particularly good, and is, like the Cholomontas mountains, an IBA.

On the coast between the Kassandra and Sithonia peninsulas is a marsh at Gerakini where migrants such as Collared Pratincoles, Stone-curlews and Glossy Ibises are common, along with larks and Spanish Sparrows in the dunes.

TIMING

Again, late spring is best, although in the highest parts the weather can only be relied upon in early to mid-summer.

SPECIES

- *Long-legged Buzzard* Particularly common at Petralona.
- *Rock Partridge* Can be heard calling from the bottom of the Petralona valley, but is very difficult to see.
- *Cretzschmar's Bunting* Found throughout, but is best located by listening for its song.
- *Rock Bunting* Inhabits the highest slopes.

ACCESS

The core of the Cholomontas range is around Taxiarchis, which is reached by driving north from Gerakini and taking the scenic road from

Polígiros towards Arnéa. The Petralona caves are signposted from the village of that name, which is 16 km north-west of Nea Moudania. Above the village a rocky valley leads up to higher ground.

Mount Itamos, on the Sithonia peninsula, is skirted by the circular coast road, but access is best gained by taking the forest roads into the interior. The road from Neos Marmaras to Parthení continues into the hills along such a track.

Mount Athos peninsula

40°10N 24°34E

Mount Athos is Chalkidiki's most famous feature and the holiest site in the country. Access is restricted and the whole area is church property: indeed, it is a semi-autonomous republic. However, this, the easternmost of the three fingers of Chalkidiki can be visited and the rewards include Golden and Short-toed Eagles, Eleonora's Falcons, Black Storks, Capercaillie, Audouin's Gulls and both shearwaters. However, you have to be male and over 18 and at present you need special authorization. This is worth the trouble for students of monastic architecture and life, but birdwatching alone probably does not justify it. Eleonora's Falcons are common around the southern cliffs and are most likely to be seen by visitors arriving by sea, as are the Audouin's Gulls, which are frequently recorded on the rocky southern coast.

Axios delta

40°30N 22°43E

This and the next site combine to create a rather peculiar IBA, in that the two rivers concerned rise in very different parts of the Balkan peninsula, but arrive at almost the same point on the coast. Their common delta is one of the most important wetlands in Greece, despite the usual assaults in the name of development. The Axios rises in the former Yugoslavia and its lower part is canalized so that it no longer floods the now-reclaimed land at the delta. Several interesting pools, a remnant branch of the river and some good riverside vegetation remain, and the river mouth is usually rewarding. Reedbeds and rice paddies are important features, the former hosting a good population of Little Bitterns, the latter attracting Squacco Herons.

The main Thessaloniki–Athens highway crosses the area, and usually there are herons, egrets, terns and raptors in evidence even as one drives along it. Collared Pratincoles, Black-winged Stilts and Avocets nest on the saltmarshes at the river mouth, as well as near the adjacent mouth of the so-called Loudias river (actually a drainage canal) to the west; Common and Little Terns also breed.

Glossy Ibises and Spoonbills breed, but these days both are more common on passage. At such times there is often a good selection of terns and there may be thousands of waders, including a scattering of rarer species such as Broad-billed Sandpipers and, very rarely, Slender-billed Curlews. Red-footed Falcons sometimes feed in flocks as they pass

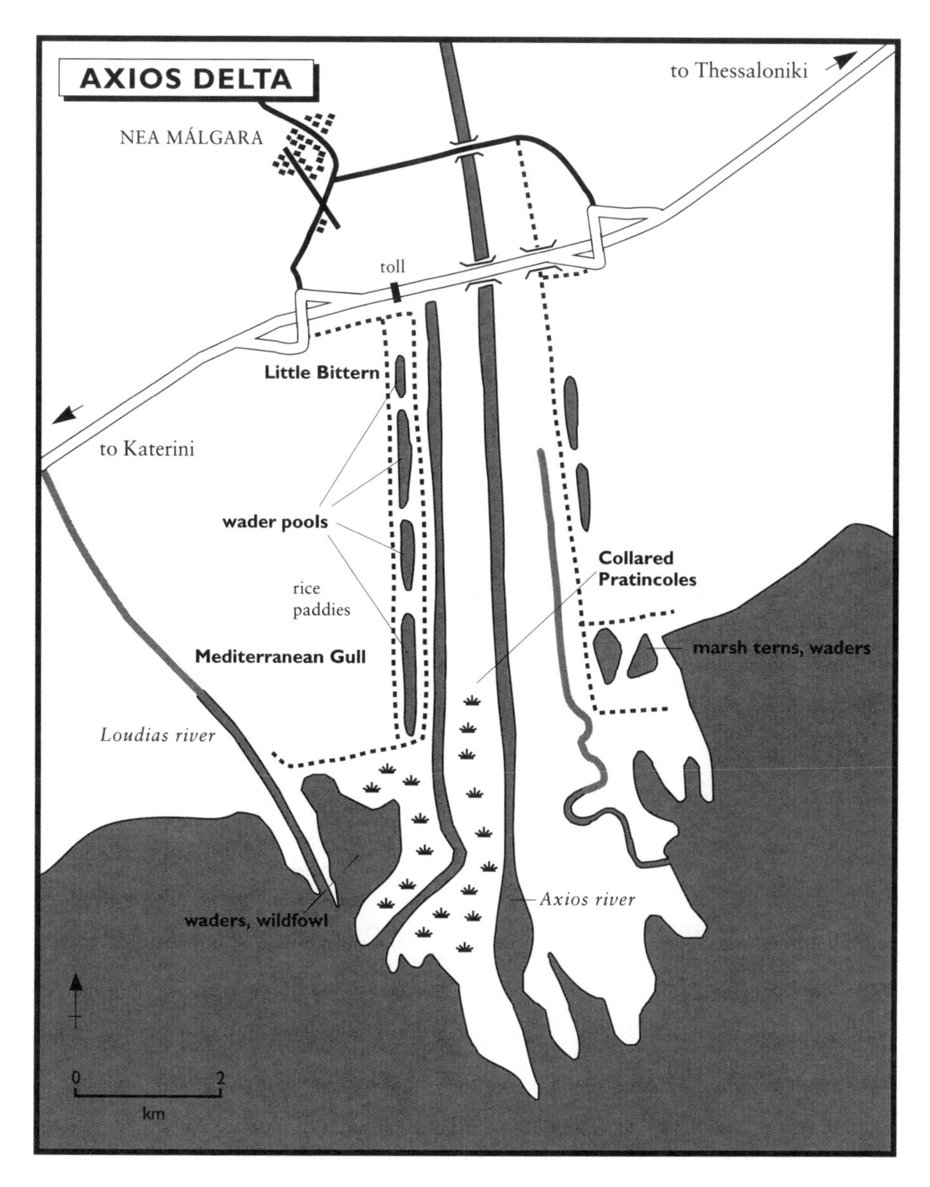

through in late April, and Red-throated Pipit should be sought at this time. Winter sees the arrival of small numbers of large raptors, notably Spotted and White-tailed Eagles, and Pygmy Cormorant and Great White Egret numbers build up.

TIMING

Bitterns are often recorded in winter, but with winter flooding now under control, wildfowl and raptor numbers have declined seriously, so spring and late summer/autumn remain the most productive times.

SPECIES

- *Collared Pratincole* Breeds in the undisturbed area between the west bank and the track.
- *Mediterranean and Slender-billed Gulls* Common at the river mouth.
- *Penduline Tit* Nests in the riverside vegetation.
- *Rufous Bush Robin* Often found in the scrub along the west track, which is also good for shrikes.

ACCESS

The embanked Axios river has reasonable tracks on both sides, but these are not directly accessible from the highway. For the east bank, it is necessary to go to Chalástro (or Halástro), and take the track from the western end of the village which leads under the highway and along the embankment. There are interesting pools and reedbeds along here. Close to the shore there are excellent pools, although the track deteriorates considerably here.

The west bank is similarly served by a good track, running under the highway from the other side of the river between Chalástro and Nea Málgara. This track can also be reached from the Nea Málgara junction. It passes good pools and excellent tamarisk scrub which attracts passerines, Rollers and Bee-eaters. After about 8 km the track bears right towards a pumping station. Here there is a coastal lagoon which is excellent for waders, herons and larks. There are hotels in Katerini to the south, and Thessaloniki is only 20 km to the north.

ALIAKMON DELTA

40°27N 22°33E

Although the Aliakmon delta is very much part of the Axios–Loudias–Aliakmon IBA complex, access is via a very different route, and therefore it is treated separately here. The bird list is very similar, and the habitats are the same, although there has been less land-claim here. A notable feature is a large lagoon near the village of Nea Agathoúpoli, south of the main delta area. This attracts Mediterranean Gulls from the nearby Kitros saltpans area. Other good birds in the lagoon include Glossy Ibises, Spoonbills and passage waders.

Access is via Nea Agathoúpoli, which is in turn just off the highway. A left turn at the village fountain leads along a road which becomes a track at the end of the village, leading to the lagoon. Lesser Grey Shrikes are worth looking for in this area. There are paths to the lagoon along the seaward edge and the southern fringe. The track continues towards the highway but smaller tracks lead off right towards the reedbeds of the delta proper.

ALYKI KITROS LAGOON

40°22N 22°40E

Between Thessaloniki and Mount Olympus there is a large coastal lagoon near the small town of Kitros. This, and the adjacent saltpans hold the most important gull colony in Greece, with over 3000 pairs of Mediterranean Gulls (the largest known colony in the Mediterranean) and 20 or so pairs of Slender-billed Gulls, apparently the only regular colony in the country. These are joined by several dozen pairs of Gull-billed Terns and 100 pairs of Collared Pratincoles. Stone-curlews, Black-winged Stilts and Avocets all breed and there are usually a few Squacco Herons. Passerines include Lesser Grey Shrikes, Calandra and Short-toed Larks, Tawny Pipits and Rufous Bush Robins.

Non-breeding visitors include Greater Flamingos, which can be present at any time of the year, Caspian Terns and Spoonbills; in winter White-tailed and Spotted Eagles occur, along with the occasional Saker. Cattle Egrets are often present at one of their few Greek haunts.

TIMING

Interesting between late August and mid-May, with late spring seeing the greatest variety among the 170 species recorded here.

SPECIES

- *Greater Flamingo* Tends to congregate at the seaward edge of the complex.
- *Gulls* The colony is among the older saltpans to the south.
- *Penduline Tit* Found along the canal which runs along the western edge of the saltworks.

ACCESS

From Thessaloniki, take the Athens highway for about 45 km and take the turn-off marked Methonia. A right turn leads to the old Thessaloniki–Athens road which leads, southwards, to the port of Pidna, 16 km to the south. From the harbour the saltpans can be explored via tracks leading due south or south-east along the shore. There is accommodation in Katerini.

MOUNT OLYMPUS

40°05N 22°20E

The magnificent setting in which stands the country's best-known mountain has guaranteed it a place in mythology and legend – and birdwatching guides. Rising dramatically from the sea to nearly 3000 m, and swathed in dense forest on its lower slopes, it is an impressive sight at a distance; closer to, its waterfalls, gorges and wild flower meadows combine to make Mount Olympus one of the aesthetic highlights of any trip to Greece.

As for its birds, Olympus boasts an array of sought-after species, and both Wallcreeper and Lammergeier are relatively easy for keen walkers. Black and Griffon Vultures, Golden, Booted and Short-toed Eagles,

Black Stork

Levant Sparrowhawks, Peregrines and Lanners make Olympus one of the better raptor sites, added to which are Eleonora's Falcons on their frequent hunting forays in autumn.

The forests are good for woodpeckers, the highlights being Grey-headed, Black, White-backed and Three-toed, one of the few sites for this species in Greece. Alpine Accentors, Alpine Choughs and Alpine Swifts are all readily visible above the tree line. The foothills are also very important, and include the Tembi valley, home to a similar range of species as well as a few pairs of Black Storks and Lesser Spotted Eagles.

TIMING

Mount Olympus is to be treated with respect at any time of the year, but from mid-June to October it is usually possible to reach the alpine zone without difficulty.

SPECIES

- *Lammergeier* Frequent sthe cliff faces and is attracted to the Spilios Agapitos refuge area, affording close views of scavenging birds.
- *Tengmalm's Owl* Present in the forests below the refuge, but rarely calls after early spring and never until after dark.
- *Three-toed Woodpecker* Said to frequent the same forests, but is probably rare, and prefers inaccessible stands of pure spruce.
- *Shore Lark* Breeds in the high alpine zones, preferring rocky ground with lichens and little vegetation.
- *Wallcreeper* Is common below the Kakí Skala ridge.

ACCESS

Mount Olympus is about 120 km south of Thessaloniki along the N-1 Lárissa highway. A local road climbs through the small town of Litochori, where there is plenty of accommodation, and on to the national park.

The most popular route among birdwatchers is probably the well-marked path from Prionia car park to the Spilios Agapitos refuge, some 6 km through dense forest, and on a further 5 km to the summit of Skolio. The refuge has 100 beds, and eating facilities, but must be booked in advance, especially at weekends. It opens in May until the end of October (tel 0532 81 800) and has English-speaking staff. This walk, allowing three hours to the refuge and a further two to the peak, is best taken in two stages, and necessitates a good level of fitness and the right footwear.

The N-1 continues south from Olympus through the Tembi valley. Tembi is 33 km from the Litochori turning and from here a road runs up the slopes of Mount Ossa. Across the valley is the village of Goni, whence the road to Kalipefki climbs Kato Olympus. This is all good raptor country.

VORAS MOUNTAINS

40°55N 21°56E

This remote border area north of Édessa has only recently been opened up for forestry exploitation, and much of it still remains a military zone. Much of it is rugged and almost inaccessible, but there are extensive pine and beech forests on the gentler slopes. Still largely unexplored ornithologically, there are records of Imperial Eagles and Lammergeiers and the latter at least probably breeds. Booted, Golden and Short-toed Eagles are apparently quite common. The forests are good for woodpeckers, including Black, White-backed and Middle Spotted.

Just to the north of Édessa is the Apsalou gorge, along which the Aridea road runs. This has breeding Egyptian Vultures and Long-legged Buzzards. The hillsides are good for Olive-tree Warblers and Lesser Grey Shrikes.

TIMING

Spring comes late to this region, and May and June are the most productive months.

SPECIES

- *Tengmalm's Owl* May inhabit the deeper forest. A check of the Promachos-Likostomo and Pefkoto Protected Forests after dark in early spring may reward the intrepid.
- *Shore Lark* Not documented for the area, but the alpine zone of Mount Tzena must be worth checking.

ACCESS

There are two protected forest areas near Aridea: Promachos-Likostomo lies between the two villages from which it is named, and at Pefkoto, about 5 km north of Vorinó. The mountain areas north to the border remain little-known, but new roads are being opened up and exploration will be rewarding. A road runs north-east out of Aridea to Períklia, 29 km distant. Smaller roads and forest tracks north of the road allow access to Mount Tzena. There is accommodation in Édessa.

Prespa lakes

40°45N 21°06E

If this spectacular National Park were more accessible, it would be crammed with tourists, and rimmed with hotels. It is a pair of stunningly beautiful lakes, set in the mountains of the far north-west corner of Greece and shared with Albania and the former Yugoslav republic of Macedonia (Skopje). The smaller lake, Mikri Prespa, is a National Park and is separated from its larger partner, Megali Prespa, by a narrow strip of land.

Prespa's is a wetland of international importance for birds: more than 260 species have been recorded. It is the only place in Europe other than the Danube delta where both pelicans breed, and one of the few places where their numbers are on the increase. Other waterbirds abound, notably herons, with all the European species represented. Particularly noteworthy are the 100 pairs or so each of Squacco Herons and Little Bitterns. There are more than 150 pairs of Pygmy Cormorants, and while Glossy Ibis appears to have disappeared as a breeding bird, it is still a regular visitor on migration.

Raptor interest includes White-tailed Eagles, which probably still breed, and Egyptian Vultures, Golden and Short-toed Eagles and Marsh Harrier. Rock Partridges are to be found above the tree-line in the

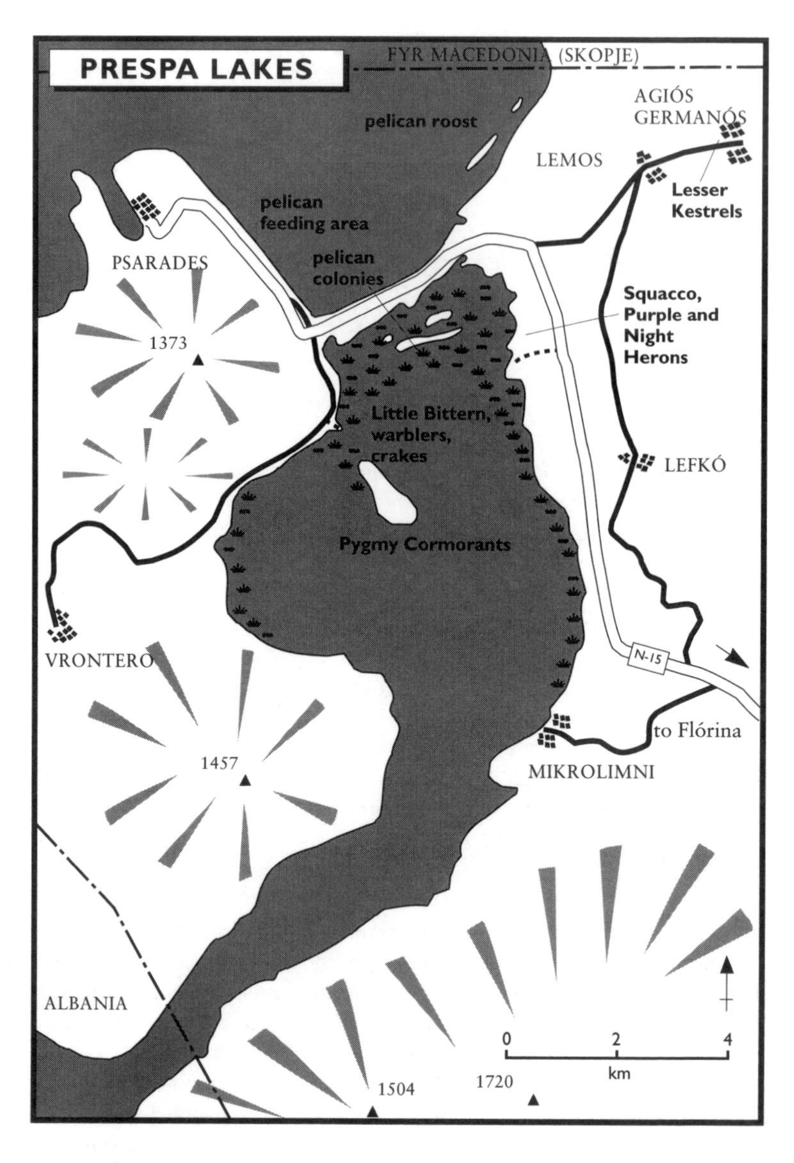

surrounding mountains and Hazel Grouse occurs in one of its few Greek sites. Notable among the breeding passerines is Barred Warbler, which has a very restricted range in Greece.

There is abundant non-bird interest provided by a host of interesting plants, including the Prespa Centaury, found nowhere else in the world. There are brown bears and wolves, as well as the occasional lynx from over the border. The larger lake – Megali Prespa – has important Byzantine relics which can best be appreciated by boat. The whole area is of cultural significance and one of the main villages in the area, Agios Germanos, has an attractive Byzantine church.

TIMING

In winter the lakes are usually frozen, although they can attract large numbers of waterfowl if not.

SPECIES

- *Dalmatian and White Pelicans* Cross between the two lakes at dusk.
- *Pygmy Cormorant* Easily seen loafing around on floating islands, drying their wings, usually alongside their obviously larger cousins.
- *Lesser Kestrel* Nest in Agios Germanos.
- *Hazel Grouse* Has been recorded in forests in the area but its present status is unknown.

ACCESS

This far corner of the country is a good 4-hour drive from Thessaloniki, along the N-2 via Florina. Some 31 km beyond Florina the N-15 runs along a causeway which separates the two lakes and leads to Psarades, where there is accommodation. Once across the causeway, a left turn onto a minor road leads to higher ground which gives a good view over Mikri Prespa, and goes on to skirt the marshes. Between Mikrolomni and Agios Germanos a track (signposted Opagia) leads to good reedy marshes on the eastern shore. Agios Germanos is another good base, and there is an information centre there run by the Society for the Protection of Prespa, (tel 0385 51452).

Lakes Petron, Vegoritis, Chaimaditis and Zazaris

40°30N 21°35E

These four very different lakes are conveniently *en route* to Prespa from Thessaloniki. Lake Vegoritis, west of Édessa, is the largest and deepest. Unless time is taken to find the shallows at the southern end, this is chiefly of interest for the cliffs and hills bordering the main road at this point, since they are the haunt of Egyptian Vultures, Long-legged Buzzards, Lesser Kestrels (nesting on the low cliffs by the road), Barred Warblers and Rollers.

The much smaller Lake Petron, nearby, has a mixed heronry which formerly included several pairs each of Glossy Ibis, Night and Squacco Herons and a few Pygmy Cormorants but which now appears to be declining. Collared Pratincoles and Black-winged Stilts breed.

Farther south and west are lakes Cheimaditis and Zazaris. The former may be the most important site in Greece for Ferruginous Duck; there are also important colonies of Little Bitterns and Whiskered Terns in the marshes to the north. The surrounding hills and forests are very important for raptors, especially where the forests remain intact. Lesser Spotted and Golden Eagles and Levant Sparrowhawks are among the inhabitants. Both lakes are important feeding and staging posts for pelicans.

TIMING

In winter the breeding birds are replaced by interesting species such as White-tailed Eagles and Red-crested Pochards.

SPECIES

- *Dalmatian Pelican* Uses the area sporadically, but April is the most important month for this species at Cheimaditis.
- *Ferruginous Duck* Tends to prefer shallow, reedy areas.
- *Montagu's Harrier* A rare bird in Greece, nesting in the floodplain north of Lake Cheimaditis.

ACCESS

The Édessa–Amíndeo–Argos road runs alongside, or close to, all four lakes. A detour to Petres from either Amíndeo or the N-2 at Kela skirts Lake Petron. Lakes Zazaris and Cheimaditis are reached via Limnochori and Pedinó, 10 km west of Amíndeo.

LAKE KASTORIÁ

40°30N 21°18E

A little to the south-west of the previous sites is Kastoriá, and the lake of the same name. Although threatened by pollution from the town, Lake Kastoriá has similar species to the other lakes in the area, including Ferruginous Duck and the two pelicans. It would appear that Lake Kastoriá comes into its own in April and early May, when fish spawning occurs. At this time, Prespa is still too cold to provide adequate food for the pelicans, and both species make daily journeys from their nesting grounds to feed. The north-east corner appears particularly attractive to them. There is a small heronry with Night and Purple Herons and Little Bitterns breed in the reedy fringe. Access is achieved just south of the village of Mavrochori on the eastern shore, or at Chlón in the north-west corner.

VIKOS-AOOS NATIONAL PARK

40°02N 20°50E

This national park is in the heart of a large and remote mountain range in the north-west of Greece, not far from the Albanian border. The sheer walls of the Vikos gorge, several hundred metres high, the Aoos ravine, with its dense forest, and the rocky peaks of Mounts Timfi and Smolikas combine to make this one of the most spectacular parts of the country. Little wonder that brown bears and lynx still inhabit its forests.

Raptors of several species occur here, including Lammergeiers and Egyptian and Griffon Vultures, Golden, Booted and Short-toed Eagles, Honey Buzzards, Peregrines and Lanners. Woodpeckers are well represented with Black, White-backed and Middle Spotted the most highly prized.

Choughs play the updrafts from the gorges, while Rock Thrushes and Ring Ouzels sing from the higher slopes. The Aoos and Vikos rivers are home to Dippers. Rock Nuthatches, Sombre Tits, Alpine Accentors and Subalpine Warblers are among the passerines breeding here.

TIMING

There are several long and rewarding hikes in the area which are only really recommended in July to September. Otherwise, May and June are the best months.

Griffon Vulture

SPECIES

◆ *Black Stork* Nests in the oak forests of the central Zagori range.

◆ *Snow Finch* Search for this bird in rocky areas at the snow-line.

ACCESS

The Vikos-Aoos National Park is immediately south of Konitsa, which is on the N-20, 59 km north of Ioannina. Mikro Papigo is a village in the heart of the park where there are several hotels. From here there is a three-hour hike to the summit of Mount Timfi. An excellent walk of similar length is possible from the old bridge in Konitsa to the Stomio monastery on the Aoos ravine.

PINDOS MOUNTAINS

39°54N 21°06E

The Pindos range forms the mountainous backbone of Greece and contains some of the country's remotest and least spoilt countryside. Brown bears enjoy a European stronghold here, along with wolves, wild boar and chamois. The Valia Kalda National Park is a small but representative corner of this magnificent range, covered in beech and black pine, with steep ravines and rocky outcrops.

Sixty-eight species of birds have been recorded breeding in the national park. Mountain species such as Wallcreepers and even Shore Larks combine with raptors and at least eight species of woodpecker (including Black, White-backed, Middle-spotted and possibly Three-toed) to make this one of the most diverse non-wetland areas for birds in the country. Several of the rarer raptors are found here, including Imperial Eagles (on passage if not breeding), Levant Sparrowhawks and Lanners.

TIMING

The main road across the range, the N-6, may be blocked by snow until well into May. Autumn migration through the passes can be spectacular for both large and small birds.

SPECIES

◆ *Imperial Eagle and Levant Sparrowhawk* Migrate through the passes such as Kataras, east of Metsovo.

◆ *White-backed Woodpecker* Favours the beechwoods around Metsovo.

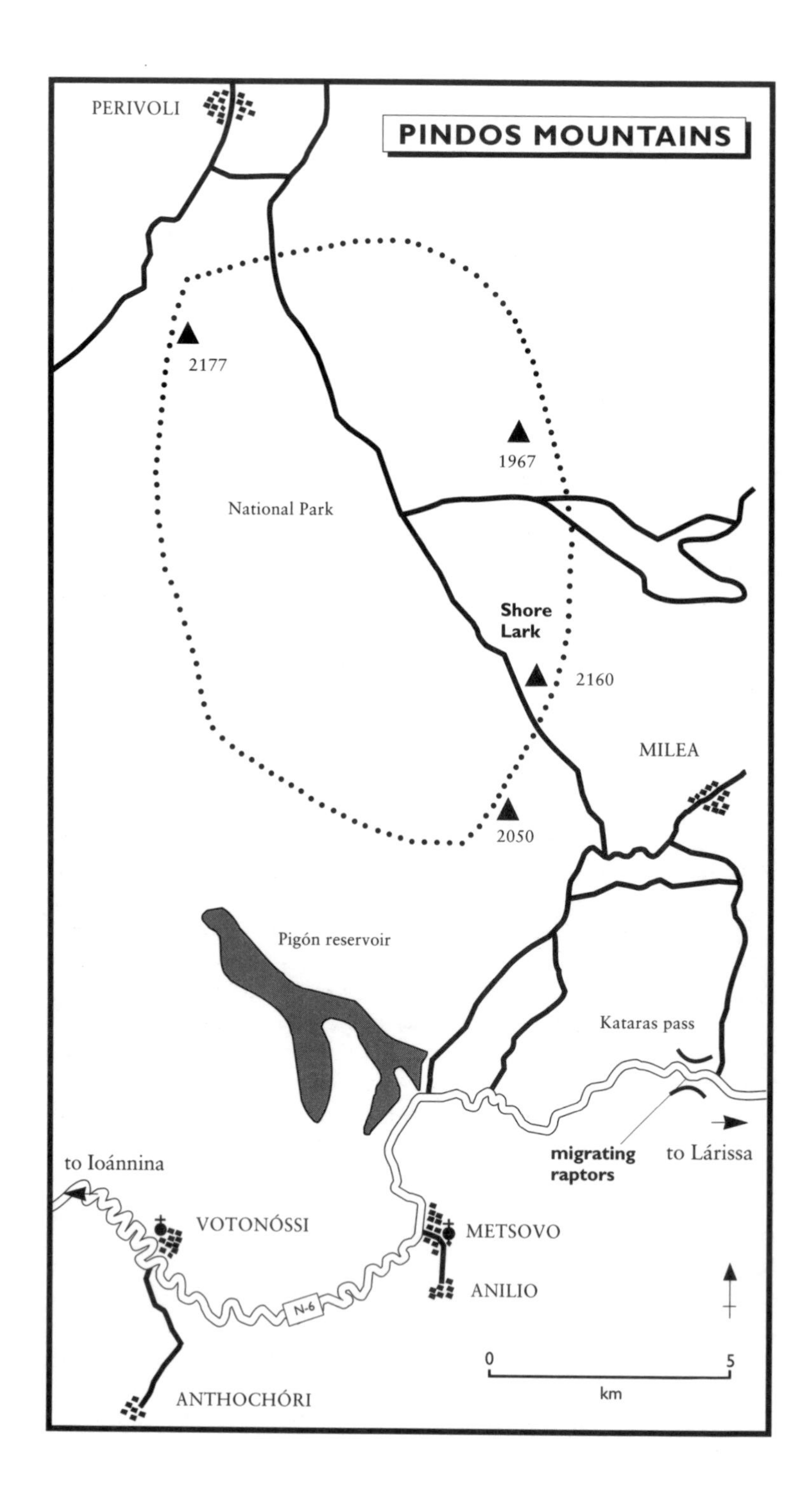
PINDOS MOUNTAINS
PERIVOLI
2177
1967
National Park
Shore Lark
2160
MILEA
2050
Pigón reservoir
Kataras pass
migrating raptors
to Lárissa
to Ioánnina
VOTONÓSSI
METSOVO
N-6
ANILIO
ANTHOCHÓRI
0
5
km

- *Shore Lark* Breeds only in the highest parts of Valia Kalda, above the tree-line.
- *Wallcreeper* Always requires patience and luck, but can often be found on old buildings outside the main breeding season.

ACCESS

There is a forest road from Metsovo on the N-6 to Perivoli, some 35 km to the north, which traverses the National Park and provides access to all the main habitats, but this is best tackled with four-wheel drive. Numerous footpaths lead to the moorland areas. There is a small hotel (open May to November) in Perivoli. This village, like several in the area, is inhabited by speakers of the ancient Walachian Greek tongue.

Metéora

39°48N 21°35E

Nestling into the Antichassia mountains east of the Pindos range, this site is famous for its towering pillars of rock topped with spectacular monasteries. Visiting culture vultures cannot fail to miss their Egyptian cousins flying overhead: this is the best site for the species in Greece with 50 or so pairs in the area. Alpine Swifts, Crag Martins, Rock Doves, Black Redstarts and Red-backed Shrikes are among the species readily seen within the site itself.

The surrounding forests are easily explored and are inhabited by Black Storks, Levant Sparrowhawks, Lesser Spotted and Booted Eagles, Honey Buzzards and Black Kites, Middle and Lesser Spotted Woodpeckers and Sombre Tits.

TIMING

Egyptian Vultures, Black Kites and Lesser Spotted Eagles arrive in late March, Levant Sparrowhawks a month or so later.

SPECIES

- *Black Stork* Frequents the quarry area about 4 km north of Metéora.
- *Rock Partridge* Calls from the drier, south-facing slopes but is difficult to see.

ACCESS

Metéora is immediately north of Kalambaka on the N-6 between Metsovo and Tríkala. There is a road north from Kalambaka into the Antichassia mountains which leads after about 10 km to good raptor forests.

Kalamás delta and gorge

39°32N 20°05

This, the most northerly wetland on the western seaboard, is hardly visited by foreign birdwatchers, but those that have explored the Kalamás delta and nearby areas report good things. The main feature is the two large lagoons on either side of the main channel, separated from the sea by sand bars which hold breeding Little Terns and Short-toed Larks. There are numerous smaller lagoons, and former branches of the delta, now isolated and reed-fringed. Black-winged Stilts, Collared Pratincoles

Lesser Spotted Eagles

and Stone-curlews nest throughout the area, and are joined during passage by up to 200 Glossy Ibises, Spoonbills and raptors. Outside the breeding season Dalmatian Pelicans feed and roost in the area, but, interestingly, there is no record of White Pelican.

Many of the raptors stay to breed on two forested hills which dominate the landscape. These include Short-toed, Golden and Lesser Spotted Eagles, while as many as eight Spotted and the occasional Imperial Eagle spend the winter.

The delta's influence stretches to the Albanian border, where there are some good marshes and lagoons at Sagiada. Passage waders and Glossy Ibises are encountered here, and a recent expedition revealed a pair of Bitterns. There are several inland, lagoons in the area, north-west of Magariti and at least one, Lake Limnopoula, has nesting Ferruginous Ducks.

There is a gorge upstream on the river Kalamás where there is a colony of Griffon Vultures, along with a few Egyptian Vultures and Short-toed and Golden Eagles. Lesser Kestrels nest in some of the villages in the area, and Rock Partridges inhabit the scrubby hillsides.

TIMING

The variety of habitats means that the area has something to offer all year. The long hunting season, August to March, brings considerable pressure to this area.

SPECIES

- ◆ *Lesser Kestrel* Nests in old buildings in towns such as Paramithia, Filiátes and Margariti.
- ◆ *Olive-tree Warbler* Inhabits the scrub-covered hills in the delta.

ACCESS

The Kalamás delta is a few kilometres west of the northern port of Igoumenitsa. Access into the area is along a complex network of tracks, and navigation is best achieved by using the nearest hill as a reference point. All the lagoons hold birds, and it is a matter of exploring all of the options, since water levels and access vary with the seasons. Lake Limnopoula is 6 km north-west of Paramithia, off the Grika road.

ACHERONDAS GORGE AND SOULIOU MOUNTAINS

39°15N 20°30E

The delta of the river Acherondas may never have been that outstanding, but recent drainage and tourist development appear to have robbed it of whatever value it once held. However, only a few kilometres upstream of the delta, the Acherondas saws its way through the Souliou mountains and the resulting gorge is good. Here there are a few pairs each of Egyptian and Griffon Vultures among a respectable raptor list which also includes Short-toed, Bonelli's and Golden Eagles. There are several small mountain ranges aligned roughly north-south and they are all worth exploring. The southern end is close to the Gulf of Amvrakikós, and several of the larger raptor species nest in the hills, visiting the wetlands to feed.

TIMING

Most of the raptors are present all year, but the gorge may be worth checking for passage Levant Sparrowhawks, Lesser Spotted Eagles and Black Storks in late April.

SPECIES

- ◆ *Rock Partridge* Inhabits the scrubby hillsides above the river.
- ◆ *Olive-tree Warbler* Found in olive groves on the Zalongo mountain.

ACCESS

The Acherondas gorge can be explored on foot, and several grades of hike are on offer, with good waymarking and well-maintained tracks. From Gliki a sign on the opposite bank to a small restaurant points to *skala Tzavélainas*. This track bears left towards a chapel and the gorge comes into view after about a kilometre. The two-hour walk to Samonida takes in most habitats.

Zalongo is an isolated mountain near the north-west corner of the Gulf of Amvrakikós, good for vultures, eagles and interesting passerines. It is reached from the minor road between Loúros and ancient Kassopi.

GULF OF AMVRAKIKÓS

39°21N 21°00E

With the gradual degradation of the more famous river deltas of the north-east, the Gulf of Amvrakikós in the west remains Greece's most intact coastal wetland, and one of the best birdwatching sites in the country. Its bounty of breeding Dalmatian Pelicans, Glossy Ibises and Spoonbills, six species of herons and vast wintering wildfowl flocks is too often overlooked by foreign birdwatchers who have yet to discover the western seaboard. Amvrakikós can be combined with visits to the Pindos range and Prespa for a week of the finest birdwatching in Greece.

In spring the breeding birds are supplemented by a tempting array of passage migrants, including most of the European raptors, all the flycatchers and a staggering selection of warblers. Winter sees the arrival of more than 150,000 waterfowl, as well as White Pelicans, Spotted Eagles, Great White Egrets and Mediterranean and Slender-billed Gulls.

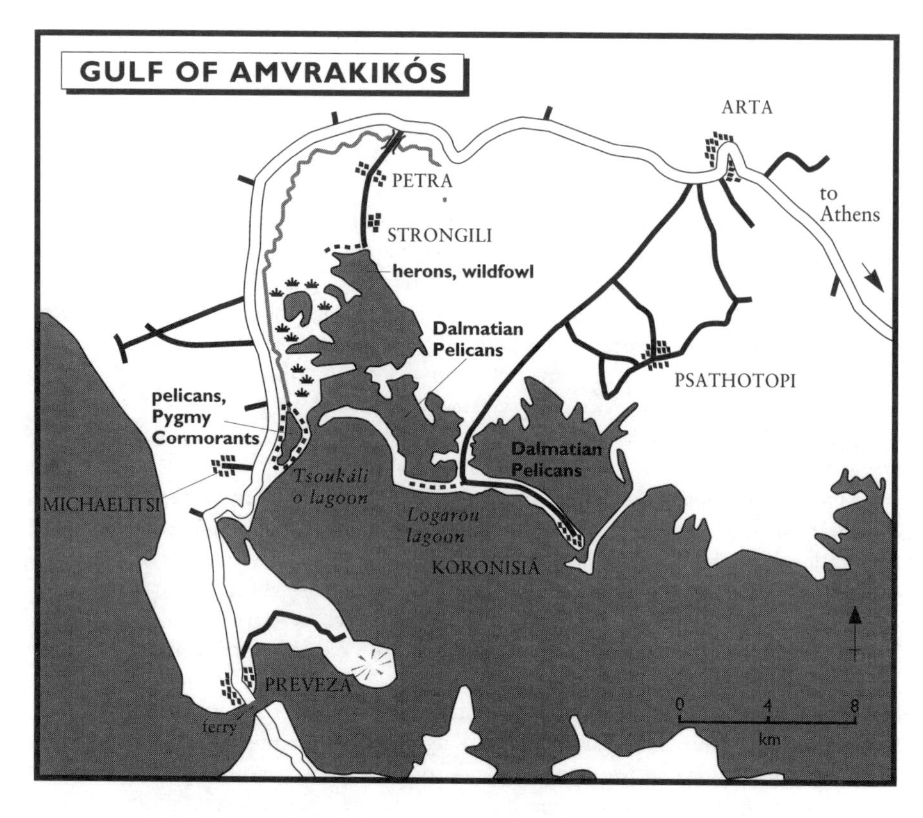

In the late 1980s the RSPB and the Hellenic Ornithological Society discovered that part of the core area of this Special Protection Area was being illegally developed with EU funds. Fortunately, the funding was cut off.

TIMING

Outstanding all year round, with peaks in spring and winter. Some tracks may be flooded in winter, especially after the abundant rain which often falls at that time.

SPECIES

- *Dalmatian Pelican* Nests, and indeed spends most of the year, in the larger Logarou and Tsoukálio lagoons but small numbers can be encountered anywhere.
- *Pallid Harrier* Worth checking for over the saltmarshes of the northern lagoons in winter, along with the more common Hen Harrier.
- *Migrant warblers, chats and flycatchers* Often abundant in the olive groves around Strongili and similar places. Olive-tree Warblers and Semi-collared Flycatchers are among those that stay to breed.

ACCESS

The northern shore is best, since it comprises several semi-enclosed lagoons and saltmarshes. The recently-surfaced road to Koronisiá affords good views over the Logarou lagoon. A sandy track runs west off this road along the southern edge of the excellent Tsoukálio lagoon, but after heavy rain I would not risk a two-wheel drive car along here.

There is a serene and beautiful lagoon beyond Strongili, the turn-off to which is 20 km west of Arta. Farther towards Préveza, near Michaelitsi, is a lagoon by the main road which is overlooked by two bird observatories (which, however, are poorly placed and usually closed). A good track skirts this lagoon giving good views of wintering wildfowl and small numbers of Pygmy Cormorants, pelicans and herons.

Another small lagoon, often good for Little Gulls in spring, is by the road about 16 km north of Amfilochia on the eastern shore. Arta and Préveza have plenty of accommodation. There is a ferry at Préveza across the mouth of the gulf.

Lefkas and Lake Voulkoriá

39°00N 20°45E

At the south-eastern corner of the Gulf of Amvrakikós is a further group of wetlands which can be reached via the Préveza ferry. Lake Voulkariá is a large, reed-fringed lake which is primarily of interest during spring passage, when all the usual reedbed warblers pass through, along with migrant raptors and Glossy Ibis. Pygmy Cormorants and both pelicans occasionally feed there after the breeding season. This area, and a nearby coastal marsh north of Páleros are occasionally visited by raptors from the Akarnanian mountains. The Páleros marsh, on the gulf of the same name, also has breeding Little Bitterns and Gull-billed Terns.

West of Voulkariá the road crosses a causeway onto the island of Lefkas. Immediately there is another lagoon which merits exploration during spring and autumn for passing waders. My own brief visit in winter yielded Great White Egrets and a range of common ducks; I felt that the breeding season might be more interesting, with Gull-billed Tern, Red-crested Pochard and Collared Pratincole possible.

Akarnanian mountains

38°45N 21°00E

Immediately to the south of the Gulf of Amvrakikós is a remote and impressive massif rising to 1589 metres. The lower slopes are cloaked in oak forest, with Greek fir and pasture at higher altitudes.

The largest mainland colony of Griffon Vultures is here, some 30–40 pairs, along with Golden Eagles, Peregrines and Eagle Owls. Olive-tree Warblers and Lesser Grey Shrikes are among the more interesting passerines, and are to be found at lower altitudes in more agricultural areas.

TIMING

Early summer sees these mountains at their best, and the weather is generally reliable from June onwards.

SPECIES

- *Griffon Vulture* Can be seen anywhere in the range, especially when thermals are rising.

ACCESS

Several small roads penetrate the area, and there are tracks of variable quality throughout, although the remotest areas are essentially cut off in enclosed valleys. The coastal road from Astakós north to Páleros runs along the cliff-tops, and can be good for raptors. There is a worthwhile diversion along a good road up to the church of Agia Dimitron for vultures, eagles and Rock Nuthatches. Inland, roads south from the N-42, which skirts the southern shore of Amvrakikos, penetrate to some extent. The road from Monastiraki south to Panagoula reaches some remote and beautiful parts. Lefkada, Préveza and Amfilochia all have accommodation.

KLISSOURA GORGE

38°30N 21°15E

This spectacular gorge, and the cliffs and outcrops nearby, form the edge of the Arákinthos mountains, in turn the boundary of the Mesolongi wetland complex (*see* below). The busy N-5 provides as good a vantage as any, and passes along the bottom of the gorge itself. Griffon Vultures nest above the road and are almost permanent features, once the air has warmed up. Other interesting raptors include Long-legged Buzzards, Lesser Spotted and Short-toed Eagle. Blue Rock Thrushes and Subalpine Warblers are among the smaller inhabitants.

TIMING

Of interest all year.

SPECIES

- *Lesser Spotted and Short-toed Eagles* Arrive in early April, and are more likely to be seen away from the main road, towards the interior of the Arákinthos range.
- *Long-legged Buzzard* Resident, but joined by migrant birds in summer; can be seen over the escarpments to the south of the gorge.
- *Wallcreeper* Is likely to occur here in winter, and possibly all year.

ACCESS

Klissoura Gorge is 16 km north of Mesolongi and just north of the turn-off to Chrissovergi. It is possible to pull off the road in the gorge with care as there are several flat areas. The southern end is the best place from which to watch. Some 4 km to the south, there are escarpments which can also be scanned from the road, just south of Kefalóvrisso.

MESOLONGI WETLANDS

38°20N 21°15E

The most accessible parts of this important wetland have been largely transformed into vast industrial saltworks or fish-farms but it is still a good place at times, and is occasionally outstanding. The saltpans still attract large numbers of waders in spring and autumn, when it is worth checking for Terek and Broad-billed Sandpipers. Collared Pratincoles and Gull-billed Terns breed in the less intensively worked areas. Dalmatian Pelicans put in the occasional appearance, sometimes dozens

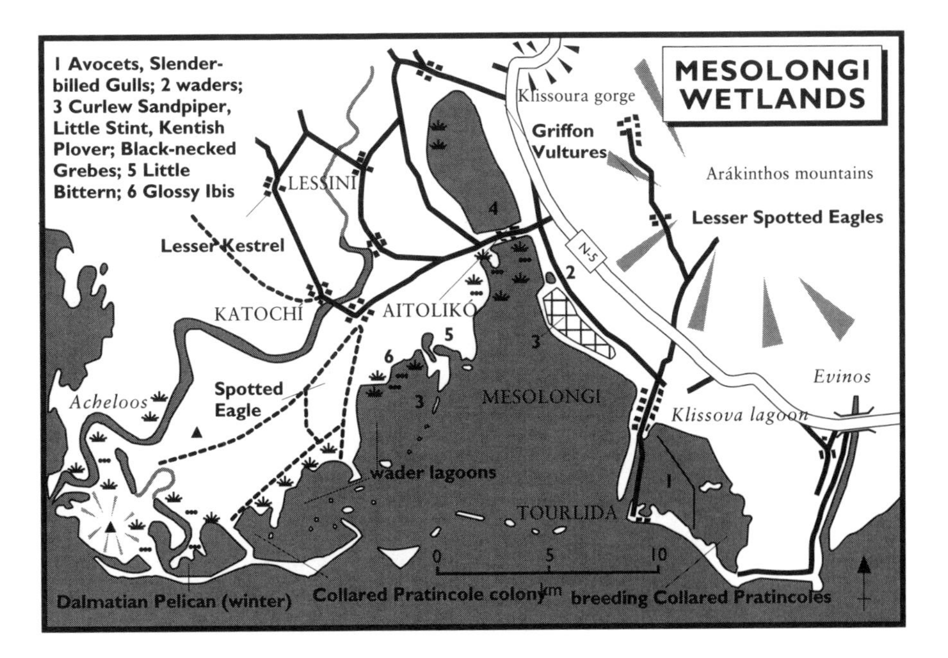

at a time, in the remaining open lagoons, and the sand bars and marshes are resting places for wintering Caspian Terns and Avocets.

Whereas this was once within easy reach, the best areas are mostly now less straightforward to get to. Best of all is probably the Acheloos delta, at least until the river is diverted, but this is a four-wheel drive job. The effort should be rewarded with Spotted and Imperial Eagles in winter and Glossy Ibis on passage. There is a superb riverine forest at Lessini consisting of Caucasian ash, smooth-leaved elm, willow and laurel. It is important for Penduline Tits and Middle Spotted Woodpeckers.

TIMING

Spring brings out the best in the Mesolongi wetlands. A hard winter in more northerly parts of the country would enhance its value at this time, although these days the area is not that good during a normal winter.

SPECIES

- *Black-necked Grebe* Winters in good numbers in the Aitolikó lagoon in particular.
- *Slender-billed Gull* Winters in the lagoons either side of the Tourlida causeway.
- *Slender-billed Curlew* Europe's most endangered species: recorded in April and may be sought in saltmarsh or undisturbed saltpans.

ACCESS

The town of Mesolongi is a short distance west of the Rio–Antirio ferry, the best route from Athens. From the town there is a causeway heading south to Tourlida which gives access to the best lagoon and saltmarsh in the eastern sector. The less accessible western sector is more intact, and may be reached via Aitolikó and Neochori. A track from the latter village leads eventually to the Acheloos delta. South of Neochori there are good brackish lagoons.

The industrial saltworks are alongside the Mesolongi-Aitolikó road, and should not be ignored in spring and autumn; from Aitolikó the lagoon of the same name can be scanned. Another way to see this lagoon is to take the road towards Kefalóvrisso at its northern end. There is accommodation in Mesolongi.

Delphi

38°30N 22°25E

Famed as one of the most evocative of the ancient sites, Delphi is not without renown among birdwatchers. Like many of the region's archaeological sites, it is an outstanding place for Rock Nuthatches and Blue Rock Thrushes. They cannot tell the difference between natural rock and ruined cities, but the latter tend to be easier for us.

The city was built into the side of a mountain and a great crag towers over the ruins. In early spring Golden Eagles display high over the heads of visitors and are usually around at other times. Peregrines, Honey Buzzards and, very occasionally, Griffon Vultures and Lammergeiers add to the raptor interest. The surrounding area is a mixture of scrubby hillside and olive groves and six buntings – Black-headed, Cirl, Corn, Cretzschmar's, Rock, and Ortolan – can be found. Warblers are also well represented, with Orphean, Rüppell's and Olive-tree particularly noteworthy.

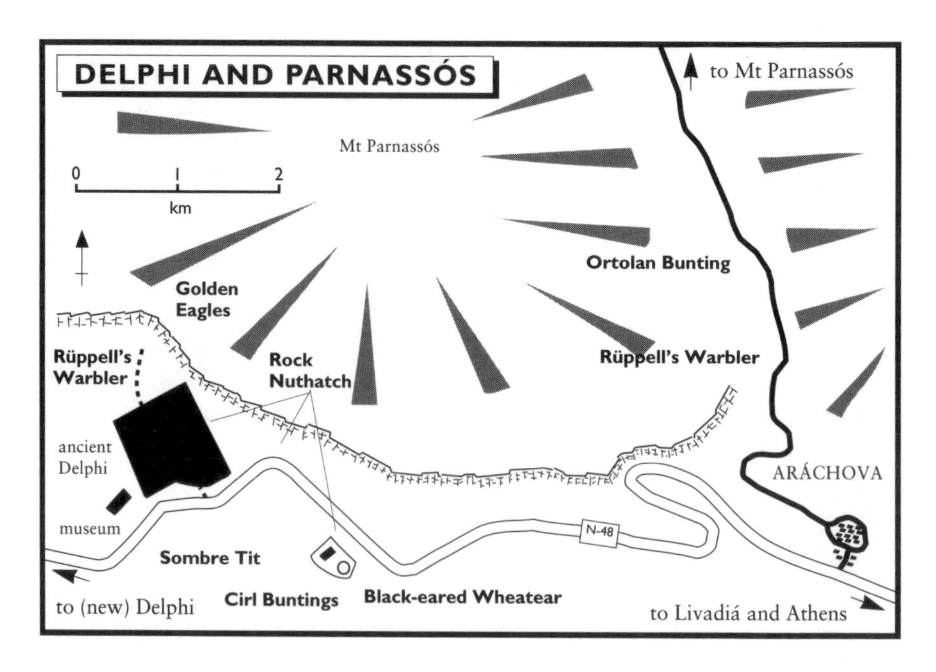

TIMING

The main problem with Delphi is that its busiest season, summer, is best for the birds. A good compromise is to go early in spring, which means fewer tourists but possibly fewer migrants. In any case, an early start is advised.

SPECIES

- *Levant Sparrowhawk* Often recorded on autumn passage in September.
- *Rock Nuthatch* Tame, but avoids crowds. Nests at the main site but is best seen below the road at the quieter Temple of Athene site.
- *Sombre Tit and Cretzschmar's Bunting* Best sought among the low trees and scrub away from the site.
- *Rüppell's Warbler* Occurs behind the site on the hillside, where there are indistinct tracks.

ACCESS

Delphi ruins are just east of the modern town of the same name, which is about 180 km west of Athens and 45 km west of Livadiá along the N-48. Delphi town has a profusion of hotels of all classe, a youth hostel and camp sites. Booking is advisable in high summer.

MOUNT PARNASSÓS

38°30N 22°37E

A few kilometres east of Delphi is a national park dominated by five peaks, usually snow-covered, and impressive unspoilt tracts of Greek fir forest. Mount Parnassós is important for its meadow flora, including one or two Parnassós endemics and 25 species which are endemic to Greece.

Lammergeiers breed, or at least have done so in recent years, but there is probably no more than one pair. Griffon and, in summer, Egyptian Vultures are more readily encountered. The forests are important for woodpeckers, with Black, White-backed and Middle Spotted all breeding. The presence of Black Woodpeckers suggests the area is probably also good for Tengmalm's Owls, which breed in their old nest holes. This would need confirmation by listening for their calls after dark in late winter. The more open areas hold Rock Partridges and the alpine meadows have Alpine Accentors.

TIMING

Snow lies for two months in the mid-winter period, and is usually present on the peaks between November and June. An abundance of flowers soon follows the retreating snow-line and May and June are excellent on all counts. After this, the area becomes rather crowded, especially at weekends.

SPECIES

- *Lammergeier* Most likely to be seen soaring along escarpments overlooking grazed alpine areas.
- *Smaller raptors* These include Goshawk in the forests and Lanner on the rocky escarpments.
- *White-backed Woodpecker* Tends to prefer lichen-rich woods and, in particular, areas with an especially high density of dead trees.
- *Black Woodpecker* Needs large trees with open ground for foraging.

ACCESS

From the main road east of Delphi a road passes through Aráchova into the park. After 14 km there is a fork. A right turn leads to the ski centre and the high alpine zone. Turning left instead, the forest thickens and there are useful forest tracks which are passable by car from late spring. The most convenient place for accommodation is nearby Delphi.

Mount Iti

38°48N 22°15E

Many would say this is the best of Greece's National Parks, and the lush meadow which carpets its central plateau, ringed by snowy peaks, is scenically perfect. Several local endemics grace its plant list, including the Iti speedwell. Chamois are found in the ravines of the Gorgopotamos.

Raptors are the main bird feature, and there are several pairs of Golden and Short-toed Eagles. The fir forests are home to several woodpecker species including Black and White-backed.

TIMING

June sees the spring flowers at their best, and July is not too hot. Autumn passage can be good, and at this time the weather and colours are perfect.

SPECIES

- ◆ *Griffon Vulture* Nests outside the national park but ranges widely in the area.
- ◆ *Black Woodpecker* Fequents the more open areas, where mature trees and bare grassland coincide.

ACCESS

Mount Iti (or Oiti) is unusually accessible. It is about 15 km south-west of Lamía and 90 km north of Delphi, and is close to the Sperchios delta. The starting point for trips into the park is Ipati, which has two hotels. From here there is a four-hour walk to the Trápeza refuge, which has beds which *must* be booked in advance (tel 0231 25 663). The walk starts from the tallest houses in the village and is marked by occasional splashes of red paint. The Livadies plateau is about 20 minutes farther up the track. Much of this is forest road driveable in a jeep in summer.

About 17 km north of Lamía is the high pass at Stená Fourkas, which is worth a stop for migrating storks and raptors in season.

Breeders include Little Bitterns, Collared Pratincoles, Black-winged Stilts and Little Terns. Spoonbills and Glossy Ibises are regular passage birds and several hundred Ferruginous Ducks arrive in autumn, staying through until December in most years. A few Spotted Eagles winter in the delta.

Sperchios delta

38°53N 22°31E

This is one of the most important wetlands outside northern Greece. There are extensive saltmarshes and sand bars as well as rice paddies. This provides a good mix of breeding, resting and feeding habitat for waders, terns and migrating herons and ibises.

Glossy Ibises

TIMING

Worth checking at almost any time, except perhaps high summer. Winter flooding may be a problem along the farm roads, though the artificial water regime of the rice paddies makes this less of a problem than it might be.

SPECIES

- *Squacco Heron* A denizen of the ricefields during spring passage, when there may be dozens together at a time.
- *Collared Pratincole, Stone-curlew and Black-winged Stilt* Nest on the saltpans.
- *Avocets* As many as 3000 winter on the saltpans and scattered pools.

ACCESS

The delta is east of the N-1 highway just south of Lamía. Access to the river mouth is good from Anthili, 8 km south of Lamía. A road from the nearby village of Roditsa leads towards the sea, via rice fields and saltpans. Access to the marshes is not easy, but the rice paddies are well served by a network of raised earth roads, some of which, however, end frustratingly at dead ends.

Cape Araxos

38°10N 21°22E

The north-west corner of the Peloponnisos is characterized by scattered lagoons and marshes, sand dunes and pinewoods. At the cape itself is the large Kalogerá lagoon; a few kilometres to the south is an area of marshland and open water near Kalógria, which is separated from the sea by the Strofilia pine forest; farther south is the brackish Lamia lake and more southerly still is the large coastal Kotichi lagoon near Varda.

Collectively, they are the most important wetland in the Peloponnese and one of the first Greek staging posts for migrants from the south. Black-winged Stilts, Stone-curlews and Collared Pratincoles nest at Kotichi along with Little Terns and Calandra Larks on the dunes. The Kalógria lagoons hold around 20 pairs of Little Bitterns and are important for passage herons and Glossy Ibis. Marsh and Hen Harriers are found there in winter. In the forest there are a few pairs of White Storks.

TIMING

The pine forest, reedbeds and scrubby hillsides attract small migrants in mid-April to early May, sometimes in huge numbers.

SPECIES

◆ *Dalmatian Pelican* Passes through Kotichi lagoon on passage and sometimes appears in winter.

ACCESS

The coast road which leaves the N-9 9 km west of Patra leads towards the cape. The southern end of Kalogerá lagoon has interesting shallows just beyond Limanaki. A right turn leads along the west shore of the lagoon, but this is a military area and access to the peninsula is barred. Turning left instead leads to Araxos village, where a right turn leads through the marshes to Kalógria; here a track leads south through the Strofilia forest towards Lamia lake.

The Kotichi lagoon is signposted at two points from the main road south to Lechena. There are hides, marked trails and a visitor centre.

Mykenai and Lake Stymfalía

37°50N 22°26E

The landscape of the north-east Peloponnese is of rolling or folded hills and occasional mountains, Mediterranean scrub and olive groves. Dotted about are ancient sites, many of which are good for birds.

Mykenai (or Mycenae), north of the port of Nafplio, is a ruined citadel among olive groves and scrub-covered hills. The most obvious bird here is the very vocal Rock Nuthatch, with several pairs building their clay-pot nests in the stone of the ruins. Rufous Bush Robins and Sombre Tits are often seen in and around the olives, where Hawfinches are common in winter. On the slopes Rüppell's Warblers sing from the scrub and Blue Rock Thrushes from the outcrops.

To the north is Lake Stymfalía, a marshy depression, reedy and sometimes filled with water. It is important for migratory birds and, at least in good water years, breeding Little Bitterns and Purple Herons. The Killini hills above hold Rock Partridges and Rüppell's Warblers.

Lake Stymfalía is circumnavigated by roads. From Xilókastro on the Corinthian Gulf coast, a road runs off into the hills through Zemenó and on, after 40 km to Stymfalía village. From Mykenai, head north to Nemea and east from there through Galatas and Psari.

Southern Peloponnese

36°49N 22°43E

The triple peninsula of the southern Peloponnese resembles the fingers of a hand reaching into the Mediterranean to grab Crete, 95 km offshore. The fingers are aligned in such a way as to funnel migrants into and out of Greece, with only Crete offering a mid-sea landfall between here and

Africa. Cape Ténaro, at the tip of the Mani peninsula and Cape Maleas, at the end of the Krithnia peninsula, are important at both seasons. All three 'pied' flycatchers, Isabelline and other wheatears, all the shrikes and warblers and larger migrants such as Rollers and Scops Owls can be seen at first light in the scrub and olive groves each April.

Both peninsulas are mountainous, sparsely forested, and with frequent cliffs both inland and at the coast. Bonelli's Eagles, Peregrines and Eagle Owls inhabit the outcrops and cliffs, along with Blue Rock Thrushes. In summer Eleonora's Falcons are often seen soaring and playing in the updraughts off the slopes, where Short-toed Eagles sometimes hover.

At the head of the Lakonikós Gulf which separates these two easterly peninsulas is the Evrotas delta, with its coastal marshes, lagoons, heathland, sandy beaches and olive groves. This is an important stop-over for migrating herons, especially Squacco, and up to 100 Glossy Ibises have been recorded. Eleonora's Falcons often hunt over the marshes.

On the western seaboard is Dinari lagoon, immediately north of Navarinos Bay, near Pilos. This is a brackish lake which attracts up to 20 pairs of Little Bitterns and an array of migrating and breeding waders, as well as occasional Greater Flamingos, Ospreys and Cranes on passage.

TIMING

All the sites mentioned are passage watchpoints. Thus April, May, August and September are the best months.

SPECIES

- *Imperial Eagle* Occurs in winter in the mountain pasture areas above Cape Ténaro.
- *Rüppell's Warbler* Found on the rocky, scrub-covered hillsides of the Taigetos Mountains.

ACCESS

The N-39 runs south down the Mani peninsula all the way to Cape Ténaro, and beyond Areópoli provides access to the spectacular foothills of the Sangias mountains. The marshes of the Evrotas delta are accessed in several places near Skála, on the N-86. The western marshes are close to the road from Githio, about 8 km west of Skála; a road running south from the N-86 leads through Limonas towards the main river mouth and coastal marshes; the coast road south of Élos is also worth exploring.

Central Corfu

39°35N 19°53E

Corfu lies in the Ionian Sea, closer to Albania than to mainland Greece. Its idyllic landscapes of low mountains and olive groves punctuated by countless cypress spires attract holiday-makers and migrants alike. At night the olive groves ring with the sound of Scops Owls and attract hordes of passerines in spring.

The capital, Kérkira (or Corfu) often has Mediterranean Gulls in its harbour and there is a lagoon (Lake Chalikiopoulou) close to the airport which can be good for herons and migrant waterbirds such as Glossy

Semi-collared Flycatcher

Ibises. Blue Rock Thrushes nest in the old fort and other monumental buildings. Paleokastritsa has cliffs overlooking the town which are good for Rock Nuthatches, Blue Rock Thrushes and Choughs. Subalpine Warblers and Lesser Grey Shrikes are frequent here, too.

Ropa plain half-way between Kérkira town and Paleokastritsa. It is bisected by a drainage ditch which can be good for reedbed warblers and herons, including Squacco. Montagu's Harriers quarter the fields from which Quails call in abundance. Three shrikes – Red-backed, Woodchat and Lesser Grey – can be found on passage and all three probably breed.

TIMING

Mid-April to early May is best when warblers, flycatchers and shrikes are particularly numerous. Autumn is just as good, except that Pied, Collared and Semi-collared Flycatchers become harder to separate.

SPECIES

- ◆ *Pygmy Cormorant and Dalmatian Pelican* Appear from time to time on Lake Chalikiopoulou.
- ◆ *Lanner* Regularly recorded quartering the cliffs above Paleokastritsa.

ACCESS

Kérkira (or Corfu) town is the main entry point to the island, by both air and, from either Patra or Italy, by sea. Paleokastritsa can be easily reached from Kérkira town by car or bus. Car hire from the airport is straightforward, but not cheap.

The road between Kérkira and Giannades crosses the area. It is worth stopping at the drainage channel and walking along it, and also scanning the damp meadows on either side.

Northern Corfu

39°45N 19°55E

The two best-known birdwatching sites in the north are Andinioti lagoon at the northernmost point of Corfu, and Mount Pandókrator. The former draws a variety of herons and waders, especially during migration.

Little Bitterns and Squacco Herons are found here, along with Whiskered and White-winged Black Terns and interesting waders such as passage Temminck's Stints.

The mountains, dominated by Pandókrator (914 m) are renowned as a Cretzschmar's Bunting site. Bonelli's Eagles, Rock Partridges, Rock Nuthatches, Black-eared Wheateasr, Rock and Blue Rock Thrushes, Subalpine and Orphean Warblers, Ortolan and Cirl Buntings and Rock Sparrows are among the consolation prizes if Cretzschmar's eludes you.

The north coast of the island, and the area just inland, are these days well watched. Sidari is a popular base for birdwatchers, although the town has thoroughly encroached on the once-excellent marsh in the area. There is, however, a small river east of the town, south-east of Megali Dris, which is worth exploring for Squacco Herons, as well as other herons and warblers.

TIMING

Red-footed Falcons and Red-throated Pipits are among the eastern migrants which can sometimes appear by the dozen in late April or early May.

SPECIES

- *Eleonora's Falcon* Often seen along the north coast between May and November.
- *Spanish Sparrow* Agios Stefanos in the north-east corner of the island is famed for its colony.
- *Cretzschmar's Bunting* Tends to haunt the higher slopes of Pandókrator, beyond the end of the road.

ACCESS

The main road north from Kérkira town encircles the Pandókrator massif and runs close to Andinioti lagoon. About 17 km from Kérkira, at Pirgí, a left turn leads to Spartilas, beyond which a right turn leads to Petalia. From here the road to the summit gets progressively rougher and most people walk from end of the paved section. From Sidari, Petalia is reached via either Karrousades, Agios Doúli and Zigós, or Andinioti lagoon and Perítha.

The lagoon is off the main coast road north of Pandókrator about 9 km west of Kassiópi, or 6 km east of Anacharási. There are straightforward tracks all round.

Southern Corfu

39°28N 19°55E

Southern Corfu differs from the more popular north in several respects, notably its relative flatness and fewer tourists. The main attraction is Lake Korission, which can be outstanding. During the migration period it has a reputation for holding different selections of birds every day, and so is worth visiting at the beginning and end of a trip. Five or six species of heron are likely on a good day, along with some bonus or other such as a migrating flock of Garganey, the occasional Glossy Ibis or Ferruginous Duck and a few good raptors. Waders may not be abundant, but there is usually a good variety, especially between late August and late May. Caspian, Gull-billed, Whiskered and Black Terns are regularly recorded.

The sand dunes around the lake hold Short-toed and Crested Larks and Tawny Pipits. There are mixed oak- and pinewoods on the more northerly dunes which are worth checking at some length for migrant passerines.

In the far south are the Alikes saltpans, where waders congregate in good numbers if the conditions are right, often joined by Collared Pratincoles and the rarer terns. Tawny Pipits and Short-toed Larks are relatively common.

TIMING

The southern wetlands are likely to be dry from June to September, and again it is during spring and autumn passage that these two sites are at their best. Both sites are subject to heavy hunting pressure during the long official season (August 25 to March 10) and to some extent during weekends at other times.

SPECIES

- *Eleonora's and Red-footed Falcons* Often seen in late April (Red-footed) or May to August (Eleonora's) around Korission lagoon.
- *Collared Pratincole* Regular migrant at Alikes and may breed.

ACCESS

Lake Korission is at the south-western bend of the island's coastline. Off the main road between Kérkira (Corfu town) and Lefkimi, there is turn westwards to Issos beach, almost opposite the turning to Chlomos. There are marshy areas and lagoons along this road, which runs close to the southern, and better, end of the lake.

The Alikes saltpans are at Lefkimi Cape, reached by taking a left turn in Ano Lefkimi. Access is not restricted. There is accommodation in Agios Giorgios and elsewhere on the coast.

ZÁKYNTHOS AND THE STROFADES

38°00N 21°00E

Now one of the most tourist-infested of all the Greek islands, a fact which has led to serious conflicts with conservationists trying to protect the important nesting beaches of Loggerhead Turtles. These are in Laganás Bay in the south, which is also good for migrating shorebirds. A good area to try is the saltpans north of the village of Alikés, north-west of Zákynthos town. These attract migrating waders and herons and in spring there are often large numbers of Red-footed Falcons there. Recent reports, however, suggest they may be declining in importance, at least in summer when they are dry.

The rocky peninsula at Keri is said to hold a small colony of Eleonora's Falcons, something of a rarity in the Ionian. They are there in summer, and a visit in early autumn would help to confirm breeding.

The Strofades are two small islets, to the south of Zákynthos, the larger of which is famous for the mass migration of Turtle Doves and other birds in spring. The main problem here is the expense of getting to the island. This can only be done by chartering a boat out of Keri or Kyparissia in the Peloponnese. However, studies so far indicate that spring migration of passerines is spectacular and the boat trip will be good for both shearwaters.

Yelkouan Shearwaters

TIMING

Most of what is known of Zákynthos and the Strofades is the result of spring studies and summer visits. An autumn passage survey would be well worth doing.

SPECIES

- *Cory's and Yelkouan Shearwaters* Common in these waters and easily seen from ferries.
- *Long-legged Buzzard* At the western edge of its range, and probably breeds in the Vrachíonas hills in the west and north of Zákynthos.

ACCESS

There are countless charter flights to Zákynthos in summer, and ferries from Killini and, in summer, Argostoli in Kefallonia and Patras. A hired moped is a good way of getting around this mostly flat island. Accommodation is plentiful in Zákynthos town and Laganás, although the latter is not to the taste of most birdwatchers, I suspect. More to the point, staying here is an affront to the turtles whose survival prospects diminish each year.

Athens City

36°50N 22°57E

Whilst not, perhaps, an obvious choice for a birdwatching trip, the capital does have one or two features which may serve to provide a glimpse of the mainland for birdwatchers *en route* to the islands. There are several parks and wooded areas which can be explored for typical birds such as Serins and Olivaceous and Sardinian Warblers. Some of the hills on which the city is built have good vegetation cover, such as Lycabettus hill, which has roads to the top. During migration periods, these hills often serve as vantage points from which to watch for Lesser Spotted Eagles and other raptors, Cranes and both storks. There are often 'falls' of small migrants such as warblers and flycatchers. Lycabettus has breeding Alpine Swifts, whilst a trip to the Acropolis should yield Blue Rock Thrushes, Rock Sparrows and Black Redstarts.

Very close to city is Mount Parnitha, a National Park to the north. Although it suffers much from its proximity to Athens, it boasts 113 species on its bird list, including breeding Short-toed Eagles and Goshawks and resident, but non-breeding, Golden Eagles. Access is via Menidi.

Marathon marshes

37°35N 23°30E

Only 40 km north-east of Athens, this small, coastal marsh is under considerable pressure, but remains important for passage waterbirds such as Glossy Ibises (up to 100 recorded), Spoonbills, Squacco Herons, Garganey, Little Crakes and Great Snipe. Late April sees Red-throated Pipits passing through and Little Bitterns, Night Herons, Black-winged Stilts, and Great Reed Warblers settling down to breed. The dry, rocky hills around the village of Marathon are good for Rock Nuthatches, Black-eared Wheatears and Cretzschmar's and Black-headed Buntings. Orphean Warblers and Rufous Bush Robins are worth looking out for.

About 36 km along the N-54 Athens–Marathon road there is a right (east) turn to Kato Souli. After 3 km a further right turn leads through the marshes towards the sea. Ditches either side of this road can be good for crakes. The road bears left alongside some wooded dunes and there are marshy areas, lagoons and reedbeds on the landward side. This is a military area, so careful with the binoculars and camera!

Northern Evvia

38°21–39°00N 23°10–23°45E

A huge island, second only to Crete, but at one point near Athens Evvia lies only 70 m from the mainland, and is connected by a bridge. Close to the town of Kími there is an area which typifies the remote eastern part of the island. The Mavrovoúni massif overlooks the town, its six bare-topped peaks cloaked on their lower slopes in fir and chestnut forests. A few pairs of Griffon Vultures reside on the sheer outcrops and the forests are the haunt of Golden Eagles. Where the forest meets farmland, Short-toed Eagles hover in search of snakes and lizards.

On the north-west coast there is a chain of hills rising to 1246 m, the Kandílio range, with a good selection of raptors including Bonelli's Eagles.

There is a small coastal wetland just east of the village of Kanatádika, north of Isteá. There is a brackish lagoon which attracts migrating Spoonbills and Glossy Ibises and breeding birds include Little Terns.

TIMING

Since Evvia and the Cyclades lie roughly in line between southern Turkey and mainland Greece, one would expect spring and autumn passage to be interesting, and the headlands would be worth checking out.

SPECIES

- *Eleonora's Falcon* Plays the updraughts in the Mavrovoúni hills during early summer before retiring to offshore islands to breed.

ACCESS

Evvia is connected to the mainland by a bridge at Chalkída. There are also ferries from Rafina, east of Athens, and ports in the Lamia area. Kími is reached by turning left 3 km before Kistos. There are small roads and tracks into the Mavrovoúni: for example between Vitala and Metóchio, or running north and south of Metóchio.

Bonelli's Eagle

Southern Evvia

38°03–38°21N 23°45–24°27E

To the south of Kími lies Lake Distos, a reedy, lake set among gentle hills and overlooked by a Venetian fortress. Pollution and water abstraction have been serious problems, and threaten this once-important wetland. In good water years, there may be a few pairs each of Little Bitterns, Night Herons, Little Egrets and Purple Herons. At the right time, there can be good numbers of passage waders and Glossy Ibises, especially in areas burned the previous year. The hills around hold a selection of raptors which sometimes hunt along the lake shore, and are home to Rüppell's Warblers and Lesser Grey Shrikes. Lake Distos is south of the village from which it takes its name, which is 60 km east of Chalkída off the N-44.

In the far south of the island there are hills and wetlands around Karystos both of which are very good for migrants. Old saltpans and a small river just to the west of the town are worth exploring during spring and autumn passage. The Ochi range above the town holds a selection of raptors including Short-toed and Bonelli's Eagles, Long-legged Buzzards, Peregrines and pre-breeding Eleonora's Falcons.

West Crete (Chaniá)

35°21N 24°16E

Crete is the largest island in Greece, and to do justice to it you need at least two bases. In the west the pleasing Venetian town of Chaniá (or Haniá) is a good place from which to explore the wetlands at Agia and Georgioúpolis, and could be used as a base for Samaria. The town itself, like the rest of the island, has Scops Owls and most of the House Sparrows are the brown-capped Italian subspecies.

The best wetland in Crete is teh Agia reservoir, *c.* 9 km south of Chaniá on the road to Samaria. This has extensive areas of open water, large reedbeds and some scrub and open shoreline. It is excellent for waders, herons, Little and Baillon's Crakes and Moustached Warblers.

In the far west is Mount Koutroulis with Lammergeiers, Griffon Vultrues and Golden Eagles. A more accessible alternative for these species, however, is the Samaria gorge (*see* below).

East of Chaniá is Georgioúpolis, where there are three wetlands of interest. Lake Kournas is *c.* 3 km south of the town, near Mouri, whilst at Georgioúpolis itself is a reed-fringed reservoir. Behind the beach is a small coastal marsh where the Almiros river flows into the sea. They are important for waders, herons and crakes on migration. Little Crakes and Squacco Herons are particularly noteworthy, with rarer waders and Glossy Ibises turning up occasionally.

TIMING

April and May can be excellent, except at Lake Kournas where water-sports start in mid-April.

SPECIES

- *Black-necked Grebe* Regular non-breeding visitor to Lake Kournas.
- *Little Crake* Can be surprisingly confiding: check out reedy ditches.

ACCESS

As well as Chaniá, Rethymnon, east of Georgioúpolis is a good base. In the south, the Kourtaliotiko and Kotsifos gorges, north of Lefkógia and Plakis respectively, are worth exploring.

SAMARIA GORGE

35°18N 24°00E

The Samaria gorge, cutting through the Lefka (White) Mountains of western Crete is, at 18 km, the longest gorge in Europe. Its width varies from 150 m to just 4 m. At its southern end, it enjoys a North African climate, while at its origins on the Omalós plateau winters are harsh and summers cool.

Samaria gorge and the Omalós plateau are important for several threatened Cretan subspecies of mammals and plants. There are 52 bird species on the official list, although visiting birdwatchers will have amassed many more, no doubt. The southern end of the gorge and coastal areas in the vicinity can be excellent for arriving spring migrants such as the three 'pied' flycatchers and Isabelline Wheatear. Prize bird is the Lammergeier. There is also a colony of Griffon Vultures (especially obvious in the Lefka Mountains at Lakos Kallergi), a pair of Golden Eagles, many Choughs and several Peregrines. Bonelli's Eagles may breed.

Cirl Buntings, Woodlarks and Black-eared Wheatears are characteristic of the plateau.

TIMING

In winter and occasionally at other times the narrowest part of the gorge may be impassable when the river is in flood and the gorge is often not open until early May.

SPECIES

- *Lammergeier* Can sometimes be watched from the top of the gorge by the entrance gate.
- *Chukar* The partridge which calls from the scrubby hillside: the Rock Partridge is absent from Crete.

ACCESS

Day trips are possible from Chaniá, by bus or car. A couple of kilometres south of Omalós is the northern entrance to the gorge. The 16-km hike to the beach is spectacular, but it is worth spending a while birdwatching at the top first. An early start is essential, especially in summer, as both the heat and the crowds can be a nuisance, and you should allow six hours.

Those not relishing making a return trip of it (you have to be truly heroic and ultra-fit) buy a ferry ticket on arrival at the beach, this connects with the return bus from Chora Sfakion to Chaniá. There are also rooms to rent in small hotels at the coast in Nea Agia Roumeli.

Central Crete

35°15N 24°45E

The main port and capital of Crete is Irakleion (Heraklion and other variants), and between here and the well-known resort at Agios Nikolaos is a wide range of birdwatching possibilities, so either town is a good base. Irakleion harbour is good for Pallid Swifts and gulls such as Mediterranean. Great Black-headed Gulls have also been recorded. Just east of the town is Gouves, where there is a degraded wetland to the east of the Creta Sun hotel, which nevertheless turns up good birds.

This has been the subject of several years' effort by British conservationists to save and improve the site for wildlife tourism. The area dries out naturally in summer but at other times can be excellent for waders and Garganey on passage. Glossy Ibises and various herons are attracted when water levels are high. The surrounding fields can be good for Red-throated Pipits, Woodchat Shrikes and other migrants.

There are several mountains and gorges in this central area which hold a good population of Lammergeiers and Griffon Vultures. The best is Mount Idi (or Mount Psiloritis), although Mount Kedros, Koutaliotiko Gorge and Prassies Gorge are all excellent. In the south of the island Mount Kofinas is also good. Mount Idi is important for both vultures, as well as Golden and Bonelli's Eagles, Peregrines, Eleonora's Falcons, Choughs and Chukasr. The juniper scrub can also be good for passerines such as Ortolan Buntings and Rüppell's Warblers.

TIMING

The Gouves lagoons are highly susceptible to fluctuations in water levels, but from December to May can usually be expected to have some water.

SPECIES

- *Bonelli's Eagle* Has been seen recently in the Zaros area.
- *Eleonora's Falcon* Hunts along the slopes of Mount Idi and the other mountains and gorges in the area.

ACCESS

Mount Idi is south-west of Irakleion above Anogia. There is a rough track leading for 13 km from Anogia to the Nida plateau. From here a path leads to the summit, a five-hour round-trip. The saltpans at Elounda, north of Agios Nikolaos, can be good.

LESITHI PLATEAU

35°10N 25°30E

This is the massif which dominates the eastern part of Crete, and is perhaps the most important area in Greece for Lammergeiers. Mount Dikti is its highest point, a rugged mountain with forests of Kermes oak and Calabrian pine. Other important areas include Mounts Thryptis and Ornon. Golden and Bonelli's Eagles and Peregrines are among the other raptors, and Griffon Vultures are rarely out of view once the thermals have started to rise. Crag Martins and Choughs are common and the stony plateau holds Black-eared Wheatears. In the orchards on the lower slopes there are Black-headed Buntings and Woodchat Shrikes. The Selinari gorge, west of Agios Nikolaos, is also good for Lammergeiers.

The main tourist attractions on the plateau are the white-sailed windmills and the Psychró cave, the latter a Lammergeier haunt. There are buses from Agios Nikolaos, and coach parties arrive by mid-morning so an early start or an overnight stay is recommended. There are rooms at Neápoli and Psychró.

CRETE: OFFSHORE ISLANDS AND HEADLANDS

35°20N 26°10E

In conservation terms, one of Crete's most important features is its Eleonora's Falcons. The largest colonies in the world are on the island of Dia, off Irakleion, with some 200 pairs, and the Dionisiades islands in the far east with over 250 pairs.

Cory's Shearwaters nest on the Dionisiades and probably on Dia; Bonelli's Eagles on Dia and Audouin's Gulls on the Dionisiades. Both are

Cory's Shearwaters

difficult to visit, but the falcons and shearwaters are easily seen on the adjacent mainland, from Irakleion and Sitía harbours and from the headland north of Vai.

TIMING

Eleonora's Falcons arrive in May and are particularly active after the young hatch in September. Cory's Shearwaters are present in the waters off the headlands from March to November.

SPECIES

◆ *Audouin's Gull* Occasionally attracted to Sitía harbour, along with the more frequent Mediterranean and Little Gulls.

ACCESS

Vai beach is well served by buses from Sitía, and is a good place from which to explore the rocky coastline nearby. Access to the islands themselves is irregular, but enquiries at the harbours may be worthwhile.

Naxos

37°00N 25°30E

Naxos is the largest of the Cyclades, and is characterized by steep, narrow ravines which run down to the sea. The main attraction here is spring and autumn passage, but Naxos is relatively unusual in the Aegean in having a reasonably healthy raptor population with a dozen or so pairs of Griffon Vultures and a few pairs of Bonelli's Eagles and Peregrines in the mountains. Eleonora's Falcons nest on the cliffs. Other breeding species include Yelkouan and, possibly, Cory's Shearwaters, Rüppell's Warblers and Cretzschmar's Buntings.

During migration interest is considerably enhanced by, in spring, Red-footed Falcons, Red-throated Pipits, Subalpine Warblers and Collared Flycatchers and in autumn by Red-backed and Lesser Grey Shrikes. Isabelline Wheatears occur at both seasons. Marmora's Warbler has been claimed in the literature as a nesting bird, almost certainly in error.

TIMING

A study carried out by the University of Athens concluded that April was the month in which the highest number of species is found with August and September seeing a smaller peak.

SPECIES

◆ *Isabelline Wheatear* Passes through early – from the first half of March, and late September to late October.

ACCESS

Naxos is served by at least three flights a day from Athens, as well as an eight-hour ferry trip three times a day. In Naxos town, cars and mopeds can be hired, but the bus service is quite good for the central mountain areas. Mount Zas (Dias or Zeus), the highest mountain in the Cyclades, is reached by way of a two–three-hour round walk from Filóti. The roads running north from Filóti to Apóllo pass along the central mountain chain. Mount Koronos is between the village of the same name and

Skadó. There is a wooded valley east of Skadó along the road to the coastal village of Lionas, which should be good for raptors and migrants.

The remotest part of the coast is south of Moutsoúna. A rocky promontory here is good for migrants. The coastal road, which requires four-wheel drive, leads to the best areas of maquis. There is accommodation in and around Naxos town, and rooms available in many of the central villages.

NORTHERN SPORADES

39°25N 24°20E

In 1986 some of the more northerly of the islands in the Sporades group were declared a Marine Park, primarily to protect the Mediterranean Monk Seal, one of Europe's most endangered mammals, which has a stronghold here.

Eleonora's Falcons are perhaps the most obvious attraction for birdwatchers, but their presence in turn indicates the islands' importance for migrating passerines, the falcons' principal prey. These include most of the region's warblers, flycatchers and chats. Audouin's Gulls nest on several islets, especially the northern island of Piperi (also the main Monk Seal area) and the rocky islets around Skandzoura in the east.

The cliffs and rocky interiors of the islands are home to Crag Martins, Blue Rock Thrushes and Rock Nuthatches. Many of the islands are covered in maquis and heath-like scrub favoured by Sardinian, Olivaceous and, in the groves, Olive-tree Warblers.

TIMING

Migration peaks in April and September/October.

SPECIES

- ◆ *Eleonora's Falcon* Arrives in May and breeds in late summer and autumn.
- ◆ *Audouin's Gull* Surveys in 1995 have shown that this species is much more common than previously realized.

ACCESS

Ships sail daily from Agios Konstantinos and Volos to the Sporades as far as Alonissos. Permission is needed to visit the core of the Marine Park, and information can be gained from the Society for the Protection of the Monk Seal at Stení Valá on Alonissos (tel 3644 146).

LIMNOS

39°50N 25°22E

Little-known ornithologically, Limnos tends to be overlooked by birdwatchers who these days flock to neighbouring Lesbos. Nevertheless, the island appears to be of major interest. Rather flat, and quite unlike Lesbos, the prime interest lies in the wetlands in the east. These comprise the large coastal lagoon Limni Alyki and Chortarolimni a little inland and to the south. Breeding species here include good numbers of Ruddy Shelducks, along with Avocet, Stone-curlew. In the south-west there is an interesting small wetland near Diapori which is also good for Ruddy Shelduck.

Lesser Kestrels appear to be relatively common on the island, especially in the flat, dry areas in the south. There are fragments of oak forest east of the airport which are good for migrants, including Red-breasted flycatchers.

TIMING
The wetlands are usually dry by mid-June, and the Ruddy Shelducks move away, although at Diapori the wetland holds water further into the summer.
SPECIES
- *Greater Flamingo* More than 1000 were recorded recently in the Alyki lagoon.

ACCESS
Flights to Limnos are available from Athens, Kavála and Lesbos, making it possible to combine these two islands in a single trip. Cars and mopeds can be hired at the main town, Mírina (also known as Kastro). East of the airport, a side road leads to Kondopoúli where a right turn leads, via Kaliópi, to Kéros beach, which stretches between the Alyki lagoon and Chortarolimni. The landward shore of Limni Alyki can be explored via the road which runs north from Kondopoúli to Plaka.

LESBOS: KALLONIS BAY

39°10N 26°15E
Lesbos has relatively recently been discovered by birdwatchers and tourists and is rapidly gaining in popularity with both. A large island close to Turkey, it boasts two species (possibly three: *see* West Lesbos, below) usually associated with that country: Krüper's Nuthatch and Cinereous Bunting (which is also found on Chios). There are other eastern influences, not least the handsome Ruddy Shelducks which frequent the wetlands around the Kallonis Gulf and the Rose-coloured Starlings which turn up most years in May. Spur-winged Plovers, Black-winged Pratincoles, River Warblers and Citrine Wagtails are among the less common but regular easterners, and the odd vagrant turns up, including Isabelline Shrike.

The Kallonis gulf is a large sea bay indenting the southern coast. There are saltpans, river mouths and marshes at the shore, and olive groves and pinewoods stretching inland. The saltpans are good for Greater Flamingos, which turn up frequently but irregularly in spring and more reliably in winter; Black Storks, Spoonbills, Glossy Ibises and marsh terns pass through each spring, while Avocets, Stone-curlews, Collared Pratincoles and Little Terns stay to breed.

Two excellent river mouths lie one either side of Skala Kallonís. The eastern one is especially good. There are raised banks from which one can watch Squacco Herons, Little Bitterns, waders and wildfowl from close range.

Some 10 km east of Kalloní, behind the eastern shore of the bay is an area dubbed 'Derbyshire' by English birdwatchers. A muddy pool here is a good spot for passage waders and Ruddy Shelducks, while the rocky outcrop and surrounding scrub attract small migrants. Rufous Bush Robins frequent the low hill by the road junction.

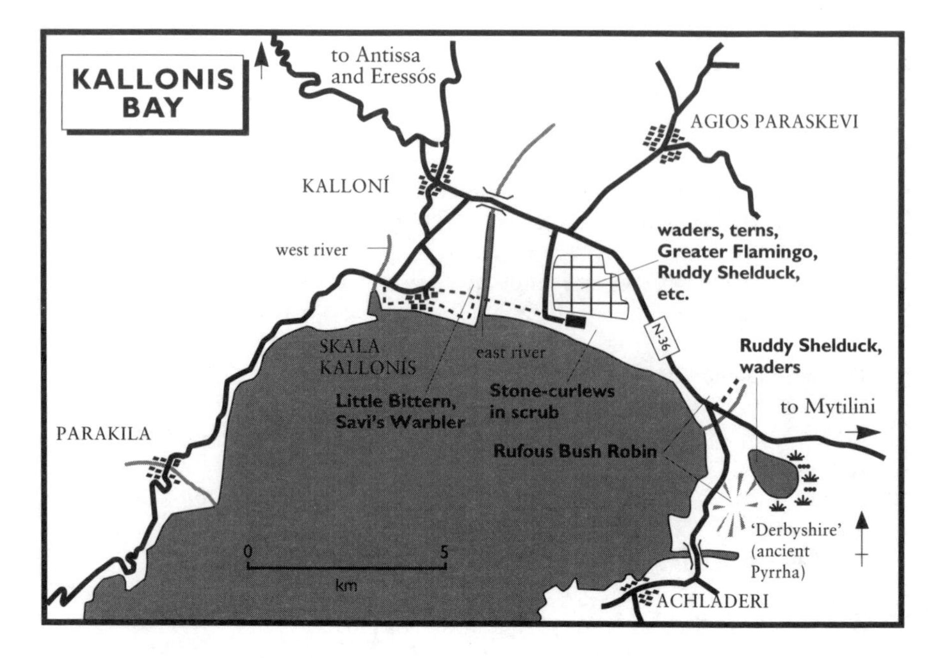

TIMING

Package tours are few in early spring, and the great majority of bird-watchers visit in May, with good results. A few pioneering early spring and autumn visits may uncover yet more attractions.

SPECIES

- *Ruddy Shelduck* Found in all the wetlands mentioned, but perhaps most reliably at the 'Derbyshire' pool.
- *Eleonora's Falcon* Nests on the north coast, on the cliffs between Mithimna (Molivos) and Eftalou cape.
- *Masked Shrike* Nests in the olive groves such as those along the Potamia valley.
- *Olive-tree Warbler* Found in the groves along the north coast, for example near Mithimna, and in the Potamia valley a kilometre or so north of the bridge.

ACCESS

Lesbos is reached by charter flight from London, and regular scheduled flights from Athens. The boat-trip from Piraeus takes 12 hours. The salt-pans are east of Skala Kallonís on the Mytilini road and are reached via a track on the right about 200 m before the turning to Agios Paraskevi. The Potamia valley is reached via a track which continues straight ahead at a sharp left-hand bend west of Skala Kallonís. The road north out of Kalloní leads to Mithimna and then eastwards towards Eftalou and the cape. The olive groves in this area hold Middle Spotted Woodpeckers, Sombre Tits and Masked Shrikes, and the road *en route* runs through scrubby hills good for Rüppell's and Orphean Warblers (e.g., east of the road out of Petra).

West Lesbos

39°00N 25°00E

Eressós is on the south-west coast of Lesbos, about 90 km from Mytilini. Above Eressós are some rugged hills which are the traditional Cinereous Bunting site, and also the haunt of Long-legged Buzzards. Cretzschmar's and Cirl Buntings are also common in the area along with Rock Sparrows and Rock Nuthatches. The same species may be seen with less exertion south of Antissa. In May 1995 at least one pair of White-throated Robins was holding territory in a western valley. This striking species is yet another Turkish bird hundreds of kilometres from its previously known

range. If observations in future years prove it to be breeding in fair numbers future editions may be in a position to reveal the details.

There is a small wetland just before Sigri which can be alive with migrants at the right time. The river mouth west of Skala Eressou is also good for marshland species and Isabelline Wheatears. The scrub behind the beach attracts passing migrants, as well as Rock Nuthatches, Rufous Bush Robins and, in the olive groves, Middle Spotted Woodpeckers.

TIMING

Cinereous Buntings are in good song in May, when most birdwatchers try for them.

SPECIES

- *Isabelline Wheatear* Apparently breeds regularly in suitable habitat west of Antissa.
- *Rufous Bush Robin* Nests in the dry river bed west of Eressós.
- *Cinereous Bunting See* directions below.

ACCESS

Eressós is about 50 km west of Kalloní, down a left turn beyond Antissa. To the north-west of the town are two distinctive peaks, with a farm between them. Above the farm on higher ground is the classic Cinereous Bunting site, but they can sometimes be found feeding around the farm itself. It is a steep climb out of Eressós town. There are other sites nearby, and Cinereous Buntings have been recorded by the road south of Antissa (try the valley on the left side of the Eressós road after the second bridge) and between Eressós and Sigri.

Agiassos

39°10N 26°30E

East of Kalloní is Agiassos, with its pine woods to the south. This is the only known site in Europe (excluding Turkey) where Krüper's Nuthatch is found. The forest here does not look much different from other areas on Lesbos, but I am not aware of any other reliable site here or on neighbouring islands. Here there is also a chance of Sombre Tits and Orphean Warblers; Subalpine Warblers and Middle Spotted Woodpeckers are common. Agiassos is reached by taking the Mytilini road east of Kalloni and turning right after 29 km. The road forks 4 km before the village, and although both ways lead to Agiassos, take the left fork and turn left again just inside the village, keeping to the metalled road until you leave Agiassos behind, heading for Plomari. Krüper's Nuthatches are found in the pines 3 km south of Agiassos, at the hairpin bend just past the sanatorium on the left.

Samos and Fourni

37°44N 26°37E

Lying only 2.5 km from Turkey at its nearest point, Samos is excellent for passage migrants of all kinds. There are several small wetlands within sight of Turkey, and waves of passing waders and herons call in from time to time. In the region of Pythagorio and the airport, and farther east at Alyki, it will be worth checking any pratincoles for Black-winged, which must turn up regularly. At Alyki Rollers breed, Greater Flamingos are regular and up to 40 Ruddy Shelducks have been recorded. If better-known Chíos and Lesbos are anything to go by, it is likely that passerine migrants such as Rose-coloured Starlings, Citrine Wagtails and other more easterly species can be expected. Cretzschmar's Buntings and Masked and Lesser Grey Shrikes breed.

In the far west, the 1433-m Mount Kerkis dominates. Honey Buzzards, Peregrines, Short-toed Eagles, Long-legged Buzzards and Eagle Owls breed on its rocky outcrops or in its cypress forests. The higher reaches are grazed and dry, and Tawny Pipits and Rock Thrushes are frequently encountered. Rüppell's Warblers are common on the lower slopes, especially east-facing, juniper-covered hillsides. Several routes up the mountain are worth trying. For the higher reaches, start in Kosmadaioí and head south, or Marathocampos and head west towards Kallithea.

Lying between Samos and Ikaría to the west are the Fournis islands, of which Fourni, the largest, is reached by car ferry from Samos. They form a group of rugged islands whose cliffs and islets are important for Eleonora's Falcons, Bonelli's Eagles and Peregrines.

Kos

36°52N 27°16E

South of Samos, and also lying close to the Turkish coast, Kos is another island whose interest increases substantially during spring passage. Two small wetlands serve to attract passing migrants, including some of the more sought-after waders such as Broad-billed Sandpipers, which are occasionally seen at the Alikes lake (comprising old saltpans which are currently unused) on the north coast in September. This is the larger of the wetlands. It is fringed with reeds to the east and west of the (usually permanent) open water, and seasonal marshes border the area to the south. The sandy heathland between the lake and the sea is good for Stone-curlews, larks, Fan-tailed Warblers and Tawny Pipits.

Nearer Kos town is a reedy lake at Psalidi. At both sites there is a small breeding population of the usual herons, supplemented in spring and late summer by migrants. Ruddy Shelducks are usually present, with counts of up to 35 at Alikes. Raptors such as Pallid Harrier, Lesser Spotted Eagle and Osprey are to be expected during spring and autumn passage.

Throughout the island the usual selection of shrikes, warblers and flycatchers can also be expected on passage, along with the odd Turkish wanderer. The spring 1995 record of a Bimaculated Lark is undoubtedly just an example of the kind of surprises in store at this time.

The mountains along the south-east coast are interesting for raptors, a particularly good population of Bonelli's Eagles on the slopes of Mount Dikios. Black Woodpecker has recently been recorded here; Long-legged Buzzards, Lesser Kestrels and Eleonora's Falcons are also to be found, the latter retiring to the cliffs at Cape Fokas in late summer to breed. Here there are also Blue Rock Thrushes and a chance of the two shearwaters offshore.

Black Woodpecker

TIMING

The island is little known in winter, when the wetlands may be worth trying for Great Snipe, White-tailed Eagles and Pallid Harriers.

SPECIES

- ◆ *Greater Flamingo* Often several hundred in the main Alikes lake.
- ◆ *Red-footed Falcon* Passes through, sometimes in large flocks, in late April and September.
- ◆ *Slender-billed Curlew* Has been recorded at the Alikes lake on three occasions, and is worth watching for in April and May.
- ◆ *Cretzschmar's Bunting* Common in the hills above Pili and Asfendiou.

ACCESS

Kos is reached by twice-daily flights from Athens, daily ferries from Athens, Rhodes and nearby islands and 1–2 sailings daily to Bodrum in Turkey. Kos town and harbour can be good for Mediterranean Gulls, shearwaters, and, on the ramparts, Blue Rock Thrushes and Pallid Swifts. Alikes Lake is about 10 km west of the town, about 2 km beyond Zipari. A left turn at Tigaki leads along the sea-front to the lake. The south-west corner of the lake has some good seasonal pools which are reached by taking the roads south of the lake by the Aslanis hotel. Mount Dikios is reached via Zipari. The mountain road to Asfendiou gives access to good forest areas such as around the small village of Zia and westwards to Pili.

Psalidi is approximately 4 km south-east of the town behind the Sun Palace hotel on the main road to Agios Fokas.

CHIOS

38°30N 26°00E

Lying within a few kilometres of the Turkish mainland, Chios comes into its own on the spring and autumn passage. Unlike many of the eastern Dodecanese islands, Chios' birds have been well documented. This is partly because of the persistent tradition of large-scale bird liming and shooting which has led to many ringing recoveries and other records.

211 species have been recorded, of which 94 are regular passage birds and 47 are accidentals. Red-backed Shrikes are the best-known, since they are a target for trappers in August and September, when they pass through in large numbers. The other three shrike species are less common, although Masked Shrikes breed in the olive groves in the south and in the Vrontados valley in the east.

Other common migrants include Bee-eaters (April, May and September), Spanish Sparrows (April, October), Short-toed Larks, Collared Flycatchers (March, April) and, in most years, Rose-coloured Starlings (May, east coast). Warblers and other insectivores congregate in large flocks in autumn at the southern headlands of Dotia and Gridia. More visits by foreign rarity-seekers would certainly add to the already impressive tally of autumn accidentals. These have included White's Thrush, Scarlet Rosefinch and Pine and Rustic Buntings.

Occasionally, birds associated only with Turkey occur, and these have included Red-fronted Serin (an irregular winter visitor) and White-breasted Kingfisher.

Interesting breeding species include Eleonora's Falcon, Rufous Bush Robin in bushy hills in the south of the island, Orphean Warbler, Hawfinch and, in a few places, Cinereous Bunting, which in Greece otherwise only breeds on Lesbos. Ortolan and Cretzschmar's Buntings and Rock Sparrows breed in the rocky hills. The few wetland areas (at Kontari, Komi, Volissos, and Langada) are most interesting in winter, when Great and Jack Snipe can be common, although there are crakes in autumn along with occasional Black-winged Pratincoles.

TIMING

March–May and August–November are the main passage periods, depending on the species. In May all the breeding birds are present but the peak of passage is over.

SPECIES

- ◆ *Eleonora's Falcon* Nests on rocky islets such as Venetiko off the island's southern tip.
- ◆ *Thrush Nightingale* Common migrant at Dotia in August and September.
- ◆ *Cinereous Bunting* Has been found breeding at Karies and is worth seeking out on grassy slopes interspersed with shrubs above this village and in the south.

ACCESS

Chios is served by charter flights from northern Europe, and regular flights from Athens. There are small remnant wetland areas at Kontari, alongside the airport, and at the river valley at Volissos in the north-west. Dotia hills and headland attract the highest density of migrants and hunters and are reached by taking the road south out of Pirgí towards Emporiós, then turning right across the hills towards the Másticho headland. The ferry to the neighbouring island of Psará can be good for Cory's Shearwaters, while the island itself is important for Eleonora's Falcons.

CYPRUS

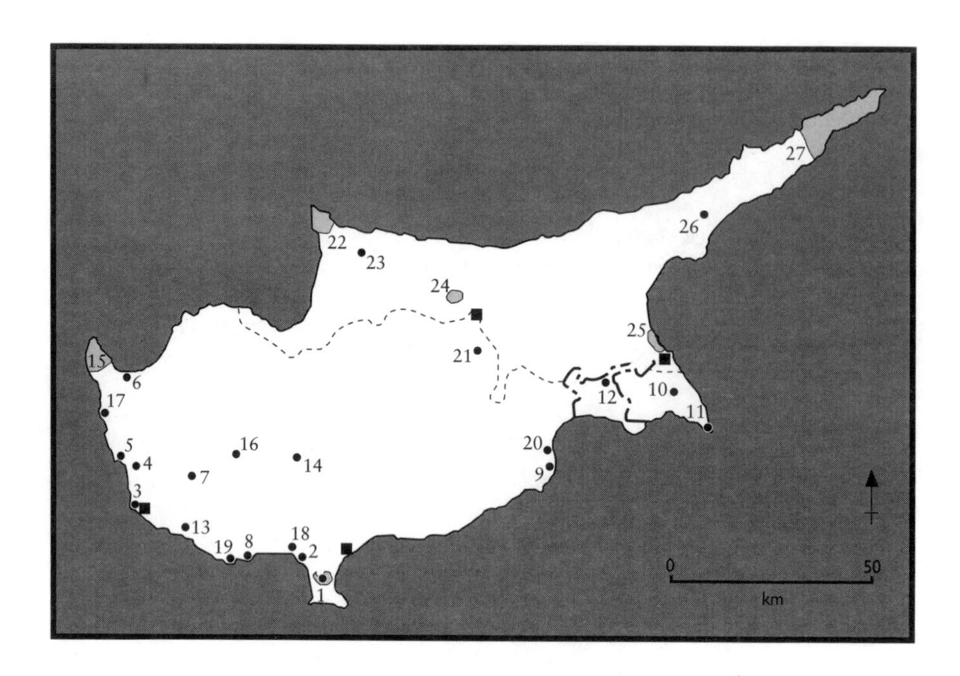

1 Akrotiri Salt-lake, 2 Phassouri Reedbeds, 3 Paphos Headland, 4 Mavrokolymbus Dam, 5 Carol Bay and Ayios Yeorios, 6 Polis, Lachi and the Baths of Aphrodite, 7 Asprokremmos Dam, 8 Kensington Cliffs and Quarry Beach, 9 Larnaca Salt-lake, 10 Paralimni Lake, 11 Cape Greco and Aya Napa, 12 Akhna Reservoir, 13 Kouklia and Dhiarizos Valley, 14 Troodos Mountains, 15 Akamas Peninsula, 16 Paphos Forest, 17 Lara, 18 Curium Beach, 19 Cape Aspro, 20 Larnaca Seafront, 21 Athlassa Dam and Forest, 22 Cape Koruçam, 23 Geçitköy Reservoir, 24 Gönyeli and Kanlıköy Reservoirs, 25 Gülseren and Glapsides Wetlands, 26 Lake Mehmetcik, 27 Karpaz Peninsula east from Dipkarpaz, with the Klidhes Islands

After the Turkish invasion of Cyprus in 1974 the island was divided and the northern part unilaterally declared the Turkish Republic of Northern Cyprus. This situation is only internationally recognized by Turkey. For the purposes of this book we shall in future refer to the northern or southern sectors. We do no seek to make any political assumptions by this decision but merely wish to make it clear to the reader which part of the island we are referring to. The tourist facilities and infrastructure, although improving, are limited on the occupied side. The fact is, though, that the myriad holiday brochures, TV adverts and travel agents exhorting us to visit Cyprus refer to the unoccupied part of the island. However, this does not mean you will inevitably have to put up with crowded beaches and unsightly developments (although there are some).

Cyprus is, quite simply, one of the most visitor-friendly places you could possibly go birding in. A long-time British military presence – still evident, especially at the garrisons at Akrotiri and Episkopi – has left several legacies of convenience for the British birder. Cars drive on the left, all signs are in English as well as Greek, and English is widely spoken by local people as well as the many ex-pats. This does not mean that you should not bother to learn any Greek or to understand the culture and concerns of the Cypriots: a naturally very hospitable people, they will treat you even more warmly if you do.

Facilities in unoccupied Cyprus are excellent. The roads are generally well-maintained, unless you get well off the beaten track (which, incidentally, we recommend you do!). The shops are well stocked, the water is safe, the food is delicious, and every kind of accommodation is available from luxury hotels to self-catering villas and bed and breakfast. The south-east coast of the island is the most developed and, whilst the birding can be very good, the ambience veers worryingly towards the 'costas'. The west end is much more attractive and, in some areas, splendidly wild. In fact, if we were asked to recommend the ideal birding trip, we would suggest a two- or possibly even three-centre holiday – Paphos or Polis in the west, Limassol in the south and Larnaca, the last being as far east as you would want to stay. Two weeks would be ideal, ten days would be fine, a week still pretty good, and if you can only manage a couple of days it would still be worth it!

In recent years, Cyprus has become very popular with birdwatchers and could even be set to rival Israel as a spring destination. For some time, probably the main thing hindering this 'progress' was the vacillation of the government in enforcing current internationally-approved conservation principles, especially by allowing the shooting of migratory birds. However, happily, in 1994 the spring shoot was officially banned, and there is every hope that the situation will continue to improve. If you want to go birding in Cyprus there are several specialist tour companies offering 'guided' tours. Many birders prefer to form their own 'unofficial' groups, or you may care to go it alone. Whichever you choose, you are guaranteed a splendid trip in a delightful country.

IMPORTANCE FOR BIRDS

Being an island – albeit a large and not particularly isolated one – Cyprus has got a few endemics that are pretty hard to see anywhere else. Most birdwatchers are anxious to tick off Cyprus Warbler and Cyprus Pied Wheatear. Fortunately, both species are ubiquitous and conspicuous (you may well see them from your hotel window!). There are also a couple of island sub-species confined to the pine forests in the Troodos Mountains: the 'Cyprus' Coal Tit looks so distinctive that you wonder why it is only a race, whilst the 'Cyprus' Short-toed Treecreeper looks so like a British Common one that you feel you need to check its toes!

Otherwise, the variety of breeding birds is not great, nor often checked, since the summers can be too hot for birding.

In winter, there are large flocks of Greater Flamingos on the salt-lakes and good numbers of wildfowl. There are also rare visitors like Finsch's Wheatear to be searched for.

However, it is undoubtedly in spring and autumn that the true importance of Cyprus can be appreciated, as literally millions of migrants pour over the island. The birds have European, Asian and African origins, and include vagrants from all directions (with increasing observer-coverage, new species are added every year). Autumn passage is more protracted but, with the weather often still hot and the terrain parched, small birds are less evident, as, indeed, are the birdwatchers. Spring passage, however, is truly immense, beginning in early March and continuing well into May. Passage is continuous, with predominant species varying from week to week, whilst certain weather conditions may produce spectacular 'falls'. Although various sites are favoured (*see* below), one of the great attractions of Cyprus is that birds occur anywhere and everywhere. A regular check of hotel gardens, parks, orchards and local fields will produce new birds nearly every day. The wetland population is also continually changing, and there are birds coasting and overhead.

Unfortunately, the same profusion that delights the birdwatchers makes migrants an easy target for hunters during the shooting seasons (*see* Conservation).

Getting there

Easy. There are many regular scheduled and charter flights from London and some provincial airports. Your only decision is whether to fly to Larnaca (in the east) or Paphos (in the west). Paphos has the advantage of being smaller, and checking out is usually very quick and easy. Both airports have excellent birding areas close by, so if your plane home is delayed you almost feel grateful (as long as it is not at night!). There is an increasing number of planes going to occupied Cyprus, but at the time of writing they are still obliged to touch down in mainland Turkey first, which prolongs the journey.

Once on the island, a hired car is undoubtedly the best way to get around and there are many companies offering a variety of cars at a variety of rates. A four-wheel drive is advisable only if you intend to tackle the unsurfaced routes, which can be very slippery after rain, or very bumpy at all times. You can also hire motor scooters, motorbikes, or bicycles. There are also inter-town buses, and taxis are much cheaper than in Britain, especially if you share.

Conservation

This is probably the most contentious and arguably the most disappointing aspect of birdwatching in Cyprus. The killing of migrant birds has long been a tradition on the island. This could be said of much of the Mediterranean region, but the sheer scale of the Cypriot slaughter has set some regrettable records, and provoked many protests from other nations. After boycotts by specialist tour companies and petitioning from bird organizations internationally there have been some considerable improvements. Bird liming and mist netting have declined and are entirely absent in some areas. During the late 1980's legislation to control shooting was introduced but not always enforced. A significant move in the early 1990's saw the government ban the shooting of birds in Spring. Sadly, a subsequent administration lifted the ban in 1993 causing an outcry in the international bird community.

More boycotts and petitions followed and fortunately funds were made available to organize a referendum which resulted in the vast majority of Cypriots declaring themselves opposed to the spring shoot. This included 70 per cent of the hunters. As a result the government commendably reversed their decision in 1994. There is now considerable optimism that this decision will stand and that conservation opportunities will be grasped. There is great scope and how marvellous it would be if some of the best birding sites could become formal nature reserves.

To achieve the best for the island's wildlife much will depend on local people and the organizations working there. There are two ornithological societies C.O.S. 1957 (mainly British) and C.O.S. 1970 (mainly Cypriot) as well as the Cypriot branch of Friends of the Earth, The Cyprus Wildlife Society and the Cyprus Foundation (formerly the Laona Project). Much encouragement is needed to unite this energy into a partnership which will influence and work with the government in ensuring the protection of the flora and fauna of this outstanding region.

At present, our feelings about the future of conservation in Cyprus are optimistic. The situation could improve further almost overnight with new legislation and better enforcement, although it seems likely that it will be some time before a, hopefully, more enlightened younger generation will insist on a total end to the slaughter. Do not be put off visiting the island. If you *do* witness any bird-killing, you will probably be appalled. Make sure you let your feelings be known to the government and the tourist board, although for your own sake, do not try to reason with the hunters themselves.

For a fuller discussion of conservation – and indeed all aspects of Cyprus birdlife – we cannot recommend too highly *The Birds of Cyprus* by Peter Flint and Peter Stewart, published by the British Ornithologists Union.

HABITATS

Nearly 50 per cent of unoccupied Cyprus is classified as 'agricultural', but much of that area is of very poor quality for crops and therefore is of wildlife interest. On lower uncultivated ground, there is extensive cover of low shrubs, but this has often been largely cleared by grazing, especially by goats. Nevertheless, particularly near the coasts, these rough fields and meadows provide valuable resting and feeding areas for migrant birds.

Extensive woodland (of Aleppo Pine and the endemic Golden Oak) occurs in the Paphos Forest in the western Troodos range. Cyprus Cedars now occur naturally only in a small part of the Paphos Forest. In the Troodos Mountains there are forests of Troodos Pine. These areas are scenically very impressive, but birds there are generally limited to the breeding species such as the endemic races of Coal Tit and Short-toed Treecreeper, along with migrant Masked Shrikes, Olivaceous Warblers, etc.

The most important wetlands are the salt-lakes at Larnaca and Akrotiri. At the latter, the extensive reedbeds and fresh-water marshes are extremely productive for birds. There are also several reservoirs created by the construction of dams. Some of these attract lots of birds, others very few. There are also several rivers that reach the sea on the south coast. Their attraction for birds depends on the water-level. If they are either dry or in full flood they are less productive than when the water is flowing slowly or there are shallow pools in the valleys.

Along the coast there are some impressively high cliffs that are home to such specialities as Eleonora's Falcon and Griffon Vulture, whilst beaches and offshore rocky outcrops are not to be ignored by passing waders, gulls, terns or birdwatchers. Also, keep looking up!

The simple rule for Cyprus is that migrants really can pop up anywhere, especially near the coast. By all means use the site guide, but also find your own 'hot spots'.

Seasons

SPRING The glorious time. The grass is green, the flowers are dazzling, and the variety and number of birds passing through are seemingly inexhaustible. Moreover, it is quite a long season. Early in March, the large lakes are used as stop-over sites by flocks of Little and Slender-billed Gulls, whilst swallows and martins increase and the first migrant warblers and wheatears appear (with Isabelline almost in the majority). Throughout April, different species seem to peak at different times – one day it is all pipits and wagtails, the next flycatchers, whilst, at the end of the month, the trees fill up with Black-headed Buntings and Olivaceous Warblers. In early May come the Bee-eaters and Rollers, and wonderful falls of several species of shrike. Throughout this time there is action along the coast – flocks of ducks, Glossy Ibises, herons and egrets – and in the air, there may be lines of cranes or soaring raptors. The latter are not numerous, but do include Pallid Harriers. There is also a relatively small but intriguing wader passage and the chance of vagrants is very high.

SUMMER *Not* the best time. June, July and August can be far too hot for birding and the variety of breeding birds is not great. Nevertheless, a visit to the mountains will produce the endemics, as well as relief from the heat. Also, the wetland areas can turn up surprises and are no doubt underwatched.

AUTUMN Can still be very hot, and the countryside is likely to be rather parched. Small birds can be hard to find, but there is an excellent raptor passage, especially in September and October. Species involved usually include good numbers of Honey Buzzards, Red-footed Falcons, Peregrines and harriers, but just about anything can float over. Keep your eyes on the skies and the telegraph poles. Also, listen out for the calls of migrating cranes, which can be passing over way up high. The rare Demoiselle Cranes migrate in late August and early September, whilst Common Cranes peak in late October. This season also sees a massive movement of wildfowl, gulls and herons, especially along the north coast.

WINTER Winters are not particularly cold in Cyprus, except up in the Troodos Mountains, which become transformed into a lively ski resort. The most spectacular attractions for the birdwatcher are the large flocks of Greater Flamingos on the salt-lakes and a good variety of wildfowl to be sorted through for the occasional rarity. There are also speciality winterers to be searched for, such as Finsch's Wheatear and Moustached Warbler. Again, more intensive coverage would probably turn up some unexpected birds.

BIRDWATCHING SITES

AKROTIRI SALT-LAKE

34°36–34°38N 32°57–33°00E

The salt-lake, which is very large and very shallow, is the most extensive feature of what is probably the best birding area in Cyprus. Having said that, the lake itself is difficult to work and can appear to be strangely devoid of birds. Although there is a metalled road along the western shore and a perfectly driveable unsurfaced track around the south and east, the water's edge always seems tantalizingly far away. Moreover, if the sun is well up, the heat shimmer can be very irritating. But do not be put off. The secret is to get there early and be prepared to get your feet wet! Park carefully (absolutely *not* on the yellow lines as this area is of military sensitivity) and set out through the salt-marsh and bushes until you get a view of the muddy shore. A cautious approach will often reveal an encouragingly large number and variety of waders, which in spring will largely consist of Little Stints, Kentish Plovers and Greenshanks, but with a good chance of Marsh, Curlew and possibly Broad-billed Sandpipers, as well as egrets and wildfowl. The same technique is not required to enjoy the huge flock of Greater Flamingos that winters on the lake, or the flocks of Slender-billed Gulls that pass through in March and April.

By autumn, the water may have dried up altogether, but the salt-flats then become resting-places for both species of crane and various raptors.

There are also several good areas immediately adjacent to the lake itself. As you drive (or walk) along the south shore check the smaller marshy pools on the opposite side to the main lake. They are particularly attractive to Wood Sandpiper, Ruff and Black-winged Stilt. Along here is the gate to Bishop's Pool. This is often listed as something of a hot spot, but the gate is usually locked and entrance is only possible by arrangement with the C.O.S. (1957). Do not let it bother you. The area is now rather overgrown and has long since seen its best days, which were probably exaggerated anyway by the fact that it used to be a ringing station!

Another area that has undoubtedly deteriorated is Zakaki. This is a network of gravel-pits, sewage lagoons and fetid ditches to the east of Lady's Mile Beach. It has been ruined by landfill, new roads and scattered development. Nevertheless, it is worth enduring the insalubrious surroundings to search for larks, pipits, wagtails and waders (if you can find any mud). White-winged Black Terns are attracted to what water is left, and you can be sure of Spectacled Warblers in the salt-marsh.

Finally, the north side of the lake is much less accessible, but there is an extensive reedbed which used to be home to a small colony of Dead Sea Sparrows. These are no longer in residence, but Bluethroats and Moustached Warblers winter here, and Penduline Tits also occur. There is also a large hirundine roost in autumn.

Our final comments on Akrotiri are that it is worth taking your time to explore it thoroughly, and that it is truly tragic that the area is not an official nature reserve, complete with visitor facilities. Both remarks also apply to Phassouri, which is essentially part of the same area (*see* below).

TIMING

A productive area at all times of the year, although in high summer it would be as inhospitable as a desert! The wintering Greater Flamingos linger well into spring, along with a selection of wildfowl. In spring, it is worth visiting the area as often as possible as the birds will change from day to day. As well as the waders, gulls and terns, there may be passerines in the maquis and bushes, and raptors overhead. To give yourself the best chance of cranes or raptors in the autumn it is essential to be there either at dawn or dusk (preferably both!).

SPECIES

- *Greater Flamingo* The wintering flock can reach 10,000.
- *Teal* The thousands that may occur in winter leave early to be replaced by good numbers of Garganey.
- *Gull-billed Tern* A small number often patrols Lady's Mile in spring.
- *Terek Sandpiper* One of the rarities that turns up now and again.
- *Cream-coloured Courser* A rare visitor but looks at home on the parched flats.
- *Blue-cheeked Bee-eater* Sometimes attracted to the reedy fringes in spring.

- *Roller* check the posts and telegraph wires.
- *Demoiselle Crane* one of the potential perks of an early autumn visit.

ACCESS

The lake is only a few miles west of Limassol and may be approached by leaving town through the New Port and turning left at the road marked Lady's Mile Beach. You will emerge from the houses with Zakaki on your right and the lake farther beyond. You may park anywhere along this (unsurfaced) road to check the pools or shoreline. Eventually the road reaches a formidable barrier of curled barbed wire. This is the boundary of the Akrotiri RAF garrison and serves to remind you that the whole area is one of military sensitivity. Do not be put off, but *do* be sensible. You may be asked to show a passport or explain your presence, although the soldiers *are* used to birdwatchers. Be polite and you will not have any trouble. In all probability you will not be stopped at all, but if you have a camera it might be as well to be discreet. The track bears right across the sand-flats at the end of Lady's Mile and continues along the southern shore of the lake. You may want to park again here and approach the shore across the salt-marsh. It can be damp but it is not dangerous.

Continuing along the road (now shale) you will pass the Bishop's Pool gate (on your left) and eventually arrive at the main surfaced road. The ground is a little higher here, so park and scan over the lake. If you turn left you will soon be stopped at the gates of the garrison and sent back, so, turn right along the western shore of the lake. On no account stop along this yellow-lined road. If you do, the military police will appear immediately, which does not make for relaxing birdwatching. As you reach the north-west corner of the lake there is a sort of grassy triangle on the right where you can safely park to explore the northern shore. Almost opposite this, a small unsignposted road veers off towards some eucalyptus trees. This leads to Phassouri reedbeds, possibly the most delightful birding spot in Cyprus and usually the highlight of the Akrotiri experience!

The area can also be approached from the west by taking the south-bound road clearly signposted to Akrotiri garrison. The salt-lake will then appear on your left: you will not miss it!

Phassouri reedbeds

34°37N 32°58E

Potentially the Minsmere of Cyprus (perhaps even better!). At least this area is a designated no-shooting 'game reserve' (although you may well encounter hunters lurking along its borders). There is also a small hide, although it is completely inaccessible if the water is high! Nevertheless, Phassouri offers wonderful birding. A narrow but surfaced road runs along over a kilometre of damp meadows that can be alive with wagtails and pipits. Beyond them – at convenient 'scoping distance – is a series of fresh-water pools that seem designed to delight waders, herons, egrets and waterfowl. Beyond the pools is an extensive reedbed. The whole area is perfectly suited to becoming Cyprus's showcase nature reserve. It should have screened nature trails, access points and perhaps even an information centre. If it did, there is no doubt that the Cypriot government would gain considerable kudos amongst the many birdwatching visitors that come here from all over Europe (on our last visit we met groups from the Netherlands, Denmark and Germany, as well as from Britain).

As it is, Phassouri remains relatively unspoiled probably only because it lies on Sovereign Base land and development is not allowed. Local farmers herd their cows across the water-meadows at regular intervals throughout the day. At first this may seem irritating, as many of the birds take to the air. However, birdwatchers soon realize that it can be something of a blessing, as rare waders are flushed that were hitherto invisible! Indeed, it is at such moments that the full magic of Phassouri can be appreciated, with flocks of Wood Sandpipers and Ruffs wheeling overhead, Garganey skidding across the water, cascades of Little Egrets, Purple Herons screeching, Black-headed Wagtails and Red-throated Pipits calling, and Marsh or Pallid Harriers soaring above the wonderful chaos.

The best technique is to drive slowly along the road, stopping now and again to scan the area carefully. It is worth revisiting the site throughout the day, as birds come and go. A peaceful vigil at Phassouri is particularly welcome after the comparatively hard going of nearby Akrotiri.

It is also worth carrying on along the road until it veers to the left and becomes unsurfaced. There are open fields, much beloved of harriers, and an area of gravel-pits with a reputation probably inflated by past ringing activities. They rarely hold much, but Armenian Gulls are reputed to occur there in winter.

TIMING

Phassouri has to be a must at any time of the year, although spring, of course, is most prolific. In autumn, flocks of Bee-eaters and Red-footed Falcons occur. If only the area were completely protected no doubt a good variety of birds would actually breed there, as well as the Reed Warblers and other common species that still do. A few years ago Night Herons attempted to establish a small colony but were, inevitably, shot.

SPECIES

- ◆ *Squacco Heron* delightfully numerous and very approachable, especially from the car!
- ◆ *Glossy Ibis* Sizeable flocks drop in to feed on spring passage.
- ◆ *Great Snipe* No doubt occurs every spring, but may not be seen unless a cow treads on it!
- ◆ *Spur-winged Plover* There are usually up to half-a-dozen of this very handsome 'lapwing' present in spring.
- ◆ *Collared Pratincole* Pratincole flocks often drop in to rest and refuel and these may include Blacked-winged. In 1993 an Oriental was spotted!
- ◆ *Citrine Wagtail* A regular spring rarity.

ACCESS

Driving north (back inland) on the Akrotiri road, pass the aerials on the left, and veer left on the narrow road before reaching the trees. Then veer left again towards the Eucalyptus trees and you emerge at the pools and reedbeds. You may choose to park in the shade of the Eucalyptae and stroll along the road, or carry on, using the car as a hide. It is possible to walk across the damp meadows thus flushing birds that could otherwise remain hidden, but you risk annoying other birders if you do. Discreet stalking, a telescope and patience are less disruptive.

PAPHOS HEADLAND

34°46N 32°27E

This area is fast becoming Cyprus's unofficial bird observatory! It even looks a bit like a British version, being a headland complete with lighthouse and garden. Most visiting birders (individuals and groups) stay at least a few days in Paphos, and it has become the habit to congregate on the headland at dawn, both to look for migrants and to exchange news of sightings in other parts of the island. It *can* be a little disconcerting for anyone hoping for a quiet time to encounter a crowd that look as though they belong in the Scillies or at Cley, but in fact the event is rather enjoyable. It is also often very productive, as this sort of intensive coverage has resulted in some very good birds being found. At the time of writing, a log book and information service is operating from the Apollo hotel at the end of the lighthouse approach-road.

The headland's prominent position on the south-west corner of the island (possibly with the added attraction of the lighthouse) draws in very good numbers of migrants. On a spring morning, the short, grazed turf is often leaping with pipits (Red-throated, Tree and Tawny), larks (Short-toed and Bimaculated), wheatears (Northern, Isabelline and Black-eared) and buntings (Ortolan and Cretzchmar's). The gardens produce warblers (including Rüppell's and Orphean), chats and shrikes. Hoopoes and Wrynecks flit along the walls, and there are hirundines and raptors in the sky. There is even excellent seawatching to be enjoyed, especially around dawn, as gulls, terns, wildfowl, herons and Glossy Ibises pass offshore.

Inevitably, rarities are found and have attracted sizeable 'twitches'! These crowds could help to make the government realize that 'green tourism' really is a going concern, and thus could help the conservation cause. Certainly a hunter would not dare raise his gun on Paphos headland with a hundred birdwatchers watching him!

TIMING

Spring has to be best, but if you are staying in Paphos you are bound to take a stroll on the headland whatever the time of year.

SPECIES

- *Great Black-headed Gull* One of the rarities that have graced a recent spring seawatch.
- *Caspian Plover* The tundra-like turf has attracted this species more than once.
- *Lesser Short-toed Lark* Worth searching through the Short-toeds.
- *Mourning Wheatear* A new bird for Cyprus, found by the authors in April 1993, caused a real good old-fashioned twitch!

Hoopoe

ACCESS

From Paphos harbour, walk past the quayside tavernas and carry on round on to the headland. Alternatively, take the road to the lighthouse, which is clearly signposted in the town. There is a car park near the lighthouse that is full of birders' vehicles soon after first light! Stroll around the headland, check the gardens, and enjoy the archaeological site while you are here!

MAVROKOLYMBUS DAM

34°50N 32°24E

This site is typical of the valleys reaching the sea along the south coast. Often there is little or no water in the river, but the vegetation – including vestigial patches of reeds – attracts migrants as well as the ubiquitous Cetti's Warbler. The flat farmland near the coast road is good for wheatears and larks (which may include Bimaculated) and there are often Black Francolins here. As the track winds up the valley, small orchards and other trees attract shrikes, Golden Orioles and Great Spotted Cuckoos. Farther up still, the scrubby bushes are excellent for Rüppell's and Subalpine Warblers, and both Cyprus Warbler and Cyprus Pied Wheatear breed in the area. As you climb, Chukars scurry or whirr ahead of you on the open rocky slopes. At the top of the valley a large and rather bleak reservoir rarely attracts more than the odd Common Sandpiper or egret but is worth a scan. If nothing else, the shoreline bushes may produce more migrants, and there could be Bonelli's Eagle or a migrating harrier soaring over the horizon.

TIMING

Spring is best, but worth a look at any time.

SPECIES

- *Black Francolin* More often heard than seen. The trick is to realize that they 'throw' their voices! They do actually often call from quite conspicuous perches, such as a pile of rocks or even a low tree branch. If you 'need' Francolin, do not panic! You will see one eventually.

- ◆ *Cinereous Bunting* Another much sought-after bird. None of the 'traditional' sites seem to work for this species, but one of us did see one along the track to Mavrokolymbus (it might not still be there!).

ACCESS

Situated 10 km north of Paphos on the road to Coral Bay and Peyia, Mavrokolymbus Dam is clearly signposted on the right. You can drive up to the dam itself, but you should certainly park and search several times on the way up. If you really want to cover it thoroughly, you should walk.

Coral Bay and Ayios Yeorios

34°51N 32°21E

Both areas are on the 'tourist' route, as it were, Coral Bay being a considerable development and Ayios Yeoryios (Agios Georgios) a village to visit. However, the coastal areas and agricultural fields between them are excellent for migrants, particularly wagtails, pipits, larks and wheatears. It is worth walking slowly through the grassier meadows, both to enjoy the wildflowers and also to flush migrating Quail. Spanish Sparrows breed nearby, Yeronisos Island has nesting Yellow-legged Gulls and there are also Peregrines. In the early morning and evenings, look out for coasting flocks of herons and Glossy Ibises.

TIMING

Best in spring

SPECIES

- ◆ *Isabelline Wheatear* One of the earlier migrants but continuing through April, they often outnumber Northern. Cyprus gives the birder an excellent opportunity to sort out several tricky wheatear species.
- ◆ *Black-eared Wheatear* Tend to be later than the Isabellines. All 'forms' occur: western (pale) and eastern (more orangey), black 'masked' and black-throated, as well as the 'difficult' females. Hours of fun!

ACCESS

Drive 'through' Coral Bay, past the latest development, park and walk out north onto the open areas near the sea. Or drive to Ayios Yeoryios, park and walk south. There are also several unsurfaced but perfectly good narrow roads criss-crossing the area.

Polis, Lachi and the Baths of Aphrodite

35°02N 32°22E

Few visitors come to Cyprus without visiting the Baths of Aphrodite, and tourist coaches come and go all day. Do not let this put you off. This stretch of the west coast offers some of the best birding on the island (and makes you wonder how good the occupied section must be!). At first glance, the area may not look particularly special, except that the fields are noticeably greener and lusher than on the south coast. However, it really is a migrant hot spot (perhaps not least because there is less shooting than in the east). Along the coast road from Polis, reedbeds and a small marsh near the camp site attract a hirundine roost which may attract a passing Hobby. Next comes the small 'resort' (a tiny harbour with a gaggle of excellent tavernas) of Lachi. The beach here has had Audouin's Gull and Greater Sand Plover. The road continues, bearing right, with agricultural fields on the seaward side, and rougher grazing ground rising inland (on the left) with scattered trees. Park anywhere along here and walk. The variety of migrants can be excellent, including comparative rarities such as Barred and Icterine Warblers, alongside Whinchats, Wood Warblers and Tree Pipits. Work the habitat thoroughly: there are pathways for Cretzchmar's and Ortolan Buntings, telegraph wires for shrikes, irrigation puddles for Red-rumped Swallows gathering mud, and so on. By late April, every tree seems to have a singing Black-headed Bunting in it. At the end of the road is the car park for the Baths of Aphrodite. The baths are, in fact, little more than a small spring. Most tourists are duly disappointed, have a drink at the taverna, and go away again! Ignore the coach parties and take your time. Just beyond the car park is a eucalyptus valley. On some days it is alive with flycatchers, giving you the chance to compare Collared, Semi-Collared and Pied. Follow the paths (they even have eco-friendly information signs!) across onto the adjacent headland, which you may have to share with a herd of goats and a number of chickens. There will almost certainly also be lots of migrants.

As a break from bush- or tree-watching, you may care to look up and enjoy the flocks of Bee-eaters that soar along the hillside later in the spring or, in the autumn, there are massive movements of herons, wildfowl, waders and gulls offshore.

TIMING

A place for all seasons but particularly productive in spring for small birds, and from August to October for the bigger ones.

SPECIES

- *Olivaceous Warbler* Suddenly the trees fill up with them in late April giving you a chance to familiarize yourself with the Reed Warbler-like song.
- *Blackcap* Yes, we know that they are not rare but their sheer abundance can be really impressive. On some days the weedy fields seem to be alive with them. Much prized by local people as a delicacy: they pickle them!
- *Bonelli's Warbler* Delightfully numerous in the later spring, often alongside Wood Warblers. The Bonelli's often burst into song whilst the Wood Warblers remain silent.
- *Thrush Nightingale* Occurs in good numbers, alongside Nightingale. Both may sing, so another chance to test your ears.
- *Red-backed Shrike* Can occur in 'falls'. One of us recalls scanning across the bushes early one May morning and counting over a hundred. Amongst these were odd Lesser Greys, Masked and Woodchats.

ACCESS

Drive along the coast road from Polis, clearly signposted to the Baths of Aphrodite. Stop, park and explore several times before finally parking at the baths and walking round the various tracks and over the headland.

ASPROKREMMOS DAM

34°45N 32°34E

This is a huge man-made reservoir. Approaching it is notoriously tricky (*see* access), but it can be worth the effort and frustration. In fact, it may turn out to be a disappointingly birdless excursion, but you will still enjoy a strange sense of achievement if you do manage to actually reach the water's edge. The atmosphere is also rather splendidly spooky, as the reservoir's creation involved flooding a valley and cutting off the small village of Phinikas, which is now derelict and deserted except for goats, chickens and a hermit-like herdsman, who may or may not be a ghost! The old buildings look as if they ought to have breeding Lesser Kestrels, but they do not. In fact, small birds seem to largely shun the place, except for the much sought-after Finsch's Wheatear that certainly winters in the area, and may linger into spring. Depending on the water-level, waders may be present. There are also Cormorants, and Pygmy Cormorant has been recorded here, and it is exactly the place a rare duck may turn up. Spectacled Warblers breed in scrub near the dam.

TIMING

One of the places definitely worth a visit in autumn and winter, which may indeed actually be better than spring.

SPECIES

- ◆ *Pygmy Cormorant* The authors confess to a salutary experience when attempting to 'tick off' a bird known to be present at the reservoir. Let's put it this way: it is a big place and size is very hard to judge. Distant Cormorants can look small; Shags look even smaller; but when, eventually, you *do* see a Pygmy Cormorant...it is *really* tiny!
- ◆ *Finsch's Wheatear* This beautiful wheatear winters in variable numbers in Cyprus and probably also occurs as a spring migrant. It prefers rocky open slopes and there is certainly some ideal habitat in the Asprokremmos area. This does not mean, however, that this is a totally reliable site. Finsch-seekers would be advised to contact local birders for information or check out the grapevine on Paphos headland!

ACCESS

Follow the road from Paphos and the reservoir is off on the inland side just after Mandria. The dam is obvious and you *can* view the reservoir from the top but you will not feel you have covered it properly! To do so, leave the main road at Timi, pass through Anarita, and look for a disused water tank just before Nata on the left-hand side of the road. Opposite this tank a track to the right takes you down to the Xeros Potamos river. The track continues parallel to the river (on your left) and eventually leads to the reservoir and the deserted village of Phinikas on its shore. It is possible to get confused because there are other water tanks in the area, and other tracks, but if you follow your nose, bearing in mind that you need to descend to the reservoir eventually, you should make it, although you may take a few wrong turnings before you do! In which case...pause and scan for good birds. The correct road IS driveable in a normal car (although it is a slow and bumpy ride) but do not try to tackle anything that looks dodgy, unless you have a four-wheel drive. There are also other tracks along the higher ground above the reservoir (look out for a pig farm and other water towers as landmarks) that lead to productive wheatear habitat.

Kensington cliffs and Quarry Beach

34°34N 32°57E

Kensington cliffs is within the boundary of the Episkopi Garrison. You cannot fail to realize you are in the area as all the houses suddenly look like a British estate, and the streets have names from Sussex and Dorset! It is also clear that military security applies, and you should not attempt to visit the cliffs unless you have made an arrangement with the C.O.S. (1957), or contacted the authorities at the garrison. Fortunately, Quarry Beach is outside the military zone and can be viewed from the clifftop, or by driving down to the beach itself and looking up at the cliffs. The specialities here are Griffon Vulture and Eleonora's Falcon. Peregrines and Alpine Swifts are also usually present. In winter, a careful search may reveal a Wallcreeper.

TIMING

The vultures are ever-present, increasing in winter, when the Wallcreepers may be around. Eleonora's Falcons arrive in late spring, and breed through summer and into early autumn.

Wallcreeper

SPECIES

- *Griffon Vulture* The garrison staff even put out meat for the birds. The stench of a dead horse was the unsavoury price we had to pay for close-up views. Despite this encouragement, the species is declining in Cyprus.
- *Eleonora's Falcon* One of the species many spring birders miss, as the birds do not arrive until the second half of April. There are other colonies on the island but the one here is probably the easiest to see.

ACCESS

On the road from Limassol to Paphos, near Curium.

LARNACA SALT-LAKE

34°53N 33°37E

If you fly in to Larnaca in daylight, this is certainly the first good birding spot you will see. The main lake is big and shallow, and there are various subsidiary areas of water nearby. A main, and very busy, road passes alongside the lake, and the local authorities have taken this chance to advertise the avian delights of Cyprus by erecting a huge sign directing you to 'Migratory Birds' (the more cynical have sarcastically enquired whether this is for the birdwatchers or the hunters). In fact, the main tourist attraction is the wintering flock of Greater Flamingos, many of which linger well into spring and can be viewed and indeed photographed right by the road. The muddy fringes of the lake also attract many waders, which may include Greater Sand Plover. Flocks of Slender-billed and Little Gulls occur, but dwindle as spring progresses. Wildfowl may include a few Ruddy Shelduck. As in all parts of Cyprus, any trees, bushes or rough ground may produce migrants. The best technique is to park at the Tekke Mosque (you cannot miss it!) and walk around the nearby woods and picnic areas.

The area of Kiti Beach and Spiro's Pool is becoming developed (a euphemism for 'a bit of a mess'!), but it is still probably even better birding than the main salt-lake. There are waders and wildfowl, and there can be migrants amongst the ramshackle holiday chalets and caravans. These birds are often probably newly arrived from the south in spring. Sadly, but not surprisingly, this is a favourite area for hunters.

TIMING

An all-year-round site, although the summer months are probably pretty bleak.

SPECIES

- *Greater Flamingo* Although the larger wintering flock is more likely to favour Akrotiri, certainly the closest views are at Larnaca. They are particularly photogenic in spring when flocks occasionally rise from the lake to set off on migration. Most of the birds are thought to come from the east (probably mainly Iran).
- *Little Stint* A few winter, but there is a constant spring passage when numbers can vary from day to day. Always worth searching through them for the occasional Temminck's.

- *Turtle Dove* One of the hunters' main quarries and one of the few species that can be shot legally. This is, in fact, iniquitous as the Turtle Dove is a quintessential example of a long-distance migrant whose numbers are decreasing alarmingly. There can be no doubt that shooting is a contributory factor.

ACCESS

The main lake is unmissable, next to Larnaca airport, a consolation if your plane home is delayed. There are signs to Kiti and Spiro's Beaches from near Meneou and the road to the sea will take you past the pools.

Paralimni Lake

35°03N 33°58E

This large, shallow lake is just west of the town of Paralimni, an area notorious as one of the main bird-liming areas in Cyprus. Fortunately, this appalling practice has diminished greatly in recent years and credit must certainly be given to the authorities for enforcing the anti-liming laws. Clearly, the limers were attracted by the abundance of birds, and this is now true of the birdwatchers. Migrant passerines may occur wherever there is cover for them, but birds on and around the lake will depend very much on the water-level. It can be very good indeed, with lots of waders, wildfowl, herons and passing flocks of terns. A telescope is essential here.

TIMING

Good in winter once the water-level has risen, and continues to be productive throughout spring until it dries out as the weather gets hotter.

SPECIES

- *Spoonbill* Never a common species in Cyprus, this is a likely site for it.
- *White-winged Black Tern* The most numerous marsh tern (although Black and Whiskered also occur). A large flock of adults in breeding plumage is an unforgettable sight.

ACCESS

Find the town of Paralimni (east of Larnaca) and the lake will be obvious (if it has not dried up). A road goes quite close to the shore at several points but eventually you will want to park, walk a little and 'scope thoroughly.

Cape Greco and Aya Napa

34°57N 34°05E

Aya Napa is the most developed holiday area in Cyprus and it would be hard to imagine any birder feeling entirely happy if they had to stay here! But if you do, take heart. The coast along here is perhaps the main landfall for spring migrants and thus, on good days, the bushes are heaving with birds. So, ignore the windsurfers and sunbathers and get out there with your binoculars (and ignore the funny looks as well). In fact, the best birding areas involve a bit of scrambling along the cliff-top paths towards Cape Greco and are generally ignored by all but the most intrepid tourists. If you drive inland a little and find any patch of bushes, especially on raised ground, you may discover a new 'hot spot'. There is one such patch known as Aya Napa forest (do not expect any real trees). This whole area has received good coverage recently (probably from 'family-bound' birders) and has turned up many rarities.

TIMING
Spring, of course. Also a good area for Finsch's Wheatear and Blue Rock Thrush in winter.
SPECIES
◆ *Red-tailed Wheatear* Just one to whet your appetite and cheer you up if you have been booked on a package holiday in the area.
◆ *Pale Rock Sparrow* Another recent 'first'.
◆ *Desert Warbler* A recent 'third'.
ACCESS
The south-east corner of Cyprus, as featured in all holiday brochures. Explore the cliff-top paths to Cape Greco (the tip of the cape itself is a prohibited area, and probably has brilliant birding!). Also try any patches of cover inland, especially if they would be visible to an incoming migrant. Think like a bird!

AKHNA RESERVOIR

35°04N 33°48E
Undoubtedly the best artificial reservoir in Cyprus, Akhna is definitely on the 'must visit' list. In fact, since the site is right on the border and Akhna village itself is occupied by Turkish troops, a trip there is something of an experience beyond birding. It comes as a bit of a shock to witness barbed-wire fences, barriers, look-out posts and armed guards. You certainly realize that the Greek/Turkish situation is far from resolved. It also means that birdwatchers should be careful where they stray, park, or photograph; and be prepared to show identification or explain their activities. Having said that, our latest visit was entirely trouble free and, ironically, it is clear that the reservoir is an accepted visitor-attraction for trippers, local anglers, and birdwatchers. The birds are excellent. The shorelines attract waders, there are muddy creeks for crakes, and the open water is perfect for wildfowl and migrant terns. The fact that the lake has been stocked with fish also explains the presence of a variety of herons and sometimes more than one species of kingfisher.

TIMING
Worth a visit at any time of year, including summer. The variation in water-level inevitably dictates which birds are present.
SPECIES
◆ *Pied Kingfisher* Recorded several times alongside its smaller cousin.
◆ *Little and Baillon's Crakes* Both species occur in Cyprus and Akhna is one of the best sites for them, especially if there are good muddy edges exposed.
◆ *Cattle Egret* Aa perhaps surprisingly scarce bird in Cyprus. Akhna seems a favoured site.

ACCESS

The reservoir is on the right of the Akhna bypass 20 km north-east of Larnaca. At the end of the bypass, a metalled track takes you to the dam, from where you can walk along the edge of the reservoir. Other tracks give access at various points. If you have time, it really is worth walking round as much of the shoreline as you can. The reservoir is not marked on available maps and it may be advisable to consult C.O.S. (1957) for more details.

KOUKLIA AND DHIARIZOS VALLEY

34°42N 32°35E

This is probably the best of the rivers that run into the sea along the south coast. On the main road from Paphos to Limassol a number of bridges pass over watercourses (which do not always hold water!). The Dhiarizos usually does. This, and its sizeable reedy fringes, make it easy to recognize. You can park off the main road near the bridge and carry on down the track leading to the sea. To your left, the river widens into a sort of mini-delta. This is frustratingly difficult to 'work' as it is overgrown with bushes and reeds and lacks any obvious pathways. There are many shallow pools hidden away, especially if the river is not running too fast. These are perfect for waders, crakes and herons, any of which may suddenly leap or scurry from cover, possibly panicked by a passing harrier. Secretive singers include Reed Warbler and Black Francolin. Returning to the bridge, cross the main road, and walk inland along the river's edge. The waterside vegetation here can be full of migrant flycatchers and warblers. Keep an eye on the wires for Bee-eaters, shrikes and Red-footed Falcons.

TIMING

Worth a visit at any time, this will be one of the last rivers to dry up.

SPECIES

- *Little Bittern* Always a hard species to see, but this is a good place to flush one.
- *Stone-curlew* A bird that is scattered round Cyprus but is rarely seen. Kouklia has a good reputation for attracting small flocks, especially in winter.
- *Great Reed Warbler* Can be delightfully common on spring passage, when it usually manages a few bursts of song.

ACCESS

Coming from Paphos, stop at the bridge just before Kouklia. Turn off the main road and park, making sure not to block the way of any farm vehicles. Explore the tracks either side of the main road (to the sea and inland).

TROODOS MOUNTAINS

34°52N 32°53E

Entering the Troodos Mountains most visitors head for Platres with its pseudo-Alpine hotels, restaurants and obligatory gift shops. This small but interesting town, full of the remnants of British influence, is an ideal centre for the birder. Wander the trails amongst splendid Troodos pines where you should find endemic races of Crossbill, Coal Tit, Short-toed Treecreeper and Jay. Mountain streams provide glimpses of Grey Wagtails, and you should keep your eyes skyward for soaring Griffon Vultures and Ravens. Around the villages both Crag Martin and Pallid Swift can be found.

The area is best explored by obtaining the trail leaflets from the Tourist Office. Trail no. 2 is especially recommended and no. 3 leads to the highly scenic Caledonian Falls.

TIMING

Excellent in spring when snow still lies on the ground. It may be worth checking in summer when Cyprus Pied Wheatear will be present.

SPECIES

- *Masked Shrike* Tthe males look simply splendid when sitting on snow-covered slopes. A relatively easy species to find in April perching in pines and dropping regularly to the ground.
- *Crag Martin* Widespread throughout the region.
- *Coal Tit* The only one of the endemic races which looks very different from those found in the rest of Europe.
- *Long-legged Buzzard* Occasionally seen in Troodos foothills.

ACCESS

The simplest route is to take the new road north of Limassol. There are other routes which wind through cultivated valleys which in themselves provide great birding opportunities.

AKAMAS PENINSULA

35°04N 32°19E

The peninsula juts out on the north-west coast between the Baths of Aphrodite and Lara beach. The best way of birding this site is to walk the 8-km track from the Baths of Aphrodite towards Cape Arnaouti. Do look out for signs warning of military exercises. This walk gives breath-taking views from elevated cliffs where a few Griffon Vultures still occur. In spring large falls of migrant passerines can be found, and in autumn special effort should be made to witness the throngs of wildfowl and herons which migrate west along the coast of Akamas.

It is certainly also worth moving inland along minor roads and tracks to the vicinity of the villages of NeoKhorio and Smyies. This area can hold many migrants and in autumn there is significant raptor movement is noted along the ridge south to Drousha village.

TIMING

Concentrate your efforts here in spring and autumn. This area is an excellent addition to a visit to Polis, Lachi and the Baths of Aphrodite with the emphasis on small migrant species in spring and particularly exciting movements of herons in autumn.

SPECIES
- *Blue Rock Thrush* Nests amongst the rocky cliffs, but sometimes a bit secretive. Fluty song brightens any day's birding.
- *Peregrine* A regular breeding area for these speedy hunters.
- *Grey Heron* A common sight throughout Europe, but autumn migrating flocks of sometimes over a hundred still take your breath away.
- *Griffon Vulture* A pair or two still nest along the remoter cliffs.

ACCESS
Follow directions as for Baths of Aphrodite.

PAPHOS FOREST

34°12N 32°44E
This well-wooded area is situated to the west of the Troodos Mountains. The forest is not normally included on a hectic spring birding schedule, but is probably worth a look, particularly from late April through to the summer. A four-wheel drive vehicle is essential to explore fully the myriad tracks which lead into the area. Naturally, raptors can be located here, including Goshawk and Bonelli's Eagle. Red-rumped Swallows, Crag Martins and Olivaceous Warblers are all numerous in the breeding season.

TIMING
Spring and early summer are undoubtedly the best times to visit, but autumn may provide views of overflying raptors.

SPECIES
- *Imperial Eagle* Rumours abound that a pair of these magnificent birds may still be present in the forest. Please find them!
- *Scops Owl* As usual, you hear them, but seeing one is hard. Try locating mobbing passerines.
- *Woodlark* Not uncommon, particularly by the forest edge.

ACCESS
The best access is gained from the Paphos to Polis road turning off to the village of Polemi and thereafter to Kannaviou where the forest begins after 2 km. Head along the Ezousas valley to the deserted Ayia Forest Station which is a good birding area. Move up farther to the Stavros Forest Station and take a detour to Cedar Valley.

Red-rumped Swallow

LARA

34°55N 32°20E

This area is the western approach to the Akamas Peninsula. The very rough road, for which a four-wheel-drive vehicle is essential, leads you parallel to the sea along scrubby hillsides and eventually to Lara beach. The taverna at the beach is a welcome sight on a hot day. The beach itself is protected for nesting turtles and access is sometimes restricted. An underwatched area, it should provide good seawatching in ideal conditions. Gulls and terns can often be seen offshore and both Cyprus Warbler and Cyprus Pied Wheatear are in surrounding scrub. Black Francolins drive you mad in spring with their incessant vocal challenge to find them if you can.

TIMING

Spring is the most productive for passerine migrants but autumn watching could produce movements of seabirds, wildfowl and herons.

SPECIES

◆ *Yellow-legged Gull* Regularly present along this stretch of coast.

◆ *Shag* Another regular here.

ACCESS

Follow the very rough track north of Ayios Yeoryios until you reach the taverna at Lara beach.

CURIUM BEACH

34°40N 32°53E

A wide beach and scrub region below the Curium antiquities and just east of Kensington cliffs and Quarry beach (*see* page xxx). An excellent site for early morning migrants particularly in spring. Follow the substantial road down to the beach running alongside one or two tavernas. Drive to the far western end and explore the ground underneath the cliffs. Chats and warblers hide in limited scrub, whilst you might see occasional Eleonora's Falcons hunting overhead. Close inspection of the cliff-face might reveal a Blue Rock Thrush or a mixed flock of buntings. In spring, search the sea for rafts of resting Garganey. Do try to visit this site in early morning or evening when, hopefully, very few other people are present.

TIMING

Spring is a good time to search for passerines but autumn could be as good.

SPECIES

◆ *Cretzchmar's Bunting* Look at all the buntings for mixed flocks which will contain Ortolans, at least, and hopefully this gorgeous creature.

◆ *Stone-curlew* Another good site for this bird early in the morning.

◆ *Rüppell's Warbler* Check every warbler carefully until the white moustaches bowl you over!

ACCESS

Follow the signs from main M1 road between Paphos and Limassol and turn right just after passing Episkopi Garrison.

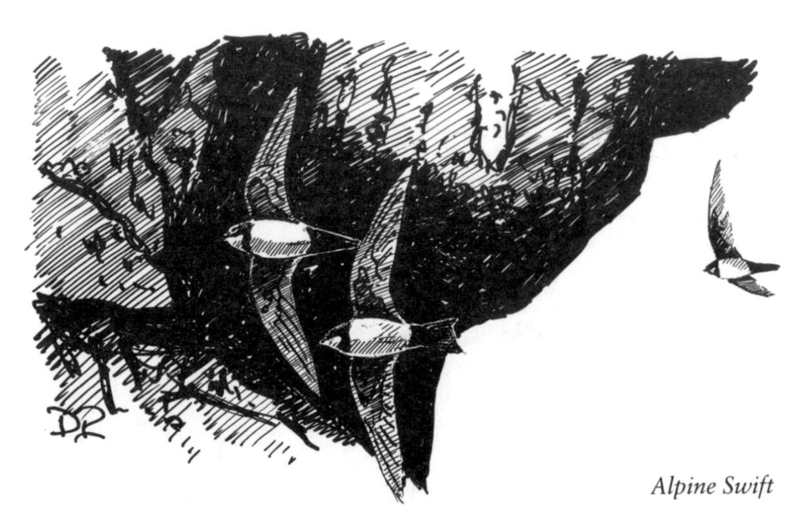

Alpine Swift

Cape Aspro

34°40N 32°44E

The cliffs can be viewed from the parking lot on top of the cliffs or from a small beach reached by a tunnel under the road. The storm-sculptured white cliffs are spectacular in themselves but also provide views of Griffon Vultures and Alpine Swifts. The main attraction, however, is the largest colony of Eleonora's Falcons in Cyprus.

TIMING

Best visited in summer to late autumn for the falcons. When the ledges are full of chicks, the total assembly of birds is breathtaking.

SPECIES

- *Eleonora's Falcon* Patience at your chosen watchpoint will reward you with stunning views of both colour phases. Why not follow the example of one of the authors? Put your bins in a plastic bag, swim along the cliff base and find a rock from which to enjoy the best views ever.

ACCESS

On the Paphos–Limassol road just 2 km east of Petra tou Romiou.

Larnaca seafront

00°00N 00°00E

Not the most aesthetic spot, but worth checking. The area is just north of Larnaca International Airport past the Sandbeach Castle Hotel as far as the fishing shelter. Gulls and terns are often here in autumn and, particularly, in winter.

TIMING

Try at any time but winter is the best time for significant numbers.

SPECIES

- *Slender-billed Gull* The most likely occupant of the groynes and rocks.
- *Mediterranean Gull* Usually present in winter.

- *Audouin's Gull* Must breed on offshore islands and not infrequently seen offshore.

ACCESS

The coast road runs south of the marina at Larnaca down to the Sandbeach Castle Hotel and beyond. A small sandy track leads south-west to Larnaca Lake.

ATHLASSA DAM AND FOREST

35°06N 33°23E

A reservoir with surrounding forest just to the south-east of Nicosia. The forest holds Long-eared Owls and the open water provides a haven for migrating waterbirds. The drier, scrubby terrain is worth checking for Calandra Lark, Spectacled Warbler and the very scarce Black-bellied Sandgrouse.

TIMING

Spring and summer are the preferred seasons but the reservoir would be worth checking in autumn for migrating waders and herons.

SPECIES

- *Calandra Lark* Search dry, stony areas or small arable fields for this large lark. Its dark underwing and wader-like flight make identification simple.
- *Black-bellied Sandgrouse* One of the few areas where this species occurs in Cyprus. Again, search the drier areas, or wait by the water in the evenings when it might come to drink.

ACCESS

Turn right off the Limassol–Nicosia road following the signs to the Experimental Farm at Athlassa. A track to the right of the farm leads to the dam and forest.

The northern part of Cyprus has escaped some of the destructive effects of mass tourism. This means that large areas of intact Mediterranean habitats can be found: unspoiled sandy beaches where, now rare, marine turtles lay their eggs and an extensive mosaic of parcelled-out land provides havens for many plant and animal species.

Because of the low population density (fewer than 50 people per km^2), moderate tourist development and the limits placed on farming by the lack of water, there are many valuable resting and feeding areas for migrants. Reservoirs and seasonal floodlands which form in years of heavy winter rain attract lots of waterbirds, compensating for the lack of extensive permanent wetlands. Certainly, some parts of the Beşparmak Dağlari (Kyrenia range) and the whole area east of Dipkarpaz are among the most important areas for birds in the island.

Getting there is easy but does take some patience. International flights still have to stop over in Turkey, but there are also several scheduled flights as well as daily ferries from Taşucu, twice-weekly ones from Marsin and occasional ones from Latakya in Syria. Car hire is easy and cheap.

While the Berne Convention has been ratified in the south, the Game and Wild Birds Protection Act, 1934 is still in force in the north of the island. Parts of this antiquated British law, which is actively hostile to wild birds, have been improved, but the current legislation does not really contribute to bird protection. The shooting, liming, netting and selling of birds are still part of the way of life and help to supplement many people's incomes. Bird catching in the north seems to be on the increase at the same time as it is declining in the south: information from various sources points to the existence of a growing illegal trade in birds between the north and south.

On a more positive note, since the Society for the Protection of Birds and Nature (KUŞKOR) came into being in 1990, the general conservation situation has improved from year to year: the shooting seasons have been shortened, a general shooting ban has been introduced around wetlands, and several endangered species and groups (e.g., Shag, Raven and raptors) have been removed from the list of shootable species. According to the President of Northern Cyprus, the spring shoot will be cancelled in 1996.

BIRDWATCHING SITES

CAPE KORUÇAM

35°24N 32°56E

The cape is also called 'Koruçam Burnu', or 'Cape Kormakitis' and lies north-west of Sadrazamköy village. The area between the village and the cape is covered with a mixture of maquis, scrub-vegetation and grassland with small strips of farmland along the road. The area is excellent for diurnal migration in spring and offers many interesting species: Marsh Harrier, Sparrowhawk, Quail, Stone-curlew, Bee-eater, Hoopoe, wagtails, Whinchat, Isabelline, Northern and Black-eared Wheatears, Red-backed and Woodchat Shrikes and Cretzschmar's Bunting.

The cape and the north coast are best for autumn coastal passage. Cory's and Yelkouan Shearwaters, Shag, various herons, waders and gulls have been reported.

TIMING

Best during spring migration from mid-March to mid-May. Sunny days with little or no wind are best for birdwatching. Autumn coastal passage occurs mainly from August until the beginning of November.

SPECIES

- ◆ *Cory's Shearwater* Scarce passage migrant but probably often overlooked offshore.
- ◆ *Stone-curlew* Fairly common passage migrant, with a few breeding records. Its present status in northern Cyprus is unknown.
- ◆ *Woodchat Shrike* Scarce to fairly common passage migrant with numbers peaking in the second half of April.

ACCESS

Cape Koruçam is the north-western point of northern Cyprus. Two roads lead from the main Girne–Güzelyurt road to the village of Sadrazamköy. The northern road leads along the coast to the village of Kayalar and from there to Sadrazamköy. If you wish to use the second road leading from Çamlibel to Koruçam and from there to Sadrazamköy you should get permission from the police station in Çamlibel. There are several military areas along this route and you may be asked to stop from time to time. The road from Sadrazamköy to Cape Koruçam is always in a very bad condition and sometimes not passable by car.

GEÇİTKÖY RESERVOIR

35°23N 33°00E

The reservoir was completed in 1989 and seems to have become a valuable stop-over site for passage migrants, with particular importance for reed-dwelling species. A dense reed-bed covers most of the reservoir. Because of its permanent water supply the reservoir may also become increasingly important for autumn migrants. Information about the species which have so far been seen at the reservoir is limited. At present more than 25 species of waterbirds are listed, including Bittern, Little Bittern, Squacco and Purple Herons, Little and Great White Egrets, Shoveler, Pochard, Marsh

Great Spotted Cuckoo

Harrier, Little Crake, Black-winged Stilt, Greenshank, Green, Wood and Common Sandpipers, White-winged Black Tern, Kingfisher and Sedge and Reed Warblers. Most of these are sightings of single birds or groups of up to five individuals. The reservoir is surrounded by grassland, maquis and open woodland abounding with spring migrants: Great Spotted Cuckoo, Bee-eater, Roller, Tree and Meadow Pipits, Northern Wheatear, Bonelli's and Wood Warblers, Woodchat Shrike and Pied Flycatcher. White Wagtail, Robin, Stonechat, thrushes and Blackcap have been recorded in winter. Breeding birds include Little Owl, Cyprus Pied Wheatear, Cetti's, Fan-tailed and Cyprus Warblers, Masked Shrike, Spanish Sparrow, and Cretzschmar's Bunting.

Around the nearby Kornos Peak (north-east of the reservoir) raptors can often be observed including Griffon Vulture and Osprey.

TIMING
Best from late March until May for passage migrants, particularly around the reservoir. Because the water supply is permanent, birdwatching is possible all year round.

SPECIES
- *Griffon Vulture* No breeding records of this species in northern Cyprus recorded since 1989. The current situation in this area is unknown but sightings of single birds have been reported regularly.
- *Masked Shrike* Common breeding migrant in wooded mountain areas.
- *Cretzschmar's Bunting* Common breeding migrant.

ACCESS
The reservoir is in the north-west of northern Cyprus next to the main Girne–Güzelyurt road. The dam is visible and easily accessible from the main road south of Geçitköy. Hunting is prohibited.

GÖNYELİ AND KANLIKÖY RESERVOIRS

35°13N 33°17E

Gönyeli Reservoir, the second largest reservoir in northern Cyprus, lies near the town of the same name. This large reservoir is usually well filled and may hold water all year round, making it of great importance for passage migrants (particularly in autumn) and winter visitors. Being close to Nicosia this reservoir is often used for recreation and can be much disturbed. The number of birds present depends largely on disturbance.

Kanlıköy Reservoir, the largest reservoir in northern Cyprus, lies in a hilly eroded landscape 4 km west of Gönyeli Reservoir. The reservoir is used for irrigating farmland, and often dries up in summer or autumn. If the water lasts until September, it becomes an excellent site for migrating waders and herons such as Squacco Heron, Little Egret, Great White Egret (occasionally), Avocet, Greenshank and Green Sandpiper. The reservoir is largely undisturbed and visited only by shepherds and their animals.

My observations suggest that there is a close relationship between these two reservoirs, which taken as a whole, represent the most important wetland of northern Cyprus.

More than 110 bird species have been observed at these two reservoirs. During spring migration many species can be seen: Bittern (rare), Little Bittern, Night, Squacco and Purple Herons, Little Egret, White Stork, Glossy Ibis, Black-winged Stilt, Spur-winged Plover, Marsh and Wood Sandpipers, White-winged Black Tern, Calandra Lark, Cyprus Pied Wheatear, Sardinian Warbler and Red-backed and Masked Shrikes. Raptors include falcons, harriers, buzzards and, occasionally, Osprey.

TIMING

Except during the hot summer months of June–August, the area is good for birdwatching all year round. In winter, anything from several hundred to 4000 birds may be present (grebes, ducks, Coot, waders and herons). Late March to mid-May and September/October are generally best for passage migrants. The number of birds during spring migration depends on water levels in the wetlands in the east of northern Cyprus. If these are low, large numbers of birds come to the Gönyeli-Kanlıköy area.

SPECIES

- *Cattle Egret* One record.
- *Great White Egret* A scarce passage migrant occurring mainly in October and November.
- *Spur-winged Plover* Small flocks can be seen regularly in April and May.
- *White-winged Black Tern* Generally a few birds in May. Scarce in northern Cyprus
- *Cyprus Pied Wheatear* Breeds only in Cyprus where it is abundant and widespread. Winters in the southern Sudan and Ethiopia.

ACCESS

Both reservoirs lie north-west of Nicosia with Gönyeli Reservoir visible from the main Nicosia–Girne road (approx. 7.5 km north-west of the centre of Nicosia). Finding the dam can be difficult. Leave Gönyeli northwards on the old road to Girne travelling uphill past a Mercedes showroom on the right. At the crest of the hill, fork right onto a narrow metalled road, turn left immediately, then sharply right onto a dirt track which leads around a hill (with a concrete water tank at the top) and on and down to the dam. Kanlıköy Reservoir is reached easily by following the track north from Kanlıköy village to the dam. Gönyeli Reservoir is extensively disturbed by picknickers and fishermen at weekends. Hunting is prohibited on and around the reservoirs.

Gülseren and Glapsides wetlands

35°09N 33°55E

This wetland lies north of Famagusta, extending from the northern edge of the city to the four-star Salamis Bay hotel farther north. Today, the remaining floodlands lie mainly to the east of the main road, and comprise three large and many smaller areas. Water from the river Kanlı (Pedhieos) forms large areas of shallow flooding, and a few deeper ponds. In the east some of the water is brackish as it is occasionally connected to the sea. In the past, the area flooded could reach several square kilometres in extent, but the building of reservoirs has reduced the amount of water reaching the area.

However, this wetland complex seems to be of great importance for passage migrants, including many species of gulls, ducks, herons and waders.

Species observed on spring migration include Black-necked Grebe, Night, Squacco and Purple Herons, Little Egret, Spoonbill (rare), Greater Flamingo (very rare), Gadwall, Shoveler, Garganey, Pallid, Hen and Marsh Harriers, Osprey, Stone-curlew, Spur-winged Plover, Sanderling, Curlew (rare but once *c.*100 together), Black-tailed Godwit, Spotted Redshank, Greenshank, Audouin's Gull, White-winged Black Tern and Kingfisher.

The land between the floodlands is also of interest. The maquis, coastal scrub, sand dunes and the forest of Salamis (with old Stone Pines) are excellent, often holding large numbers of migrants, such as Great Spotted Cuckoo, Bee-eater, Roller, Spotted and Pied Flycatchers, Golden Oriole and Red-backed Shrike.

Resident breeders in the area include Black Francolin, Cyprus, Cetti's, Fan-tailed and Spectacled Warblers, Spanish Sparrow, Barn Owl and, probably, Long-eared Owl.

TIMING

The number of birds and species here is very variable and can change from day to day.

In winter the floodlands may hold a considerable number of gulls, ducks and other waterbirds. The best period is spring migration – from mid-March until mid-May with a peak in mid-April, when tens of thousands of birds use the area to refuel and may stay to breed.

SPECIES

- ◆ *Greater Flamingo* A common winter visitor to the salt-lakes in southern Cyprus. Occasionally recorded here in very wet winters when large parts of the area are flooded.
- ◆ *Great Spotted Cuckoo* Recorded on passage with some birds staying to breed. Found mainly in the Salamis forest and its surroundings.
- ◆ *Long-eared Owl* Recorded breeding records in Salamis forest since 1968.
- ◆ *Cyprus Warbler* Very common in the Salamis ruins.

ACCESS

Gülseren wetland is located on the northern edge of Famagusta, to the east of the main Dipkarpaz road. Most of the site lies within the Gülseren military camp where entry, photography and videos are strictly forbidden. There is access to a small part of the wetland outside the military camp. Take the last public road to the right on the edge of the city, turn right again and then next left and the wetland will become visible. If there is water this area is excellent for waders and herons as well as gulls and terns. Do not take photographs here or attempt to enter the area from the coast.

The two main parts of Glapsides wetland are farther north, between the two junctions leading to the village of Tuzla (*c.* 2.5 km north of Famagusta to the east of the main road). Several roads and tracks lead to the area from the main road giving good views. Further smaller wetlands can be found between the main road and the coast as far north as the Salamis Bay hotel (*c.* 5 km north of Famagusta). For the old Salamis forest take the road to the Salamis ruins, clearly marked from the main road. The forest is north of the restaurant near the entry to the ruins. At weekends the Salamis forest and its surroundings are disturbed by tourists and local picknickers. Hunting is banned in the area.

LAKE MEHMETCİK

35°25N 34°04E

A shallow, natural lake. The size of this seasonal lake depends on the winter rainfall and may reach a maximum extent of about 1 x 0.5 km. If rainfall is heavy in winter, the lake may hold water from January until May. Because of its extensive areas of shallower water, this is a valuable stop-over site for migrants in spring, particularly waders and herons. Migrant visitors include Little Bittern, Night, Squacco and Purple Herons, Little Egrets, Glossy Ibis, Garganey, Pintail, Black-Winged Stilt, Spur-winged Plover, Little Stint, Curlew Sandpiper, Spotted Redshank and Greenshank, Common, Wood, Green and Marsh Sandpipers. Various terns occur and raptors include falcons (mainly Kestrels) and Marsh and Hen Harriers.

The surroundings of the lake are a mosaic of Olive and Carob plantations, maquis, grassland and small areas under regular cultivation. The area attracts many songbirds to remain throughout the winter (thrushes, Blue Rock Thrush and warblers) and migrants such as Common Crane, Bee-eater, Roller and Hoopoe. It is also a breeding area for a few pairs of Black Francolin, Chukar, Cyprus Pied Wheatear and, probably, Cyprus Warbler.

TIMING

In winter, wildfowl, Grey Heron and waders can be found on the lake and thrushes in its surroundings. Mid-March until May is best for passage herons and waders. The surroundings of the lake also attract many other passage migrants during both migration periods. Summer visitors like Cretzschmar's and Black-headed Buntings mainly arrive around mid- to late April.

SPECIES

- *Glossy Ibis* A regular visitor to the lake from mid-March until the end of April with flocks of up to 12 individuals.
- *Hoopoe* A rare breeder with more occurring on passage.

ACCESS

This lake lies west–south-west of Mehmetcik on the Karpaz peninsula. From Famagusta take the main road to Dipkarpaz. About 3 km after the village of Çayırova, leave the main road to the left towards Mehmetcik.

Spur-winged Plovers

The lake is visible on the left shortly before you arrive at the village. Hunting is banned on and around the lake when there is enough water in it for the birds.

Karpaz peninsula east from Dipkarpaz, with the Klidhes islands

35°37N 34°27E

A long, narrow peninsula north-east of Dipkarpaz with sandy and rocky shores and cliffs. The centre of the peninsula is dominated by a mosaic of grass and scrub-covered hills, with small strips of farmland and maquis towards the coast. Apart from a few tourist facilities, the peninsula is uninhabited. The area of the north coast has much open woodland providing cover and a first landfall for many autumn migrants. Large numbers of passage birds occur in both seasons and movement is often particularly spectacular in spring. The number of species can be very high and includes raptors, Stone-curlew, Bee-eater, Roller, Hoopoe, Red-backed and Woodchat Shrikes, various larks, pipits, wagtails, warblers and wheatears. It is an important breeding area for Chukar and Black Francolin, both of which have increased in numbers following a shooting ban introduced more than 20 years ago. As well as many residents, breeding migrants like Bee-eater, Red-rumped Swallow, Cretzschmar's and Black-headed Buntings breed in the area.

Cape Zafer (Zafer Burnu/Cape Andreas) is one of the finest sites on the island for visible migration. Waterbirds pass north offshore in spring and seawatching can be rewarding at any season. A considerable raptor passage including falcons (mainly Red-footed, Hobby and Peregrine) harriers, buzzards and a few Lesser Spotted Eagles also occur at the cape in spring.

The Klidhes Islands are a chain of nine small, rocky islands off the north-east point of Cyprus. The main island holds breeding Shags, Peregrines and Audouin's and Yellow-legged Gulls.

TIMING

Late March–mid-May is best for passage migrants on the Kırpasa peninsula. On the north coast autumn migration can be observed during September and October. Cape Zafer offers interesting birds throughout the year and during the main migration periods movement is always very apparent and often spectacular. During the breeding season (late April–end of July), Audouin's Gull may occasionally be seen flying past. Shag is present at or near the colony all year.

SPECIES

- ◆ *Audouin's Gull* Breeds on the main Klidhes island.
- ◆ *Shag* The breeding population is the sub-species *P.a. desmarestii.*
- ◆ *Peregrine* Probably one or two pairs on the main Klidhes island.
- ◆ *Black-headed Bunting* Quite a common breeding migrant with the first birds usually arriving in mid-April.

ACCESS

Only two roads lead north-eastwards into the area from Dipkarpaz. A left turn in the village leads to Ayios Philon and then along the north coast to Aphendrika. The metalled road along the south coast leads to the Apostolos Andreas Monastery, where the police will ask to see either your passport or your driving licence. From the monastery a track continues to Cape Zafer. There is a small hotel/restaurant where the road reaches the southern coast (*c.* 5.5 km north-east of Dipkarpaz in the direction of the monastery). The whole area is designated as a national park.

Bibliography and Further Reading

Birds of Turkey series, published by Max Kasparek Verlag, Heidelberg and available through OSME's sales list*, covering the following sites:

1 *Erçek Gölü*
2 *Seyfe Gölü*
3 *Kızılcahamam*
4 *Kızılırmak Deltası*
5 *Kulu Gölü*
6 *Yeniçağa Gölü* (not included in this book)
7 *Acıgöl*
8 *Köyceğiz-Dalyan*
9 *Hotamış Marshes*
10 *Çöl Gölü*
11 *Uludağ*
Further titles are in preparation.

Flint, P.R., and Stewart, P.F., *The Birds of Cyprus, An annotated check-list*, British Ornithologists' Union, Tring 1983, 1992

Gosney, D., *Finding Birds in Western Turkey*, Gostours, Sheffield, 1996

Gosney, D., *Finding Birds in Eastern Turkey*, Gostours, Sheffield, 1993

Gosney, D., *Finding Birds in Turkey–Ankara to Birecik*, Gostours, Sheffield, 1992

Green, I., and Moorhouse, N., *A Birdwatchers' Guide to Turkey*, Prion Ltd, Perry, 1995

Grimmet, R.F.A., and Jones, T.A., *Important Bird Areas in Europe*, ICBP, Cambridge, 1989

Kasparek, Aygün, and Max, *Reiseführer Natur Türkei*, BLV Verlagsgesellschaft, Germany, 1990

Kasparek, M, *Die Vögel der Türkei*, Max Kasparek Verlag, Heidelberg, 1992

Roselaar, C S, *Songbirds of Turkey: an atlas of biodiversity of Turkish passerine birds*, Pica Press, 1995

Tsunis, G., *An ecotouristic Guide to Greece*, HSPN, 1993

Turkey Bird Reports. Published by OSME*

WIWO (The Foundation Working Group for International Wader and Waterfowl Research) has published several reports on ornithological surveys of wetlands in Turkey. These include:

22 *A survey of waders and waterfowl in the Çukurova deltas, spring 1987*

45 *Bird census in the Kızılırmak delta, Turkey, in 1992*

48 *Wader and waterfowl migration in the Çukurova deltas, South Turkey, spring 1990*

A full list of publications (with prices) is available on request from WIWO, c/o Driebergsweg 16 C, 3708 JB Zeist, The Netherlands

*See p. 14 for OSME's address

Scientific names

Black-throated Diver *Gavia arctica*
Great Northern Diver *Gavia immer*
Red-necked Grebe *Podiceps grisegna*
Black-necked Grebe *Prodiceps nigricollis*
Cory's Shearwater *Calonectris diomedea*
Yelkouan Shearwater *Puffinus yelkouan*
British Storm-petrel *Hydrobates pelagicus*
Cormorant *Phalacrocorax carbo*
Shag *Phalacrocorax aristotelis*
Pygmy Cormorant *Phalacrocorax pygmaeus*
Darter *Anhinga melanogaster*
White Pelican *Pelecanus onocratalus*
Dalmatian Pelican *Pelecanus crispus*
Bittern *Botaurus stellaris*
Little Bittern *Ixobrychus minutus*
Night Heron *Nycticorax nycticorax*
Squacco Heron *Ardeola ralloides*
Cattle Egret *Bubulcus ibis*
Little Egret *Egretta garzetta*
Great White Egret *Egretta alba*
Grey Heron *Ardea cinerea*
Purple Heron *Ardea purpurea*
Yellow-billed Stork *Mycteria ibis*
Black Stork *Ciconia nigra*
White Stork *Ciconia ciconia*
Glossy Ibis *Plegadis falcinellus*
Bald Ibis *Geronticus eremita*
Spoonbill *Platalea leucorodia*
Greater Flamingo *Phoenicopterus ruber*
Bewick's Swan *cygnus bewickii*
White-fronted Goose *Anser albifrons*
Lesser White-fronted Goose *Anser erythropus*
Greylag Goose *Anser anser*
Red-breasted Goose *Branta ruficollis*
Ruddy Shelduck *Tadorna ferruginea*
Shelduck *Tadorna tadorna*
Gadwall *Anas streptera*
Teal *Anas crecca*
Pintail *Anas acuta*
Garganey *Anas querquedula*
Shoveler *Anas clypeata*
Marbled Duck *Marmaronetta angustirostris*
Red-crested Pochard *Netta rufina*
Pochard *Aythya ferina*
Ferruginous Duck *Aytha nyoca*
Tufted Duck *Aythya fuligula*
Velvet Scoter *Melanitta fusca*
Goldeneye *Bucephala clangula*
Smew *Mergus albellus*
Red-breasted Merganser *Mergus serrator*
White-headed Duck *Oxyura leucocephala*
Honey Buzzard *Pernus apivorus*
Black Kite *Milvus migrans*
Red Kite *Milvus milvus*
White-tailed Eagle *Haliaeetus albicilla*
Lammergeier *Gypaetus barbatus*
Egyptian Vulture *Neophron percnopterus*
Griffon Vulture *Gyps fulvus*

Black Vulture *Aegypius monachus*
Short-toed Eagle *Circaetus gallicus*
Marsh Harrier *Circus aeruginosus*
Hen Harrier *Circus cyaneus*
Pallid Harrier *Circus macrourus*
Montagu's Harrier *Circus pygargus*
Goshawk *Accipiter gentilis*
Sparrowhawk *Accipiter nisus*
Levant Sparrowhawk *Accipiter brevipes*
Buzzard *Buteo buteo*
Steppe Buzzard *Buteo buteo vulpinus*
Long-legged Buzzard *Buteo rufinus*
Lesser Spotted Eagle *Aquila pomarina*
Spotted Eagle *Aquila clanga*
Steppe Eagle *Aquila rapax*
Imperial Eagle *Aquila heliaca*
Golden Eagle *Aquila chrysaetos*
Booted Eagle *Hieraeetus pennatus*
Bonelli's Eagle *Hieraeetus pennatus*
Osprey *Pandion haliaetus*
Lesser Kestrel *Falco naumanni*
Red-footed Falcon *Falco vespertinus*
Merlin *Falco columbarius*
Hobby *Falco subbuteo*
Eleonora's Falcon *Falco eleonorae*
Sooty Falcon *Falco concolor*
Lanner *Falco biarmicus*
Saker *Falco cherrug*
Peregrine *Falco peregrinus*
Barbary Falcon *Falco peregrinoides*
Hazel Grouse *Tetrastes bonasia*
Caucasian Black Grouse *Lyurus mlokosiewiczi*
Capercaillie *Tetrao urogallus*
Caspian Snowcock *Tetraogallus caspius*
Chukar *Alectoris chukar*
Rock Partridge *Alextoris graeca*
See-see *Ammoperdix griseogularis*
Black Francolin *Francolinus francolinus*
Quail *Coturnix coturnix*
Water Rail *Rallus aquaticus*
Spotted Crake *Porzana porzana*
Little Crake *Porzana parva*
Baillon's Crake *Porzana pusilla*
Corncrake *Crex crex*
Purple Gallinule *Porphyrio porphyrio*
Coot *Fulica atra*
Common Crane *Grus grus*
Demoiselle Crane *Anthropoides virgo*
Little Bustard *Otis tetrax*
Great Bustard *Otis tarda*
Black-winged Stilt *Himantopus himantopus*
Avocet *Recurvirostra avosetta*
Crab Plover *Dromas ardeola*
Stone-curlew *Burhinus oedicnemus*
Cream-coloured Courser *Cursorius cursor*
Collared Pratincole *Glareola pratincola*
Oriental Pratincole *Glareola maldivarum*
Black-winged Pratincole *Glareola nordmanni*
Little Ringed Plover *Charadrius dubius*
Kentish Plover *Charadrius alexandrinus*
Lesser Sand Plover *Charadrius mongolus*
Greater Sand Plover *Charadrius leschenaultii*
Caspian Plover *Charadrius asiaticus*
Pied Kingfisher *Ceryle rudis*

Dotterel *Eudromias morinellus*
Golden Plover *Pluvialis apricaria*
Spur-winged Plover *Vanellus spinosus*
Red-wattled Plover *Vanellus indicus*
Sociable Plover *Vanellus gregarius*
White-tailed Plover *Vanellus leucurus*
Lapwing *Vanellus vanellus*
Sanderling *Calidris alba*
Little Stint *Calidris minuta*
Crossbill *Loxia curvirostra*
Temminck's Stint *Calidris temminckii*
Curlew Sandpiper *Calidris ferruginia*
Broad-billed Sandpiper *Limicola falcinellus*
Ruff *Philomachus pugnax*
Jack Snipe *Lymnocryptes minimus*
Great Snipe *Gallinago media*
Snipe *Gallinago gallinago*
Black-tailed Godwit *Limosa limosa*
Whimbrel *Numenius phaeopus*
Slender-billed Curlew *Numenius tenuirostris*
Curlew *Numenius arquata*
Spotted Redshank *Tringa erythropus*
Redshank *Tringa totanus*
Marsh Sandpiper *Tringa stagnatilis*
Greenshank *Tringa nebularia*
Green Sandpiper *Tringa ochropus*
Wood Sandpiper *Tringa glareola*
Terek Sandpiper *Xenus cinereus*
Common Sandpiper *Actitis hypoleucos*
Spotted Sandpiper *Actitis macularia*
Wilson's Phalarope *Phalaropus tricolor*
Red-necked Phalarope *Phalaropus lobatus*
Great Black-headed Gull *Larus ichthyaetus*
Mediterranean Gull *Larus melanocephalus*
Little Gull *Larus minutus*
Slender-billed Gull *Larus genei*
Audouin's Gull *Larus audouinii*
Yellow-legged Gull *Larus cachinnans*
Armenian Gull *Larus armenicus*
Kittiwake *Rissa tridactyla*
Gull-billed Tern *Gelochelidon nilotica*
Caspian Tern *Sterna caspia*
Sandwich Tern *Sterna sandvicensis*
Common Tern *Sterna hirundo*
Little Tern *Sterna albifrons*
Whiskered Tern *Chlidonias hybridus*
Black Tern *Childonias niger*
White-winged Black Tern *Chlidonias leucopterus*
Spotted Sandgrouse *Pterocles senegallus*
Black-bellied Sandgrouse *Pterocles orientalis*
Pin-tailed Sandgrouse *Pterocles alchata*
Rock Dove *Columba livia*
Turtle Dove *Streptopelia turtur*
Laughing Dove *Streptopelia senegalensis*
Great Spotted Cuckoo *Clamator glandarius*
Barn Owl *Tyto alba*
Striated Scops Owl *Otus brucei*
Scops Owl *Otus scops*
Eagle Owl *Bubo bubo*
Pygmy Owl *Glancidium passerinum*
Little Owl *Athene noctua*
Tawny Owl *Strix aluco*
Long-eared Owl *Asio otus*
Short-eared Owl *Asio flammeus*

Tengmalm's Owl *Aegolius funereus*
Nightjar *Caprimulgus europaeus*
Pallid Swift *Apus pallidus*
Alpine Swift *Apus melba*
Little Swift *Apus affinis*
White-breasted Kingfisher *Halcyon smyrnensis*
Kingfisher *Alcedo atthis*
Blue-cheeked Bee-eater *Merops superciliosus*
Bee-eater *Merops apiaster*
Roller *Coracias garrulus*
Hoopoe *Upupa epops*
Wryneck *Jynx torquilla*
Grey-headed Woodpecker *Picus canus*
Green Woodpecker *Picus viridis*
Black Woodpecker *Drycopus martius*
Syrian Woodpecker *Dendrocopos syriacus*
Middle Spotted Woodpecker *Dendrocopos medius*
White-backed Woodpecker *Dendrocopos leucotos*
Lesser Spotted Woodpecker *Dendrocopos minor*
Three-toed Woodpecker *Picoides tridactylus*
Bar-tailed Desert Lark *Ammomanes cincturus*
Desert Lark *Ammomanes deserti*
Thick-billed Lark *Calandrella cheleensis niethammeri*
Calandra Lark *Melanocorypha calandra*
Bimaculated Lark *Melanocorypha bimaculata*
Short-toed Lark *Calandrella brachydactyla*
Lesser Short-toed Lark *Calandrella rufescens*
Crested Lark *Galerida cristata*
Woodlark *Lullula arborea*
Shore Lark *Eremophila alpestris*
Crag Martin *Hirundo rupestris*
Red-rumped Swallow *Hirundo daurica*
Tawny Pipit *Anthus campestris*
Olive-backed Pipit *Anthus hodgsoni*
Tree Pipet *Anthus trivialis*
Red-throated Pipet *Anthus cervinus*
Water Pipit *Anthus spinoletta* (mountains)
Yellow Wagtail *Motacilla flava*
Black-headed Wagtail *Motacilla flava feldegg*
Citrine Wagtail *Motacilla citreola*
Grey Wagtail *Motacilla cinerea*
White Wagtail *Motacilla alba*
Yellow-vented Bulbul *Pycnonotus goiavier*
Dipper *Cinclus cinclus*
Radde's Accentor *Prunella ocularis*
Alpine Accentor *Prunella collaris subalpina*
Rufous Bush Robin *Cercotrichas galactotes*
Robin *Erithacus rubecula*
Thrush Nightingale *Luscinia luscinia*
Nightingale *Luscinia megarhynchos*
Bluethroat *Luscinia calliope*
Bluethroat *Luscinia svecica*
White-throated Robin *Irania gutturalis*
Black Redstart *Phoenicurus phoenicurus*
Redstart *Phoenicurus phoenicurus*
Whinchat *Saxicola rubetra*
Stonechat *Saxicola torquata*
Isabelline Wheatear *Oenanthe isabellina*
Northern Wheatear *Oenanthe oenanthe*
Pied Wheatear *Oenanthe pleschanka*

Cyprus Pied Wheatear *Oenanthe cypriaca*
Black-eared Wheatear *Oeanthe hispanica*
Desert Wheatear *Oenanthe deserti*
Finsch's Wheatear *Oenanthe finschii*
Red-rumped Wheatear *Oenanthe moesta*
Red-tailed Wheatear *Oenanthe xanthoprymna*
Mourning Wheatear *Oenanthe lugens*
Rock Thrush *Monticola saxatilis*
Blue Rock Thrush *Monticola solitarius*
White's Thrush *Zoothera dauma*
Ring Ouzel *Turdus torquatus*
Cetti's Warbler *Cettia cetti*
Fan-tailed Warbler *Cisticola juncidis*
Graceful Warbler *Prinia gracilis*
River Warbler *Locustella fluviatilis*
Savi's Warbler *Locustella luscinioides*
Moustached Warbler *Acrocephalus melanopogon*
Aquatic Warbler *Acrocephalus schoenobaenus*
Sedge Warbler *Acrocephalus Schoenobaenus*
Paddyfield Warbler *Acrocephalus agricola*
Marsh Warbler *Acrocephalus palustris*
Reed Warbler *Acrocephalus scirapceus*
Great Reed Warbler *Acrocephalus arundinaceus*
Olivaceous Warbler *Hippolais pallida*
Upcher's Warbler *Hippolais languida*
Olive-tree Warbler *Hippolais olivetorum*
Icterine Warbler *Hippolais icterina*
Marmora's Warbler *Sylvia sarda*
Spectacled Warbler *Sylvia conspicillata*
Subalpine Warbler *Sylvia cantillans*
Ménétries' Warbler *Sylvia mystacea*
Sardinian Warbler *Sylvia nelanocephala*
Cyprus Warbler *Sylvia melanothorax*
Rüppell's Warbler *Sylvia rueppelli*
Desert Warbler *Sylvia nana*
Orphean Warbler *Sylvia hortensis*
Barred Warbler *Sylvia nisoria*
Blackcap *Sylvia atricapilla*
Green Warbler *Phylloscopus nitidus*
Greenish Warbler *Phylloscopus trochiloides*
Bonelli's Warbler *Phylloscopus bonelli*
Wood Warbler *Phylloscopus sibilatrix*
Mountain Chiffchaff *Phylloscopus sindianus*
Firecrest *Regulus ignicapillus*
Spotted Flycatcher *Musciapa striata*
Red-breasted Flycatcher *Ficedula parva*
Semi-collared Flycatcher *Ficedula semitorquata*
Collared Flycatcher *Ficedula albicollis*
Pied Flycatcher *Ficedula hypoleuca*
Bearded Tit *Panurus biarmicus*
Marsh Tit *Parus palustris*
Sombre Tit *Parus lugubris*
'Cyprus' Coal Tit *Parus ater*
Krüper's Nuthatch *Sitta krüperi*

Great Rock Nuthatch *Sitta neumayer*
Rock Nuthatch *Sitta neumayer*
Wallcreeper *Tichodroma muraria*
Short-toed Treecreeper *Certhia brachydactyla*
'Cyprus' Short-toed Treecreeper *Certhia brachydactyla*
Penduline Tit *Remiz pendulinus*
Golden Oriole *Oriolus oriolus*
Isabelline Shrike *Lanius isabellinus*
Red-backed Shrike *Lanius collurio*
Lesser Grey Shrike *Lanius minor*
Great Grey Shrike *Lanius excubitor*
Woodchat Shrike *Lanius senator*
Masked Shrike *Lanius nubicus*
Jay *Garrulus glandarius*
Alpine Chough *Pyrrhocorax graculus*
Chough *Pyrrhocorax pyrrhocorax*
Brown-necked Raven *Corvus ruficollis*
Raven *Corvus corax*
Rose-coloured Starling *Sturnus roseus*
House Sparrow (It sub-sp) *Passer domesticus italiae*
Spanish Sparrow *Passer hispaniolensis*
Dead Sea Sparrow *Passer moabiticus*
Pale Rock Sparrow *Petronia brachydactyla*
Yellow-throated Sparrow *Petronia xanthocollis*
Rock Sparrow *Petronia petronia*
Snow Finch *Montifringilla nivalis*
Red-fronted Serin *Serinus pusillus*
Serin *Serinus serinus*
Syrian Serin *Serinus syriacus*
Twite *Acanthis flavirostris*
Crimson-winged Finch *Rhodopechys sanguinea*
Desert Finch *Rhodopechys obsoleta*
Mongolian Trumpeter Finch *Rhdopechys mongolica*
Trumpeter Finch *Rhodopechys githaginea*
Scarlet Rosefinch *Carpodacus erythrinus*
Bullfinch *Pyrrhula pyrrhula*
Hawfinch *Coccothraustes coccothraustes*
Pine Bunting *Emberiza leucocephalos*
Cirl Bunting *Emberiza cirlus*
Rock Bunting *Emberiza cia*
Cinereous Bunting *Emberiza cineracea*
Ortolan Bunting *Emberiza hortulana*
Grey-necked Bunting *Emberiza buchanani*
Cretzschmar's Bunting *Emberiza caesia*
Rustic Bunting *Emberiza rustica*
Little Bunting *Emberiza pusilla*
Black-headed Bunting *Emberiza melanocephala*
Corn Bunting *Emberiza calandra*

INDEX

Accentor, Alpine 18, 23, 51, 80, 92, 94, 103, 136, 140, 151
Accentor, Radde's 13, 18, 79, 84, 86, 94
Avocet 27, 58, 67, 112, 122, 130, 132, 135, 149, 166, 167, 200
Bee-eater 7, 15, 21, 31, 39, 53, 59, 86, 91, 110, 130, 134, 173, 178, 182, 186, 192, 198, 200, 202, 203, 204
Bee-eater, Blue-cheeked 82, 85, 86, 87, 91, 180
Bittern 28, 46, 65, 95, 144, 199, 201
Bittern, Little 20, 24, 27, 28, 32, 57, 63, 78, 88, 122, 126, 129, 132, 137, 139, 140, 147, 152, 153, 154, 155, 157, 160, 161, 167, 192, 199, 201, 203
Blackcap 7, 186, 200
Bluethroat 49, 82, 180
Bulbul, Yellow-vented 19, 36, 38, 40, 84
Bullfinch 42
Bunting, Black-headed 15, 79, 101, 128, 130, 150, 160, 178, 186, 203, 204, 205
Bunting, Cinereous 17, 82, 84, 85, 87, 94, 101, 167, 169, 170, 173, 185
Bunting, Cirl 16, 31, 59, 150, 157, 162, 169
Bunting, Corn 15, 150
Bunting, Cretzschmar's 15, 17, 19, 33, 84, 101, 103, 130, 131, 150, 151, 157, 160, 165, 169, 171, 172, 173, 183, 186, 195, 198, 200, 203, 204
Bunting, Grey-necked 13, 82, 90, 92, 97
Bunting, Little 46
Bunting, Ortolan 79, 121, 130, 150, 157, 163, 173, 183, 186
Bunting, Pine 173
Bunting, Rock 17, 18, 31, 51, 59, 79, 131, 150
Bunting, Rustic 173
Bustard, Great 34, 50, 58, 60, 61, 65, 68, 74, 88, 89, 93, 95, 96
Bustard, Little 34, 88, 93
Buzzard 24, 43
Buzzard, Honey 22, 25, 41, 42, 43, 45, 52, 70, 109, 131, 140, 143, 150, 171, 179
Buzzard, Long-legged 15, 53, 58, 60, 129, 131, 137, 139, 148, 159, 161, 169, 171, 193
Buzzard, Steppe 52
Capercaillie 124, 132
Chiffchaff, Mountain 42, 51
Chough 18, 23, 51, 63, 79, 140, 156, 163, 164
Chough, Alpine 18, 23, 51, 79, 136
Chukar 84, 87, 162, 163, 203, 204
Coot 13, 24, 59, 62, 201
Cormorant 22, 126, 127, 187
Cormorant, Pygmy 24, 25, 27, 31, 34, 57, 64, 65, 72, 73, 77, 82, 91, 92, 95, 104, 110, 123, 126, 133, 137, 139, 147, 156, 187
Corncrake 35
Courser, Cream-coloured 82, 85, 86, 180
Crake, Baillon's 49, 161, 191
Crake, Little 27, 28, 39, 49, 57, 66, 68, 72, 76, 78, 82, 123, 160, 161, 162, 191, 200
Crake, Spotted 65, 89, 93
Crane, Common 34, 35, 45, 50, 54, 58, 70, 73, 78, 88, 91, 93, 95, 159, 179, 203
Crane, Demoiselle 73, 90, 91, 92, 93, 179, 181
Crossbill 193
Cuckoo, Great Spotted 19, 28, 35, 184, 200, 202
Curlew 80, 202
Curlew, Slender-billed 101, 104, 110, 111, 128, 132, 149, 172
Darter 82
Dipper 17, 140
Diver, Black-throated 20, 22, 34, 46
Diver, Great Northern
Dotterel 70
Dove, Laughing 21
Dove, Rock 143
Dove, Turtle 190
Duck, Ferruginous 13, 26, 34, 45, 57, 63, 66, 91, 97, 101, 109, 110, 124, 126, 139, 140, 144, 152, 157
Duck, Marbled 7, 12, 13, 34, 39, 40, 68, 72, 73, 78, 97
Duck, Tufted 62
Duck, White-headed 7, 13, 39, 46, 56, 59, 66, 67, 68, 72, 73, 78, 79, 90, 95, 97, 101, 109, 110, 124, 129
Eagle, Bonelli's 30, 85, 124, 145, 155, 157, 160, 161, 162, 163, 164, 165, 171, 184, 194
Eagle, Booted 30, 41, 53, 109, 124, 126, 129, 131, 136, 137, 140, 143
Eagle, Golden 18, 23, 42, 53, 57, 58, 60, 62, 63, 79, 92, 95, 108, 109, 121, 124, 126, 129, 131, 132, 136, 137, 139, 140, 144, 145, 147, 150, 152, 159, 160, 161, 162, 163, 164
Eagle, Imperial 35, 52, 53, 63, 101, 108, 109, 124, 137, 141, 144, 149, 155, 194
Eagle, Lesser Spotted 22, 23, 25, 45, 53, 89, 101, 108, 121, 123, 124, 126, 129, 131, 136, 139, 143, 144, 145, 148, 159, 171, 204
Eagle, Short-toed 26, 30, 41, 53, 60, 62, 109, 124, 126, 129, 131, 132, 136, 137, 140, 144, 145, 148, 152, 155, 159, 160, 161, 171
Eagle, Spotted 19, 35, 53, 63, 101, 104, 108, 123, 133, 135, 144, 145, 149, 152
Eagle, Steppe 53, 108
Eagle, White-tailed 27, 29, 32, 35, 45, 63, 104, 108, 123, 126, 133, 135, 137, 139, 172
Egret, Cattle 35, 48, 91, 93, 135, 191, 201
Egret, Great White 24, 29, 31, 45, 46, 58, 65, 82, 133, 145, 147, 199, 200, 201
Egret, Little 15, 62, 77, 126, 129, 161, 182, 199, 200, 201, 202, 203
Falcon, Barbary 85
Falcon, Eleonora's 7, 19, 28, 29, 31, 32, 35, 89, 101, 102, 103, 108, 123, 130, 131, 132, 136, 155, 157, 158, 160, 161, 163, 164, 165, 166, 168, 171, 173, 178, 188, 189, 195, 196
Falcon, Red-footed 23, 24, 32, 45, 53, 57, 70, 104, 130, 132, 157, 158, 165, 172, 179, 182, 192, 204
Falcon, Sooty 85
Finch, Crimson-winged 17, 18, 51, 64, 79, 90, 92, 95, 96, 98

Finch, Desert 82, 84, 85, 87, 94
Finch, Mongolian Trumpeter 90, 91, 92
Finch, Snow 17, 18, 51, 79, 92, 96, 141
Finch, Trumpeter 84, 91, 94
Firecrest 23
Flamingo, Greater 7, 13, 27, 35, 39, 48, 56, 58, 60, 69, 70, 74, 78, 96, 110, 111, 112, 122, 135, 155, 167, 171, 172, 176, 179, 180, 189, 202
Flycatcher, Collared 42, 85, 124, 130, 156, 165, 173, 184, 186
Flycatcher, Pied 156, 184, 186, 200, 202
Flycatcher, Red-breasted 17, 42, 43, 45, 124, 167
Flycatcher, Semi-collared 42, 52, 85, 101, 108, 130, 146, 156, 184, 186
Flycatcher, Spotted 202
Francolin, Black 19, 34, 36, 38, 39, 40, 89, 184–5, 192, 195, 202, 203, 204
Gadwall 202
Gallinule, Purple 19, 34, 36, 40
Garganey 15, 56, 58, 65, 76, 157, 160, 163, 182, 195, 202, 203
Godwit, Black-tailed 58, 67, 202
Goldeneye 96
Goose, Greylag 45, 60, 78, 110
Goose, Lesser White-fronted 7, 101, 104, 109, 110, 123
Goose, Red-breasted 34, 101, 123, 128
Goose, White-fronted 29, 45, 57, 60, 64, 66, 68, 69, 72, 73, 74, 78
Goshawk 23, 43, 53, 108, 151, 159, 194
Grebe, Black-necked 27, 56, 57, 58, 59, 63, 68, 90, 95, 96, 110, 149, 162, 202
Grebe, Red-necked 50, 73, 78, 79, 90, 96, 97, 109
Greenshank 179, 200, 202, 203
Grouse, Caucasian Black 13, 18, 42, 51, 52
Grouse, Hazel 124, 138, 139
Gull, Armenian 54, 90, 96, 97, 182
Gull, Audouin's 7, 36, 37, 101, 102, 103, 132, 164, 165, 166, 171, 186, 197, 202, 205
Gull, Great Black-headed 15, 24, 34, 37, 39, 46, 104, 163, 183
Gull, Little 45, 46, 58, 147, 165, 178, 189
Gull, Mediterranean 23, 28, 56, 68, 123, 128, 134, 145, 155, 163, 165, 172, 196
Gull, Slender-billed 34, 56, 68, 70, 74, 78, 128, 134, 145, 149, 178, 179, 189, 196
Gull, Yellow-legged 185, 195, 205
Harrier, Hen 29, 53, 61, 82, 154, 202, 203
Harrier, Marsh 15, 35, 53, 82, 137–8, 154, 182, 198, 199–200, 202, 203
Harrier, Montagu's 17, 24, 53, 65, 70, 82, 88, 89, 91, 93, 95, 98, 140, 156
Harrier, Pallid 53, 82, 88, 104, 146, 171, 172, 178, 182, 202
Hawfinch 16, 31, 44, 45, 124, 154, 173
Heron, Grey 109, 126, 194, 203
Heron, Night 20, 24, 32, 61, 65, 77, 85, 109, 126, 129, 139, 140, 160, 161, 182, 201, 202, 203
Heron, Purple 24, 27, 32, 54, 57, 63, 76, 88, 97, 109, 122, 126, 129, 130, 140, 154, 161, 182, 199, 201, 202, 203
Heron, Squacco 24, 30, 49, 57, 62, 77, 97, 109, 124, 126, 129, 130, 132, 135, 137, 139, 153, 155, 156, 157, 160, 162, 167, 182, 199, 200, 201, 202, 203
Hobby 32, 45, 48, 53, 130, 186, 204
Hoopoe 15, 16, 30, 183, 198, 203, 204
Ibis, Bald 82, 85, 87
Ibis, Glossy 29, 31, 35, 57, 64, 76, 77, 109, 123, 126, 128, 130, 131, 132, 137, 139, 144, 145, 147, 149, 152, 154, 155–6, 157, 160, 161, 162, 163, 167, 178, 182, 183, 185, 201, 203
Jay 193
Kestrel, Lesser 15, 29, 30, 53, 57, 60, 63, 64, 66, 70, 72, 73, 74, 99, 101, 109, 139, 144, 167, 171, 187
Kingfisher 34, 36, 200, 202
Kingfisher, Pied 7, 31, 32, 36, 86, 89, 191
Kingfisher, White-breasted 7, 19, 32, 36, 37, 38, 39, 173
Kite, Black 41, 44, 50, 52, 109, 143
Kite, Red
Kittiwake 22
Lammergeier 18, 24, 51, 52, 53, 79, 95, 101, 108, 135, 136, 137, 140, 150, 151, 161, 162, 163, 164
Lanner 36, 108, 109, 136, 140, 141, 156
Lapwing 54
Lark, Asian Short-toed 56, 66, 72
Lark, Bar-tailed Desert 82
Lark, Bimaculated 15, 17, 72, 90, 95, 171, 183, 184
Lark, Calandra 15, 17, 39, 49, 57, 59, 60, 121, 128, 135, 153, 197, 201
Lark, Crested 15, 158
Lark, Desert 82, 85, 87
Lark, Lesser Short-toed 56, 90, 183
Lark, Shore 15, 17, 18, 23, 51, 61, 78, 79, 92, 94, 103, 136, 137, 141, 143
Lark, Short-toed 57, 121, 128, 135, 143, 183
Lark, Thick-billed 82
Martin, Crag 18, 79, 143, 164, 166, 193, 194
Merganser, Red-breasted
Merlin 61, 108
Nightingale 39, 64, 124, 186
Nightingale, Thrush 39, 110, 173, 186
Nightjar 45, 126, 130
Nuthatch, Great Rock 13, 82, 83, 84, 85, 87, 90
Nuthatch, Krüper's 16, 18, 19, 24, 31, 33, 42, 44, 101, 167, 170
Nuthatch, Rock 15, 31, 38, 41, 59, 61, 73, 79, 84, 101, 103, 109, 121, 131, 140, 148, 150, 151, 154, 156, 157, 160, 166, 169, 170
Oriole, Golden 16, 25, 45, 52, 184, 202
Osprey 46, 49, 53, 112, 155, 171, 200, 201, 202
Ouzel, Ring 18, 94, 140
Owl, Barn 202
Owl, Eagle 38, 59, 87, 94, 96, 97, 99, 109, 129, 147, 155, 171
Owl, Little 200
Owl, Long-eared 87, 197, 202
Owl, Pygmy 125
Owl, Scops 16, 30, 32, 80, 87, 130, 155, 161, 194
Owl, Short-eared 49, 93
Owl, Striated Scops 13, 81, 85, 87
Owl, Tawny 82
Owl, Tengmalm's 23, 124, 136, 137, 151
Partridge, Rock 101, 131, 138, 143, 144, 145, 151, 154
Pelican, Dalmatian 13, 24, 26, 27, 29, 35, 45, 46, 64, 73,

101, 104, 109, 110, 111, 112, 123, 126, 129, 139, 140, 144, 145, 146, 147, 148, 154, 156
Pelican, White 24, 25, 26, 35, 38, 41, 72, 74, 78, 97, 104, 126, 129, 139, 140, 144, 145, 147
Peregrine 30, 53, 109, 121, 136, 140, 147, 150, 161, 162, 163, 164, 165, 171, 179, 185, 188, 194, 204, 205
Petrel, British Storm 102
Phalarope, Red-necked 39, 41, 45, 66, 82, 90, 96, 97, 98, 128
Phalarope, Wilson's 46
Pintail 58, 203
Pipit, Meadow 200
Pipit, Olive-backed 46
Pipit, Red-throated 35, 45, 69, 112, 130, 133, 157, 160, 163, 165, 182, 183, 186
Pipit, Tawny 17, 63, 94, 128, 130, 135, 171, 183
Pipit, Tree 64, 183, 200
Pipit, Water 18, 23
Plover, Caspian 93, 96, 104, 183
Plover, Crab 34
Plover, Golden 70
Plover, Greater Sand 34, 37, 40, 56, 66, 71, 72, 74, 76, 78, 82, 104, 186, 189
Plover, Kentish 15, 40, 122, 130, 179
Plover, Lesser Sand 34
Plover, Little Ringed 17
Plover, Red-wattled 82, 88, 89
Plover, Sociable 90, 104
Plover, Spur-winged 24, 26, 27, 31, 37, 61, 78, 85, 104, 110, 111, 112, 122, 123, 167, 182, 200, 202, 203
Plover, White-tailed 71, 73, 85, 104
Pochard 24, 59, 199
Pochard, Red-crested 13, 45, 50, 57, 139, 147
Pratincole, Black-winged 39, 50, 90, 93, 97, 167, 171, 173, 182
Pratincole, Collared 24, 27, 28, 30, 37, 40, 46, 69, 70, 72, 74, 78, 112, 122, 125, 128, 130, 131, 132, 134, 135, 139, 143, 147, 148, 153, 158, 167, 182
Pratincole, Oriental 182
Quail 53, 54, 59, 93, 98, 156, 185, 198
Rail, Water 34
Raven 43, 193, 198
Raven, Brown-necked 89
Redshank 89, 95, 96
Redshank, Spotted 202, 203
Redstart 64
Redstart, Black 18, 79, 90, 92, 95, 143, 159
Robin 200
Robin, Rufous Bush 19, 25, 32, 40, 84, 109, 125, 128, 134, 135, 154, 160, 167, 170, 173
Robin, White-throated 17, 57, 59, 61, 63, 64, 79, 84, 87, 94, 95, 169
Roller 15, 32, 45, 52, 90, 108, 109, 110, 134, 139, 155, 171, 178, 181, 200, 202, 203, 204
Rosefinch, Scarlet 42, 44, 51, 99, 173
Ruff 15, 56, 58, 65, 70, 76, 78, 180, 182
Saker 36, 53, 54, 89, 95, 96, 108, 135
Sanderling 202
Sandgrouse, Black-bellied 17, 68, 72, 78, 85, 89, 93, 197
Sandgrouse, Pin-tailed 85, 88, 89
Sandgrouse, Spotted 85
Sandpiper, Broad-billed 35, 39, 41, 45, 56, 63, 69, 76, 95, 96, 97, 104, 123, 132, 148, 171, 179
Sandpiper, Common 184, 200, 203
Sandpiper, Curlew 179, 203
Sandpiper, Green 200, 203
Sandpiper, Marsh 35, 39, 58, 63, 64, 67, 72–3, 82, 95, 96, 123, 179, 201, 203
Sandpiper, Spotted 34
Sandpiper, Terek 34, 39, 69, 96, 97, 104, 128, 148, 180
Sandpiper, Wood 64, 67, 123, 180, 182, 200, 201, 203
Scoter, Velvet 94
See-see 81, 84, 85, 87, 88
Serin 159
Serin, Red-fronted 17, 18, 24, 51, 59, 61, 79, 94, 173
Serin, Syrian
Shag 187, 195, 198, 205
Shearwater, Cory's 19, 28, 102, 130, 159, 164, 165, 171, 172, 173, 198, 199
Shearwater, Yelkouan 20, 22, 28, 111, 125, 130, 159, 165, 171, 172, 198
Shelduck 96
Shelduck, Ruddy 12, 13, 15, 25, 26, 27, 48, 50, 54, 57, 59, 60, 61, 68, 73, 78, 95, 96, 104, 109, 123, 129, 166, 167, 168, 171, 189
Shoveler 78, 199, 202
Shrike, Great Grey
Shrike, Isabelline 85, 167
Shrike, Lesser Grey 15, 59, 111, 130, 134, 135, 137, 147, 156, 161, 165, 171, 173, 186
Shrike, Masked 7, 19, 25, 28, 31, 101, 105, 108, 109, 168, 171, 173, 178, 186, 193, 200, 201
Shrike, Red-backed 15, 53, 121, 130, 143, 156, 165, 173, 186, 198, 201, 202, 204
Shrike, Woodchat 19, 87, 130, 156, 163, 164, 173, 186, 198, 199, 200, 204
Smew 14, 23, 24, 26, 45, 46
Snipe 58
Snipe, Great 24, 34, 39, 93, 96, 97, 160, 172, 173, 182
Snipe, Jack 173
Snowcock, Caspian 13, 18, 42, 51, 52, 79, 80, 89
Sparrow, Dead Sea 39, 81, 82, 85, 87, 88, 180
Sparrow, House 161
Sparrow, Pale Rock 82, 84, 85, 87, 88, 191
Sparrow, Rock 60, 79, 87, 90, 157, 159, 169, 173
Sparrow, Spanish 30, 39, 129, 131, 157, 173, 185, 200, 202
Sparrow, Yellow-throated 82, 85, 87, 89, 99
Sparrowhawk 53, 108, 198
Sparrowhawk, Levant 22, 41, 53, 89, 101, 108, 109, 121, 123, 124, 126, 129, 136, 139, 141, 143, 145, 151
Spoonbill 24, 41, 45, 61, 64, 70, 73, 78, 93, 109, 126, 128, 132, 134, 135, 144, 145, 152, 160, 167, 190
Starling, Rose-coloured 35, 45, 52, 90, 167, 171, 173
Stilt, Black-winged 15, 26, 27, 31, 46, 63, 67, 95, 112, 122, 128, 130, 132, 135, 139, 143, 152, 153, 160, 180, 200, 201, 203
Stint, Little 15, 56, 58, 64, 70, 76, 95, 123, 179, 189, 203
Stint, Temminck's 123, 128, 157, 189
Stonechat 90, 200
Stone-curlew 28, 31, 40, 45, 73, 85, 112, 122, 125, 128, 130, 131, 135, 144, 153, 166, 167, 171, 192, 195, 198, 199, 202, 204
Stork, Black 22, 25, 41, 42, 44, 45, 67, 104, 108, 121, 124, 126, 129, 131, 136, 141, 143, 145, 159, 167

Stork, White 7, 15, 20, 22, 30, 35, 38, 41, 63, 65, 67, 70, 82, 104, 129, 154, 159, 201
Stork, Yellow-billed 34, 82
Swallow, Red-rumped 16, 19, 39, 186, 194, 204
Swan, Bewick's 25, 46
Swift, Alpine 21, 31, 79, 99, 136, 143, 159, 188, 196
Swift, Little 41, 82, 85, 86
Swift, Pallid 21, 24, 84, 163, 172, 193
Teal 69, 180
Tern, Black 109, 126, 190
Tern, Caspian 27, 28, 70, 95, 99, 128, 135, 149, 157
Tern, Common 123, 132
Tern, Gull-billed 25, 26, 28, 46, 50, 56, 57, 68, 73, 74, 78, 85, 93, 104, 128, 135, 147, 148, 157, 180
Tern, Little 85, 123, 125, 128, 132, 143, 152, 153, 160, 167
Tern, Sandwich 123
Tern, Whiskered 24, 56, 57, 62, 63, 66, 78, 95, 109, 126, 139, 157, 190
Tern, White-winged Black 45, 50, 54, 56, 66, 90, 92, 95, 157, 180, 190, 200, 201, 202
Thrush, Blue Rock 23, 31, 38, 41, 59, 79, 121, 148, 150, 154, 155, 156, 157, 159, 166, 171, 172, 191, 194, 195, 203
Thrush, Rock 17, 23, 52, 79, 92, 94, 95, 99, 125, 140, 157, 171
Thrush, White's 173
Tit, 'Cyprus' Coal 175, 178, 193
Tit, Bearded 63, 65, 78, 99, 123
Tit, Marsh 43
Tit, Penduline 15, 24, 30, 32, 48, 49, 62, 65, 90, 110, 127, 129, 134, 135, 149, 180
Tit, Sombre 16, 33, 44, 59, 101, 109, 140, 143, 151, 154, 168, 170
Treecreeper, 'Cyprus' Short-toed 175, 178, 193
Treecreeper, Short-toed 44
Twite 18, 42, 51, 96
Vulture, Black 18, 44, 52, 101, 107, 109, 136
Vulture, Egyptian 18, 23, 41, 44, 53, 62, 73, 107, 109, 121, 124, 129, 137, 139, 140, 143, 144, 145, 151
Vulture, Griffon 18, 38, 51, 52, 53, 57, 62, 107, 109, 121, 136, 140, 144, 145, 147, 148, 150, 151, 152, 160, 161, 162, 163, 164, 165, 178, 188, 189, 193, 194, 196, 200
Wagtail, Black-headed 182
Wagtail, Citrine 39, 45, 50, 54, 57, 64, 69, 76, 82, 90, 92, 98, 167, 171, 182
Wagtail, Grey 193
Wagtail, White 200
Wagtail, Yellow 112
Wallcreeper 18, 38, 41, 51, 80, 86, 135, 136, 141, 143, 188
Warbler, Aquatic 101
Warbler, Barred 42, 64, 85, 138, 139, 186
Warbler, Bonelli's 16, 33, 44, 62, 109, 186, 200
Warbler, Cetti's 30, 32, 85, 184, 200, 202
Warbler, Cyprus 7, 175, 184, 195, 200, 202, 203
Warbler, Desert 191
Warbler, Fan-tailed 19, 171, 200, 202
Warbler, Graceful 19, 34, 38, 40, 82
Warbler, Great Reed 15, 28, 32, 49, 62, 78, 160, 192
Warbler, Green 17, 42, 43, 51
Warbler, Greenish 13
Warbler, Icterine 186
Warbler, Marmora's 165
Warbler, Marsh 42, 51, 93
Warbler, Ménétries' 82, 83, 85, 87, 91
Warbler, Moustached 15, 49, 91, 161, 179, 180
Warbler, Olivaceous 15, 44, 159, 166, 178, 186, 194
Warbler, Olive-tree 7, 16, 19, 33, 84, 101, 105, 108, 129, 130, 137, 144, 145, 146, 147, 150, 166, 168
Warbler, Orphean 16, 19, 28, 31, 33, 85, 108, 109, 124, 125, 150, 157, 160, 168, 170, 173, 183
Warbler, Paddyfield 34, 90, 92, 93, 96, 99
Warbler, Reed 182, 192, 200
Warbler, River 48, 64, 110, 167
Warbler, Rüppell's 7, 19, 31, 32, 33, 101, 103, 150, 151, 154, 155, 161, 163, 165, 168, 171, 183, 184, 195
Warbler, Sardinian 16, 38, 159, 166, 200
Warbler, Savi's 99
Warbler, Sedge 200
Warbler, Spectacled 180, 187, 197, 202
Warbler, Subalpine 16, 19, 31, 124, 131, 140, 148, 156, 157, 165, 170, 184
Warbler, Upcher's 38, 82, 84, 87
Warbler, Wood 44, 186, 200
Wheatear, Black-eared 15, 157, 160, 162, 164, 183, 185, 198
Wheatear, Common
Wheatear, Cyprus Pied 7, 19, 34, 39, 175, 184, 193, 195, 200, 201, 203
Wheatear, Desert 82, 85, 87, 96
Wheatear, Finsch's 17, 59, 73, 79, 90, 176, 179, 187, 191
Wheatear, Isabelline 15, 105, 109, 155, 165, 170, 178, 183, 185, 198
Wheatear, Mourning 82, 183
Wheatear, Northern 183, 185, 198, 200
Wheatear, Pied 39, 90
Wheatear, Red-rumped 82
Wheatear, Red-tailed 13, 15, 17, 82, 83, 84, 85, 87, 191
Whimbrel 35
Whinchat 64, 186, 198
Woodlark 16, 60, 63, 94, 162, 194
Woodpecker, Black 17, 23, 42, 43, 44, 124, 131, 136, 137, 140, 141, 151, 152, 171
Woodpecker, Green 33
Woodpecker, Grey-headed 33, 43, 44, 53, 124, 136
Woodpecker, Lesser Spotted 45, 143
Woodpecker, Middle Spotted 16, 19, 31, 33, 43, 62, 124, 128, 137, 140, 141, 143, 149, 151, 168, 170
Woodpecker, Syrian 15, 30, 84, 128
Woodpecker, Three-toed 124, 136, 141
Woodpecker, White-backed 25, 33, 53, 124, 136, 137, 140, 141, 151, 152
Wryneck 23, 33, 44, 183